Chances and Choices

Chances and Choices

EXPLORING THE IMPACT
OF MUSIC EDUCATION

STEPHANIE PITTS

OXFORD
UNIVERSITY PRESS

OXFORD
UNIVERSITY PRESS

Oxford University Press, Inc., publishes works that further
Oxford University's objective of excellence
in research, scholarship, and education.

Oxford   New York
Auckland   Cape Town   Dar es Salaam   Hong Kong   Karachi
Kuala Lumpur   Madrid   Melbourne   Mexico City   Nairobi
New Delhi   Shanghai   Taipei   Toronto

With offices in
Argentina   Austria   Brazil   Chile   Czech Republic   France   Greece
Guatemala   Hungary   Italy   Japan   Poland   Portugal   Singapore
South Korea   Switzerland   Thailand   Turkey   Ukraine   Vietnam

Copyright © 2012 by Oxford University Press

Published by Oxford University Press, Inc.
198 Madison Avenue, New York, New York 10016

www.oup.com

Oxford is a registered trademark of Oxford University Press

Library of Congress Cataloging-in-Publication Data
Pitts, Stephanie
Chances and choices: exploring the impact of music education / Stephanie E. Pitts.
   p. cm.
Includes bibliographical references and index.
ISBN 978-0-19-983875-2 (hardback)—ISBN 978-0-19-983877-6 (pbk.)
1. Music—Instruction and study—Social aspects. I. Title.
MT1.P595 2012
780.71—dc23   2011039299

9 8 7 6 5 4 3 2 1

Printed in the United States of America
on acid-free paper

CONTENTS

ACKNOWLEDGEMENTS

The first and greatest acknowledgement in this book is due to all the people who have told their musical life histories as part of this project, and particularly to those who have allowed them to be included in full as "Interludes" in the book. I collected over one hundred fascinating and sometimes moving stories and am grateful to all those who wrote them, and who helped encourage their friends and colleagues to do the same.

My research has been supported by funding from the Worldwide Universities Network, which enabled me to visit the University of Illinois at Urbana-Champaign. There I experienced the warmth and wisdom of Liora Bresler and had valuable conversations with her colleagues and students. During a trip to Italy, funded by the University of Sheffield, I was generously hosted and advised by Anna Rita Addessi, Johannella Tafuri, Fred and Dilys Seddon, and Michele and Cristina Biasutti. For Italian language teaching and translation, I thank Liz White and Anna Ferrarese.

A period of research leave from the University of Sheffield made the writing of this book possible, and I am grateful to colleagues for covering my absence during that time, especially Andrew Killick, Renee Timmers, Vicki Rowe, and Jo Burrows. Thanks also to Suzanne Ryan, Adam Cohen, Caelyn Cobb, and colleagues at Oxford University Press for their support and efficiency throughout the publication process.

For friends and family who provided suggestions, support, and welcome distractions during the writing process, I am hugely grateful; particular thanks go to Matthew Redfearn, Betty Porter, Karen Burland, Oscar and Rich Clark, Katie van Buren, Nikki Dibben, Chris Spencer, Melissa Dobson, and Kate Gee. Finally, love and thanks as always to my parents, for helping to make my own musical life history such a fulfilling one.

ABOUT THE COMPANION WEBSITE

http://www.oup.com/us/chancesandchoices

The companion website for *Chances and Choices* features detailed analysis of the musical life histories in this book, including the coding system that was used to generate the quantitative aspects of the analysis and so to guide the focus of the qualitative discussion. Profiles of all the life history respondents are also provided, with a table of their quoted materials that helps to connect comments from across the book's chapters, and to link these with the formative musical experiences and current activity of the respondents. The summary of initial findings (referred to in Chapter 1) that was sent to participants in the first phase of research is also available, offering both a brief view of the research and an illustration of the consultation with respondents that formed part of the project.

Readers are also invited to contribute their own musical life histories through an online forum hosted at the University of Sheffield, which is intended to form the next phase of this research. Perspectives from all backgrounds—musical, cultural, and geographical—are warmly welcomed, and it is hoped that this online collection of life histories will become a resource for all researchers and practitioners with an interest in the impact of music education.

Chances and Choices

1 | Investigating the Impact of Music Education

1.1 Whose Story? Defining and Interpreting Musical Life Histories

GETTING AT THE "TRUTH" of what happens during a school day is no easy task. Parents ask their children what they have done at school and are told "nothing much" or "it was fine". Quality assurance inspectors compile statistics on pupil attendance and attainment and make observations of teachers, whose stress at the inspection process causes them to behave unnaturally. Researchers run focus groups, distribute questionnaires, interview students and teachers, but still gain only an outsider's perspective on the multiple experiences of education in any classroom. The students themselves, meanwhile, might perceive the intentions and even the content of a lesson quite differently from their teacher, relating their school experience to their wider social world in individual and unpredictable ways. The experiences and effects of learning in school are understood differently by all involved and are recalled through many layers of interpretation in later years.

Harder still, then, is to understand the impact of what happened during those school days upon later life experience, attitudes, and ambitions. The influences of childhood are closely intertwined, such that the attitudes of an encouraging (or discouraging) teacher are mediated by the response (or lack of) in the home to news of successes (or disappointments) in school. Parental experiences of education and their life ambitions and social values—as well as their genetic material—shape children's expectations of school and teachers, heightening or limiting a child's responsiveness to the stimuli that are deliberately provided or accidentally encountered in the course of every-day life. In their adult lives, the same children will look back on their school years with a mixture of gratitude, blame, or indifference, interpreting the intentions of their teachers, the attitudes of their peers, and their own be-haviour in ways that make sense of their adult identities and destinations.

This book uses retrospective accounts of formative musical experiences to examine the long-term impact of music education and to evaluate its place among the many influences upon children's motivation to engage with music throughout their lives. As respondents reflect on events that occurred sometimes as long as 70 years earlier, the day-to-day details of lessons, people, and activities will inevitably be partial, but amongst the blurred mem-ories will be significant moments that have come to form part of that per-son's musical and educational narrative. These stories are subjectively factual: they offer not so much a record of how music education has changed across generations—though this is certainly evident in the responses—but of how it has been experienced, understood, and acted upon by the individuals involved. Through the stories and selections offered as part of a life history, the highlights, regrets, and opportunities of a range of musical childhoods become apparent, and their long-term effects can be traced through to adult musical lives as teachers, amateur players, concert-goers, and parents, of-fering a new perspective on the many valuable reasons for embedding music in childhood and in education.

The process of constructing an autobiographical narrative makes its own contribution to identity, affirming and making sense of those aspects of past life that are most helpful in rationalising current experience, and allowing storytellers to present a coherent account of themselves to their listeners. In telling their stories, "people selectively appropriate aspects of their experi-ence and imaginatively construe both past and future to construct stories that make sense to them and to their audiences, that vivify and integrate life and make it more or less meaningful" (McAdams, 2001, p. 101). Several writers have suggested that "musicians may be predisposed to interpreting their childhood as one full of music and/or longing for music" (Gavin, 2001, p. 59), sometimes placing too much emphasis on early experiences as deter-mining "everything that will happen later, what we can be, what we can do" (Holt, 1978, p. 4). While John Holt agrees that "musical people are particu-larly prone to talk this way" (ibid., p. 4), life stories collected from influential scientists show that musicians do not have the monopoly on this: "I always replied, when asked the standard question, that I was going to be a scientist when I grew up" (Brockman, 2004, p. 92). Helen Gavin's study, in which she compared the childhood recollections of musicians with those who did not pursue music in adulthood, offers a nice counter-example to the belief that early influences necessarily have a life-determining effect: she reports a professional flautist recalling how her parents "bought me a flute when I asked, so I suppose that set me off to where I am today, but they also bought me a bike, and I'm not in the Tour de France" (Gavin, 2001, p. 57).

Theories of autobiographical memory confirm that the impact of significant encounters is not predetermined: a discouraging conversation with a piano teacher will motivate some young musicians to practise more determinedly for future success, even while it convinces others that a musical future is not for them (cf. Pillemer, 2001, p. 131). Such tendencies to tell "redemption" or "contamination" stories—the extent to which negative events are interpreted positively with hindsight—are a feature of personal identity and can be a marker of wellbeing, optimism, and satisfaction with life, as well as being influenced by age, gender, and relative distance from the events being narrated (McAdams, Reynolds, Lewis, Patten, & Bowman, 2001). Autobiographical narratives are also prone to "self-enhancement" (Bluck, 2003), whereby individuals view their past selves as inferior to their current state, so asserting the implicit belief that they would now behave more effectively in a given situation. In the musical life stories on which this book draws, these traits are all in evidence: the actions of parents, teachers, and other role models are similar across a range of narratives but are interpreted differently as individuals attribute influences and values to particular events and people in ways that make sense of their own musical identities.

Autobiographical reflection offers a particular perspective on educational experiences, one that is shaped by events and opportunities through the lifespan, and by the strength of the storyteller's sense of self as a musician. Some musical journeys have been recounted many times, perhaps reinforced by parents or others, and so individuals have come to know themselves as people who have always been musicians: "I'm told I could sing before I could talk, but I can't remember this!" [UK26, aged 52; see Section 1.3 for explanation of participant codes]. Such narratives are full of "self-defining memories" (Moffitt & Singer, 1994, p. 26), in which a sequence of musical goals and achievements is traced from formative years through to adult life. Others present their musical histories as having been more serendipitous, dependent on particular people or opportunities for the formation of a musical identity that is seen as anomalous within the family context: "no member of my extended family is in any way 'musical', none could play an instrument or ever went to concerts" [UK19, aged 74].

Within these different kinds of life narrative, experiences of music education are interpreted by the storyteller on two levels: first by their impact at the time, and secondly by the retrospective contribution they are seen to have made to long-term engagement in music. Both aspects can be profoundly influential on the musical lives of individuals, but the latter is rarely considered in educational policy, debate, and practice, emphasis tending to fall instead on the more immediately evident outcomes of music education—exam results, youthful performing successes, a thriving school musical culture. This book aims to investigate what happens to young people's musical engagement once they leave school, and to consider how teachers and parents can inspire and nurture musical learning in such a way that it can be sustained beyond formal education.

1.2 Aims, Scope, and Limitations

This book has six principal aims:

- To investigate the long-term impact of childhood musical learning through empirical accounts of lifelong musical involvement
- To evaluate the contribution of school music education to lifelong involvement and attitudes to music, considering the impact of teachers, peers, and opportunities
- To consider the influence of other locations for learning, including childhood home and community, and adult learning and activity
- To highlight particular strengths of music education, including opportunities for skill development, inspiration, and self-identity as a musician
- To question the drawbacks of educational systems for music, and the ways in which learning might be inhibited through criticism or perceived lack of relevance or opportunity
- To propose ways in which awareness of the long-term impact of music education might help to shape the rationale and realities of future practice

These are ambitious aims within a relatively neglected area of music education research, and some clarifying remarks about the origins, scope, and limitations of the study are necessary at this point.

The idea of investigating the long-term impact of music education grew from my previous studies of adult musical participation (Pitts, 2005), during which it became evident that people for whom music was a central part of their adult lives often traced their interests back to influential people or opportunities in their childhood, and particularly to the extracurricular music-making they had experienced in school. The participants in those studies, who included regular concert-goers, singers in Gilbert and Sullivan societies, and composers pursuing an interest in contemporary music, all expressed a commitment to the role of music in education, seeking to share their own enthusiasms with the next generation and sometimes expressing concern about diminishing levels of interest in the genres and activities that they most valued. Some participants evaluated their educational experiences as part of their explanations for why they made music as adults, recalling specific performances, lessons, or teachers as moments in which they realised the importance of music in their own lives. Others expressed regret at not having persisted with instrumental lessons, or encouraged their children to do the same. These hints at the long-term impact of childhood musical encounters offered a fascinating glimpse into a new perspective on music education, which represented a move away from the measurability and accountability of contemporary school life towards a recognition of the lasting effects of learning, and a potentially richer understanding of the contribution made by teachers and parents in shaping future generations of musicians and listeners.

In deciding to pursue this area of research, I began with participants who were similar to those in the *Valuing Musical Participation* (Pitts, 2005) studies: adults who were regularly engaged in music as players, listeners, or teachers, and who were therefore likely to have articulate opinions on their educational experiences and the ways in which these had affected their musical attitudes, skills, and priorities. (Further details of how I recruited these participants and elicited and analysed their musical life histories are given in Section 1.3.) As anticipated, these respondents offered rich, varied stories, by no means overwhelmingly positive in their views of music education, and revealing complex interrelationships between many factors: parental attitudes and expectations, the extent of listening and playing in the home, opportunities at school, instrumental lessons, self-directed listening and learning, the seeking out of performing and tuition in adulthood, and the consolidation of musical priorities and levels of involvement in later life. The analysis of these narratives raised many questions about music education, prompting discussion of the role of the home environment, the characteristics of effective classroom and instrumental teachers, and the relationship between school music learning and longer-term attitudes and engagement in the arts. In other ways, however, the sample was somewhat narrow, being recruited largely in Britain, and amongst those who were musically active— not from the much greater proportion of the population who might judge their school music to have had little effect on their leisure use and continued personal development in adulthood.

Some of the limitations of the sample were addressed within the boundaries of this study. Firstly, to counter the UK focus of the data, a further survey was conducted in Italy, chosen to represent those central European countries where music has traditionally been taught principally in conservatoires, with more limited provision of classroom lessons and extracurricular music-making within mainstream education (Tafuri, 2001). I had intended to recruit additional participants in North America, where band and choral programmes are dominant in the curriculum, giving young people a different kind of preparation for adult involvement in music (Kelly, 2009). This phase of recruitment was unsuccessful, however, and also raised doubts in my mind about the extent to which I would be able, as an outsider to the educational system, to interpret the life histories as being typical or otherwise, and to relate them to a detailed knowledge of the aims and trends in US music education over recent decades. These doubts apply equally to the Italian responses, leading to the cautious use of these data mainly to illustrate the extent to which this research method might be applied in other contexts, and the cultural and educational differences that are raised by doing so. In the absence of more internationally diverse data, existing research literature is used to draw attention to features of the UK responses that are not universal in music education, and to stimulate debate about the broader applicability of thinking about musical learning from a lifespan perspective.

A second limitation of the participant group was the prevalence of classical musicians, which arose partly from having recruited through professional magazines read mainly by music teachers and classical music listeners (see Section 1.3 for further details), and also because of the conventional educational pathways followed by many of the older respondents. To balance this, I undertook a final phase of recruitment targeted at popular musicians, gaining a small but indicative sample that helped to bring some of the assumptions of the main data set into sharper focus, and to raise new questions about the effectiveness of music education as a foundation for different kinds of lifelong engagement. Once again, though, this expansion of the scope of the study does not fully embrace the range of musical life histories that could be investigated—nor indeed the many potential "non-musical" narratives and the perspectives upon music education that such respondents could offer. I readily acknowledge the limitations of this study, doing so at this early stage in the book in order to invite readers to consider how the stories of these particular participants could illuminate those of other players, teachers, and listeners, and perhaps prompt research in a wider range of educational and social contexts. Nonetheless, this study makes a new contribution in illuminating the "chances and choices" of ordinary musical lives, showing how small decisions and opportunities in childhood can have a lasting impact, and questioning whether there might be more effective ways of ensuring that the foundations for lifelong engagement with music are embedded within mainstream musical education.

1.3 Approaches to Data Collection and Analysis

This project sought to collect retrospective accounts of formative musical influences and opportunities from adults who had sustained an active interest in music throughout their lives. To enable the collection and analysis of a relatively large data set, written responses were used in preference to interviews, and many of these were detailed and extensive. Such accounts were loosely termed "life histories" in my correspondence with participants but did not follow strictly the methods of life history research, which typically features detailed, multiple interviews with a small number of participants (see Goodson & Sikes, 2001). Here, narratives were sought from a larger sample of participants (134 in total), aiming for an exploratory overview of trends in music education experience, as well as individual accounts of formative events and influences. The written form used in this study, whilst offering less interactive opportunity than an interview, was true to the essence of life history research in allowing respondents to "speak for and about themselves" (Atkinson, 1998, p. 5). Respondents constructed their own finished account and submitted this to me when they were satisfied with the story they had told—so, arguably, removing the layer of researcher interpretation and construction that would come with transcribing multiple interviews. Rineke Smilde (2009a) uses the term "biographical narratives" to describe her interviews with professional musicians; those in this book are more properly labeled "autobiographical narratives", constructed by the respondents themselves and providing insight on those memories that have lasted and become part of a narrative—sometimes newly discovered in the telling, at other times apparently well rehearsed. Throughout this book, the term "life history" has been retained as a readily understood shorthand for the autobiographical data that underpin this study, reflecting my intention to preserve in this larger-scale study the aims of in-depth life history research—namely by "comprehending the complexities of a person's day-to-day decision making and the ultimate consequences that play out in that life so that insights into the broader, collective experience may be achieved" (Cole & Knowles, 2001, p. 11).

The first phase of data collection took place mainly between March and July 2007, when responses were received from 72 participants, distributed by age as shown in the Phase 1 column of Table 1.1. Each response was given an anonymous reference (UK1–72) and coded in full to enable quantitative analysis of trends across the data, as well as grounded qualitative analysis of the individual narratives. Phase 1 participants were recruited through letters and articles published in professional magazines: *Music Teacher*, which has an audience of classroom teachers; the *Incorporated Society of Musicians (ISM) Music Journal*, read mainly by instrumental teachers; and the *British Broadcasting Corporation (BBC) Music Magazine*, which has a wider circulation amongst regular listeners and concert-goers. The survey was also advertised on the University of Sheffield website, attracting responses from current music students, researchers, and their friends.

These methods of recruitment were effective in targeting a range of age groups and in locating people likely to be active amateur or semiprofessional performers, regular concert or recorded music listeners, or music educators working in classrooms or instrumental studios. As discussed in Section 1.2, these targets focused mainly on those with principal interests in classical music, a bias that is justified in some measure since so little is currently known about the long-term musical destinations of those who have taken

TABLE 1.1 Age Distribution of Participants Across All Phases of Data Collection

AGE RANGE	NUMBER OF RESPONDENTS			SOURCES (SEE EXPLANATIONS BELOW)			
	PHASE 1 [UK1–72]	PHASE 2 [UKP73–81]	PHASE 3 [IA1–25 & IS1–28]	PHASE 1 ONLY			WWW/E-MAIL
				BBC	MT	ISM	
<18	0	1	26	0	0	0	27
19–25	6	2	6	1	1	0	12
26–35	9	1	14	0	0	0	24
36–45	8	2	2	0	3	1	8
46–55	15	3	1	7	2	1	8
56–65	21	0	1	3	6	6	6
66–75	8	0	1	5	2	1	0
75+	5	0	0	2	1	1	1
No age given	0	0	2	0	0	0	2
Total:	**72**	**9**	**53**				

SOURCES: BBC = *British Broadcasting Corporation (BBC) Music Magazine*; MT = *Music Teacher* magazine; ISM = *Incorporated Society of Musicians (ISM) Journal*; www/e-mail = University of Sheffield website survey/personal e-mail and participant networks

this "conventional" route through UK music education. For the older partici-pants particularly, the dominance of classical music in the curriculum meant that professional magazines relating to music education and engagement as classical listeners were sources most likely to reach those for whom music education had had a lasting impact. Attempts to reach a more general popu-lation, including those for whom musical learning had not been significant in the longer term, proved more difficult, and other research in this area (Lamont, 2011) has concluded likewise that locating respondents able to talk about an absence of influential music education is problematic, and this remains a challenge for future research.

To balance this classical music focus to some degree, a targeted phase of data collection took place from May to July 2010, in which additional partici-pants were recruited through the contact networks of friends and colleagues working in popular music (see Phase 2 column in Table 1.1). Several pop music lecturers and band members circulated the online survey link to stu-dents and musicians of their acquaintance, resulting in a focused sample of nine respondents who were studying or working in popular music as ama-teurs or semiprofessionals. These responses have been numbered UKP73–81, following on from the UK Phase 1 data, with the P indicating their status as popular musicians and thus their distinctive contribution to the evidence and discussion. A further three respondents were identified from the Phase 1 data as being popular musicians and have been coded similarly—UKP14, UKP30, and UKP41—giving a total of twelve popular musicians. Recruiting in sub-stantial numbers amongst this population proved to be a further challenge: those working within popular music advised against targeting pop-related magazines, judging these to be read mainly by younger fans rather than active adult pop musicians who would have the long-term perspective on their music education that I was seeking. An additional number of incomplete re-sponses were discarded, and this greater trend towards non-completion among this group raises questions about whether the written form of data collection was appropriate for all types of respondents. These methodological implications—and the scope for extending this research into a wider popula-tion—will be discussed further in an evaluation of the study in Chapter 7.

The project also sought to include an international dimension, and while it proved too great an undertaking to replicate the study in full outside the UK (see Section 1.2), a smaller-scale survey in Italy helped to illuminate the distinctive characteristics of musical learning in another country and there-fore to question some of the assumptions inherent in the UK data and its analysis. Italian respondents were recruited through visits to music educa-tors at the Universities of Bologna and Padova, who distributed the survey to

TABLE 1.2 Stimulus Questions for Life History Responses

1. What kind of music was going on in your home as a child? How influential do you think this was in your development?
2. What are your memories of school music? (These might include people, activities, opportunities . . .)
3. Who has been influential on your musical behaviour at various stages of your life?
4. What have been the highlights of your musical life history so far?
5. Do you have any regrets about missed opportunities in music?

---

their students and colleagues; by this method the survey also reached a class-room teacher, who elicited responses from students aged 14 to 19 in her school. The sample was further increased through the networks of Italian students and academics known to me in the UK, who sent the survey to friends and relatives at home. In total, 53 Italian responses were received, translated in full, and analysed following the same procedure as for the UK data. The Italian respondents were allocated a participant code: IA1–25 for the adults and IS1–28 for the school students (see Phase 3 column in Table 1.1). In addition to this Italian focus, the Phase 1 group included four participants of other nationalities who had been educated outside the UK before pursuing careers or higher education in Britain. Since the number of responses of this kind was too small to form a representative group, they have been integrated with the Phase 1 analysis, but their responses have been coded as "outside-UK" [OUK] so that their different perspectives are evident in the discussion.

All respondents were asked to provide brief details of their age, musical education, and current activities and then to respond to the stimulus questions shown in Table 1.2. Some writers addressed these questions systematically, while others provided a freeform narrative that focused in more or less depth on each area. The transcribed responses were broadly categorised into the areas of home, school, and adult involvement. As the data set grew, these categories were subdivided, and the following six fields of influence and opportunity emerged as central to the narratives:

- Home influences and opportunities—including parent/sibling activities and attitudes, extended family, resources in the home, and family cultural activities such as concert-going and church attendance
- Education influences and opportunities—including primary, secondary, and higher education; organised youth ensembles (such as county orchestras); and instrumental lessons

- Self-directed learning in childhood—self-taught instrumental learning, organising ensembles, composing outside school
- Adult learning and/or performing—including taking up or resuming instrumental learning, academic study of music, summer schools, membership of ensembles, involvement in church music, making music with friends, and reflecting on skill levels and opportunities
- Experiences as a parent and/or teacher—learning from own teachers' practice, motivation to provide opportunities for young people, supporting own children
- Broader social/cultural influences in adulthood—concert-going, recorded music listening, and supporting local musical opportunities

Within these categories, the narratives were coded in more detail to produce individual outlines, showing the influences and events mentioned by each respondent (see example in Table 1.3). The coded responses were then compiled to give percentage calculations of the most widely reported influences. From these numerical overviews, the strongest themes across all the responses could be derived, and the qualitative data were then reintroduced to shed light on the reported experiences and to suggest reasons for the prominence and absence of particular themes.

In coding and interpreting the data, care was taken not to add inferences to the narratives, since the aim was to capture the respondents' interpretation of their life histories, not to impose the researcher's. It could reasonably have been inferred, for instance, that those respondents who mentioned having piano lessons also had a piano in the home, but this fact was noted only when it was described as a significant feature of childhood life. The omission of a particular influence—even a potentially substantial one such as listening in the home or primary school education—was not necessarily an indication of its absence in participants' lives, but rather its relative unimportance in the life narrative they were offering for the purposes of the research. Caution is therefore needed in interpreting the quantitative data derived from the written narratives, since omissions may assume undue significance when removed from the context of the qualitative responses. The inclusion of quantitative coding in the analysis process was intended to illuminate general trends in the data, following David Silverman's recommendation that "simple counting techniques, theoretically derived and ideally based on participants' own categories, can offer a means to survey the whole corpus of data ordinarily lost in intensive, qualitative research" (Silverman, 2001, p. 37). However, this remains principally a qualitative study, in which the distinctiveness of individual responses is central to understanding the

TABLE 1.3 An Example of Coded Data

UK3: AGED 52, LEFT SCHOOL 1972. MA STUDENT, PIANO TEACHER, SINGER IN CHOIR.

CONTEXT		EVENTS
Home influences and opportunities	Parents' musical tastes	Father listening
	Parents' musical attitudes	Support for lessons/practice
		Parents recognising musical potential
	Resources in the home	Instruments in the home
		Radio/gramophone
Education influences and opportunities	Primary school	Trips to concerts
	Secondary school	Class lessons
		Performing opportunities
		School choir: belonging
		Inspiring teachers
		Off-putting teachers
		Studying for exams
		Judging skills as superior to peers
		Making decisions about musical future
Self-directed learning in childhood	Playing/performing	Self-taught instrumental playing
Adult learning and/or performing	Learning in adulthood	Continuing/resuming lessons
		Performance qualifications
		Academic study of music

relative influence of home, school, and independent learning across different generations and circumstances.

Towards the end of the Phase 1 data collection, all participants who had expressed an interest in hearing about the outcomes of the research were sent a summary of the initial analysis and invited to comment on my interim analysis and conclusions. (This summary is provided online as an accessible overview of the initial findings.) A few respondents were prompted by the summary to provide additional recollections of their own experience, which were then added to their original response. Further consultation with some respondents took place as the book neared completion, as those who had indicated a keen interest were invited to read drafts of chapters, and permission was sought to use some responses in their entirety as "Interludes" within

Box 1.3.1

"I've really enjoyed writing this. It's Monday, my 'housework' day, so perhaps it's just been an avoidance technique! I have realised how important my family and teachers have been in my life. They are nearly all dead now and I hope they all realised how much they meant." [UK33, aged 56]

"I hope some of this is useful to you. I feel better for having written it! I think I sound more bitter and regretful than I actually am—it is only recently that any of this has really occurred to me." [UK37, aged 42]

the book (see Section 1.6 for further explanation). These stages of consulting with participants were felt to be important on ethical grounds and also enriched the research through providing additional insight and validation.

As part of the data collection, some respondents had spontaneously commented on the process of contributing their life history to the project, reporting the sometimes cathartic insights of their storytelling (see Box 1.3.1). Their reactions illustrate the therapeutic value of storytelling, whereby "we increase our working knowledge of ourselves because we discover deeper meaning in our lives through the process of reflecting [on] events, experiences and feelings" (Atkinson, 1998, p. 1). Relating musical life histories therefore appears to be a purposeful activity for participants, allowing them to make sense of the influential people and formative experiences that have contributed to their present engagement in music. Such interpretations are at the heart of this project, which seeks to determine not just the characteristics of supportive home and effective educational contexts for music, but also the factors that bring them to the forefront of young people's consciousness, such that music becomes a significant part of their future lives.

1.4 Existing Research on Musical Life Histories

The musical lives that are most often represented in the research literature, as well as in popular biographies, are those of professional musicians—composers, conductors, and performers who have achieved notable success in their chosen genre. These lives are scrutinised for early indicators of musical promise and enter popular discourse as evidence for musical "genius" or "talent"—Mozart's impeccable recall of Allegri's *Miserere* after one hearing, or Arthur Rubenstein's claim to have been able to play the piano before he could speak becoming the measure of what it means to be "musically gifted" (cf. Howe, Davidson, & Sloboda, 1998). Gift and talent are problematic terms in music, since they bring with them the notion that while some children will be intrinsically musical, others will lack the ability to acquire such skills or interests. While children can certainly lack the encouragement, inclination, or persistence to achieve a high level of performance skill, research in musical development increasingly asserts that the potential to do so is present in the vast majority of the population, as demonstrated through the human capacity to make sense of music in infancy (Trehub, 2006) and even before birth (Parncutt, 2006). To assume otherwise risks creating a hierarchy of musical provision, where the indicators of interest and ability in some children are supported and reinforced, whilst those of children viewed as "unmusical" go unnoticed (Sloboda, 2005, p. 300). If the notion of musical talent "in no way accounts for the very wide range of adult musical accomplishment that exists in industrialized societies" (Sloboda, 2005, p. 301), alternative explanations for variations in musical aptitude must be sought in the exposure to musical opportunity and learning that is made available to young people.

Whilst the emphasis on documenting the lives of successful or famous musicians risks distorting perceptions of what it means to be musical, there are nonetheless some interesting insights to be gained from the interpretations of these musical trajectories, which might in turn shed light on a more generalist experience of musical learning. Several recent collections of interviews offer a useful starting point: Elizabeth Haddon's (2005) *Making Music in Britain*, in which the author was prompted by reading a performer's concert programme biography into investigating the journeys that lie behind a list of musical achievements; Rineke Smilde's (2009a) *Musicians as Lifelong Learners*, which portrays the lives of professional musicians mainly working in the Netherlands with reference to their experiences in higher education (with the interviews reproduced in a companion volume; Smilde, 2009b); and two books on jazz musicians by Chris Horne (2004) and W. Royal Stokes (2005), exploring the British and American jazz scenes, respectively, through the life stories of prominent performers. Of these, Smilde's is the most systematic study, eliciting "learning biographies" from a focused group of 32 professional musicians and considering the implications of their career paths and experiences for policy and practice in musical training. Smilde notes that "contrary to some of the 'myths' about musicians", not all of her respondents were sure of their musical pathway from childhood: "a few were aware of their passion from an early age, others not at all" (2009a, p. 126). However, many of the musicians had improvised spontaneously in childhood (p. 146) or had experienced critical incidents such as hearing a particular recording or giving a memorable performance, findings consistent with Sloboda and Howe's (1991) investigations of the formative years of advanced performers.

Although Smilde's account shows no "standard biography" for the route into professional musicianship, it does suggest a sense of the separateness of future professionals from mainstream music education: school music was recalled mainly as being "hopeless and demotivating" (ibid., p. 211), the exceptions occurring when singing and performing events left more positive impressions. She also reports frequent examples of informal learning, showing that young musicians' independent responses to opportunity are as important as the provision of direct tuition. If school music therefore has little to offer those who will attain professional success in music, two clear questions are raised: (1) Is this a satisfactory admission to be made of mainstream music provision? and (2) What are the alternative purposes served by school music education? This book will provide new evidence to address both of these questions by evaluating the aims and impact of musical provision for all as demonstrated in the life histories.

Haddon (2005) also reflects on the formative musical experiences of her interviewees, who are a more diverse group of British performers, educators, and composers, and finds that while the family and school contexts of her interviewees varied through age and circumstance, there were similarities in the positive attitudes towards music shown by influential adults:

> A common factor is having been brought up in an environment where music was present and was taken seriously, although the family might not necessarily be musicians. Somehow, often as a result of a particular experience, music becomes a passion, even an obsession, and regardless of what kind of formal tuition is received, meaningful experiences are sought and gained. (Haddon, 2005, p. 3)

Learning, rather than teaching, is thus highlighted as the critical factor, providing further evidence for the argument that some degree of self-education and motivation is vital for success in all kinds of music. Formal education alone is generally insufficient in advanced musical development: "Using a variety of learning methods and seeking the support and advice of other musicians is a successful strategy which all the musicians have adopted" (ibid., p. 3). Although "informal learning" has come only recently to the attention of music education researchers (e.g., Folkestad, 2006; Green, 2008), its presence as a motivating force in the lives of successful musicians is apparent in many of Haddon's interviews: examples include folk musician Kathryn Tickell neglecting her classical violin practice in favour of trying "to pick out a Northumbrian traditional tune because I knew it inside my head and that's what I really wanted to play" (Haddon, 2005, p. 211), and composer Howard Goodall sitting with a school friend and writing his first pieces of music, later reflecting that "I'm not sure I really knew what it all sounded like, but I loved the idea of making music on the lines" (ibid., p. 73). In both of these cases, and in others in the book, these young musicians had adult role models around them, and their early forays into a creative musical world were recognised and encouraged.

Like Smilde's (2009a, 2009b) interviewees, many of Haddon's report an unpredictability in their musical careers rather than a strongly ambitious drive: composer and broadcaster Antony Hopkins claims that "I failed at everything I set out to do but have succeeded wildly at things I'd never thought I would do" (ibid., p. 99). Haddon concludes that "the love of music and the need to be involved with it are the most powerful motivators of all" (p. 9): for those who go on to become professional musicians, motivation and opportunity tend to be in ready supply, and there is limited evidence that school music alone could provide the stimulus for a "first-generation" musician to embark upon a professional career. Nonetheless, the provision of opportunity and the recognition of potential in childhood both appear to be vital to lifelong engagement in music, at whatever level of public success: this book will include many examples of these elements being successfully supported in schools—and sadly some others where this has not been the case.

Informal and self-directed learning strategies are even more evident in the biographies of jazz musicians, particularly in "the teenage years of rapid musical absorption" (Horne, 2004, p. 2). Since many of the most prominent jazz musicians in the UK and US today grew up in the decades when the classical genre dominated school music, their own musical learning was by definition on the edge of the mainstream; even in the more musically diverse curriculum of recent decades, jazz remains somewhat marginalised (Riley & Laing, 2006). Many of Horne's interviewees, however, felt that they had benefited from a classical education, acquiring their musical skills within the instrumental and extracurricular opportunities available through school and college while simultaneously pursuing their own listening and playing, often encouraged by influential adults. Jazz pianist Steve Melling confirms that "having a classical grounding with lots of theory in it too, which I had, was invaluable in making sense of jazz" (Horne, 2004, p. 167). Other jazz musicians interviewed by Horne (2004) and Stokes (2005) reflect on the enormous amount learned through listening, exploring their instrument, and the chance encounters with professional musicians that could be the start of a successful career. Bassist and arranger Geoff Gascoyne suggests that "in some ways, jazz education is a bit of a contradiction" (Horne, 2004, p. 119), but like many of his fellow interviewees he is committed to guiding and supporting young jazz musicians. Tim Garland, saxophonist and composer, argues that providing access to live music is one of the most compelling routes into learning jazz: "if people can see a saxophone player playing, six feet in front of them, for the first time ever, they can feel the air coming out of the horn, it's incredible and always worth doing" (ibid., p. 109).

It is striking in these accounts that the process of learning jazz is closely connected to the "real" performing world of gigs, improvising sessions, and recordings: musical education in this sphere is genuinely part of the "art world" (Becker, 1982) and has an authenticity that can sometimes be lost in the transference of musical practices into educational settings. Lucy Green (2002) provides further evidence for the self-directed, peer-supported learning of popular musicians and has begun to explore the applicability of such approaches for school music, devising and evaluating lessons based on the strategy of "purposive listening" (Green, 2008) that underpins the learning of many pop and jazz musicians. The life history accounts from popular musicians included in this book show similar tendencies towards a self-motivated musical education rooted in the available classical training and strongly supplemented with independent listening and playing.

This review of existing research has not aimed to be comprehensive: other studies of lifespan development (e.g., Gembris, 2006; Manturzewska, 1990) will be discussed alongside the empirical data throughout the book. I end here with a study that comes closest to exploring "ordinary" musical lives—the Music in Daily Life Project, in which the musical tastes and activities of 41 American citizens are documented through unstructured interviews exploring the question "What is music about for you?" (Crafts, Cavicchi, Keil, & the Music in Daily Life Project, 1993). Writing a few years before Tia DeNora's (2000) study of *Music in Everyday Life*, which demonstrated the sophistication of the choices and musical judgements made in everyday music listening, Crafts et al. express concern about the "passive consumerism" revealed by many of their participants: "looked at as a social phenomenon, aren't all these headphoned people alienated, enjoying mediated 'my music' at the expense of a live and more spontaneous 'our music'?" (ibid., p. 3). Since the focus of their project was on recorded music listening, mentions of school and instrumental learning are infrequent; where they do occur they reinforce themes that will become familiar throughout this book, of influential adults, chance opportunities for performance, and memorable incidents that stimulate or underpin musical learning. Crafts et al. aimed to contribute to "the still small shelf of books where people not ordinarily heard from get to have their say at last", and in doing so to challenge the assumptions of musical experts and authorities about "who they are writing for and why" (p. 3). This book serves a similar purpose for music education, by highlighting the many ways in which musical learning is experienced in different contexts throughout the lifespan, and bringing into question the centrality of formal, institutional education in shaping the musical lives of the majority of the population.

1.5 Global Perspectives on Music Education

For reasons already outlined (Section 1.2), the majority of the life histories upon which this book draws are those of British citizens, whose experience has inevitably been shaped by the changing educational policies and practice of the UK, and by the social and cultural specificities of their childhood and adult years. To set these life histories and their analysis in context, this section offers a brief literature review of international differences in approaches to music education, so highlighting the aims and intentions that transcend the practices of different countries and raising questions relevant to music educators and researchers everywhere.

When attempting a comparison of global practices in music education, it is immediately striking that the discourse of international researchers is similar, even when the practice across their countries is notably different. Steven Kelly's (2009) assertion that "learning music's value requires active experience through music participation" (p. 42) would support the British emphasis on learning through composing (Paynter & Mills, 2008), as well as Kelly's own American perspective, which places ensemble performance at the heart of the curriculum. The long-established US system of band and choral programmes has a stability that the history of British music education has arguably lacked (see Section 2.1; also Pitts, 2000), being closely linked to the popularity of wind bands in late-19th-century America (Kirchhoff, 1988), and offering students the opportunity to acquire and display performance skills in ways that are readily understood and valued by parents and the wider community. Prominent North American writers on music education have, however, expressed serious doubts about the aims and effectiveness of these programmes, suggesting that they inhibit creativity in the music curriculum and risk making students teacher-dependent in their opportunities for musical expression: "The focus on technical proficiency, necessary when public performance is perceived to be the be-all and end-all of the endeavor, throws the delicate balance between technique and understanding out of kilter, leaving many if not most students with skills unusable after high school and meager musical sensitivity to the nature of the art in which they have been engaged so mechanically" (Reimer, 1989, p. 183). Some writers have focused on guiding band programme directors "to construct a coherent, sequential, yet multifaceted experience for students" (Morrison, 2008, p. 168), while others have proposed a new emphasis on music technology (Webster, 2007) and composing (Hickey, 2003), although with reportedly variable success in persuading teachers of the value and practicalities of new methods (Strand, 2006).

International differences in music education go beyond curriculum content and classroom practice, being affected also by teachers' roles and attitudes and the extent of governmental influence through curriculum prescription and inspection systems (for a useful overview of national differences and priorities see Campbell, 2008, pp. 60–85). Alexandra Kertz-Welzel (2004) offers a provocative comparison of how American pedagogy compares to the German concept of *Didaktik*, defined as "the science and art of teaching music in terms of determining goals, contents and methods" (p. 277). Kertz-Welzel asserts that whilst American teachers have a clearly defined performance-based curriculum and can therefore become expert in specific aspects of music pedagogy, the German music curriculum, which is determined at school level and does not follow a standard approach or textbook, requires "a broader perspective rather than adherence to a methodology" (p. 282). Although this portrayal suggests a more reflective practitioner culture where the curriculum is less strongly defined, Kertz-Welzel acknowledges that American philosophical writing on music education encourages lines of thought that are close to *Didaktik*, theorising about the role of musical learning in society and questioning the traditional methods of achieving these ends (see, e.g., Elliott, 1995).

A similar dichotomy can be observed in British scholarship and practice, where explicitly philosophical theorising about music education is relatively rare—with the obvious exception of Keith Swanwick's work (e.g., 1979; 1999)—and research tends to focus on the reflective experience of varied classroom approaches and their implications. Such debates are in themselves a philosophical act, embracing what Estelle Jorgensen calls "the philosopher's crucial role in clarifying ideas and practices, interrogating commonplaces, and suggesting applications to practice" (Jorgensen, 2003a, p. 212), but the framing of these ideas as theories or systems of music education is less commonplace among British researchers than their North American counterparts (cf. Elliott, 1995; Reimer, 2003). Before drawing worrying conclusions about the disjunction between policy, practice, and research, we might reflect that where curriculum structures seem histori-cally fixed and relatively uncontested (as in America and Australia), philo-sophical writing can assume a common understanding of what music education means and therefore reach more complex theoretical planes; where researchers must start by engaging with a shifting definition of what music education aims to include and achieve (as in Britain and Germany), their writing is likely to be more exploratory and grounded in varied practice rather than agreed policy. Both approaches have value in reflecting and chal-lenging the state of music education, but their unspoken differences in out-look can be a further barrier to effective global debate.

This distinction between the ideals of philosophical writings, the re-quirements of national policy documents, and the reality of classroom life means that local understanding within a global perspective is necessary for effective music education research. Recent edited books by multiple na-tional authors (e.g., Hargreaves & North, 2001) have helped to advance in-ternational awareness among researchers, with Gordon Cox and Robin Stevens' (2010) collection offering an additional historical dimension intended to "enrich our understanding of the ways in which music can act as a powerful educational force and also question our taken-for-granted pedagogies and our assumptions about the place of music in compulsory schooling" (p. 1). Göran Folkestad extends the challenge of understanding global musical experience to include the "process of interaction between the participants' musical experience and competence, their cultural practice, the tools, the instruments, and the instructions" (Folkestad, 2005, p. 284)—recognising, in other words, that comparisons of school curricula offer only a partial picture of the arts in children's lives (see Boynton & Kok, 2006; Bresler & Thompson, 2002). Lucy Green's (2011) edited collection begins to explore these broadly defined musical identities, providing snapshots of musical learning in locations as diverse as an Aboriginal homelands school in the Northern Territory of Australia (Marsh, 2011) and the Philharmonic Society Wind Bands of Corfu (Dionyssiou, 2011). The case studies of Green's book illustrate the strong influence of national context on music education practices, showing that the understanding of any education system (partic-ularly one that is unfamiliar) needs to include awareness of its interactions with parenting styles, attitudes to the arts, provision for community music-making, and so on.

As this life history study will show, interpretations of the effects and impact of musical education need to take account of cultural context and family circumstances, not to mention the wide variation between schools, teachers, and the pupils themselves. Perhaps it is not surprising, therefore, that music education researchers most often look to their own locality to understand musical teaching and learning, just as teachers too "must know their own systems and standards, but they can also be enlightened, refreshed, and inspired by knowing approaches and practices to music making and teaching beyond their own perspective" (Campbell, 2008, p. 61).

1.6 Structures and Voices in This Book

Within the contexts outlined in this chapter, this book aims to re-evaluate the purposes and effects of musical learning across generations and musical traditions. It will consider respondents' retrospective understanding of what they were taught and why, and interrogate the values and skills that were acquired as a result of experiences in classrooms, homes, and beyond. It will imagine how today's music education, in the UK and beyond, might affect the current generation, and will question the extent to which music educators can prepare their students for the musical, technological, and cultural plurality they will encounter in their lives. Finally, it will consider the place of music education in the wider context of a lifetime of musical experience, examining the roles of teachers, parents, and others in enabling students to become musically active, enquiring, and critical, all qualities essential to the flourishing of music in schools, homes, and wider society.

One of the great pleasures of this project has been reading the diverse and fascinating life history accounts submitted by respondents. So that readers can experience the richness of these narratives, twelve selected accounts are included here as "Interludes" between chapters, chosen to represent a range of ages, educational and home experiences, and levels of lifelong musical activity. These life histories were edited in consultation with their authors, and references to specific schools, teachers, and friends were anonymised for publication. Other details of local colour, such as mentions of regional concert halls or ensembles, have been retained, with explanatory footnotes added where necessary. The writers were asked for permission to publish their accounts, to which their responses were entirely positive; the majority chose to appear under their own names, but pseudonyms were chosen in consultation with the writers where this was their preferred option. Elsewhere in the chapters, quotes from the full sample of submitted life histories have been referred to by their participant code, which although slightly impersonal saves the confusion of using over one hundred pseudonyms. Sidebars are used from time to time to create space for longer quotes that illustrate the experiences being discussed in each chapter. On the companion website, the quotes featured in the book are presented alongside details of the respondents' past and current involvement in music so that their reflections are linked more closely with their biography. In these various ways, the voices of the respondents are strongly present in the book, in keeping with the spirit and aims of life history research.

After the first two interludes, the discussion begins in Chapter 2 with an overview of the UK data, analysed by generation in order to identify key themes that are investigated more closely in the subsequent chapters. Chapter 3 considers "locations for learning"—home, school, and the amorphous areas in between—and includes a focus on the Italian respondents, whose experiences highlight different possibilities in the balance between teacher and parent influence in musical decision making. These themes are explored further in Chapter 4, where the characteristics of significant musical mentors and role models are examined. Chapter 5 analyses the life history accounts by outcome, tracing the journeys and experiences of adult listeners, teachers, and performers and exploring the effects of learning throughout the lifespan. The final chapters consider the implications of the life history narratives for researchers and practitioners: Chapter 6 evaluates the extent to which the respondents' experiences fulfil the claims made by 20th-century writers for the value and impact of music education, and Chapter 7 reflects on the usefulness of the life history approach to research and the messages it has for those seeking to provide musical foundations for the next generation of young people.

Interlude A: MW [UK36]
Aged 81, left school 1947

Childhood piano lessons, an influential mother, and a lifelong love of classical music

I was a child who would not keep still it seems. My mother, who was probably a Grade 2 pianist and largely self taught, decided I should have piano lessons to keep me still for a couple of ten minute sessions each day. My gem of a teacher (trained with Kathleen Ferrier of Blackburn) said she had left it two years too late. I was 7 years old. She eventually confided that if I attained Grade 5 by 11 years of age, then it was up to me to go for gold and that I would have a lifelong interest. I achieved Grade 5 by age 11 and went on to obtain Grade 8 by the late teens after distractions of schooling and girls along the way. Some of the grades were good. After national service, marriage and professional exams, and two children I started having lessons again from my same teacher who indicated that I could have passed the diplomas if I practised a lot more. I think she meant the teacher's diplomas and not the performer's. Until a few years ago there were several of her diploma pupils dotted about the town.

My memories of school music are that there was only one period per week. However, the music master was a vocalist and so we all sang. Later, he retired and the Master appointed was FRCO[1]. Bliss! I remember going into the dedicated music room and while he waited for us all to settle, he just casually played Chopin's black key study. That I still remember tells you that it influenced me. I took an interest in the school organ and had a few lessons

---

[1] Fellow of the Royal College of Organists: an advanced diploma in organ playing

there and at our church. We were encouraged at school to do extra curricular music and other activities as it was a very successful independent grammar school[2]. However, it was war time and there were many restrictions that would not be tolerated these days. Our grandson recently left that same school and we were able to attend concerts. I was more than impressed by the standard, the range and the depth of achievement. Suffice it to say that this school recently gave a full evening concert of all ages, talents and disciplines at the Bridgewater Hall[3] for the second time. The opportunities are virtually limitless for those who want to take advantage of them now. I was also privileged to attend lunch time events while at school with a good friend and a maths master, when they played Beethoven transcriptions of his symphonies on two pianos. This friend gained his FRCO, and became a tutor in harmony and associated subjects at the Royal Northern College of Music.[4] He retired to Aldeburgh[5] where he was honorary organist. We have kept in touch all these years and he has been a great encouragement to me without perhaps being aware of this. I am still in touch with his widow.

The highlights of musical experience are difficult to detail. I never go a day without music of some sort. Always classical, but I can enjoy Kenny Ball. At least it is structured music. I find it frustrating that there is never sufficient time to practise even now—at my age I will never get to where I always wanted to be. When the Theatre in the Forest in Grizedale was in existence, I was lucky to have conversations with the likes of John Lill and John Ogdon and Hepzibah Menuhin and many others. They all want a drink at the bar afterwards! John Lill was quite happy to talk to two or three of us when we described ourselves as failed pianists. Without hesitation he said that it did not matter. Being involved with music was all that mattered. That sums it all up I think. (How you get to that stage is perhaps the key.) Had it not been for my mother I may have never had such an enjoyable and fulfilling experience in my life.

My current involvement in music is for private amusement at the piano. I have a season ticket for the Bridgewater Hall for the Hallé[6] Thursday series concerts and enjoy the visiting concert pianists and the great acoustics. I

---

[2] A fee-paying, selective high school
[3] A large concert hall in Manchester, in the North West of England
[4] A music conservatoire in Manchester, which trains performers, composers, and conductors at undergraduate and postgraduate level. See http://www.rncm.ac.uk
[5] A coastal town in Suffolk, South East England, best known as the home of the Snape Maltings Concert Hall, and the Aldeburgh Festival, founded by composer Benjamin Britten and tenor Peter Pears. See http://www.aldeburgh.co.uk
[6] The resident orchestra of the Bridgewater Hall, Manchester

have three or four friends who are musically involved with their communities and we enjoy many musical conversations. I hope to work on Schubert's piano duets with one of them.

It seems to me that it all depends on an early start, aptitude, parental encouragement, personal interest, a very good teacher with insight, and also in my case, a tolerant wife. There is no other talent in my immediate family of wife and two children although my brother would have progressed had he persevered. However, one of my five grandchildren has an interest but no decent piano. He enjoys playing my 100-year-old Steinway.

From an early age therefore I have been involved in classical music just for personal enjoyment. All beginning with my mother trying to keep me still for a few minutes every day. I do not doubt that there was a talent on her side of the family which was never given a chance. My maternal grandfather was a church organist and a poor violinist, I was told. I suspect it is all in the genes to start with.

Interlude B: Piers Spencer [UK47]
Aged 62, left school 1963

Influential parents, supportive school environment with elements of self-directed learning; now retired from music teaching and lecturing career

Each of my parents fitted into the two different definitions of the word 'musical' given in most dictionaries: 'fond of' and 'skilled in' music. Of the two, my mother had a more acute ear and greater natural ability as a pianist. My father was a rather ham-fisted piano player, yet of my parents, it was my father who, it seemed, loved music more. My mother had a 'take-it-or-leave-it' attitude to music; she never worked at developing her natural musical talent and had a limited range of 'classical' pieces in her repertoire. It was my father who, to me, seemed really passionate about music and who was also intellectually fascinated by musical ideas. His tastes ranged widely—he liked jazz and classical music equally. I remember him (in 1955) bringing home a 78 record of Bill Haley's 'Rock around the Clock', of which both my mother and I (a rather priggish 10-year-old) heartily disapproved. Although I was fortunate to inherit my mother's musical genes (playing by ear and doing aural tests have never been a problem for me), I feel that it was my father who was culturally the greater influence. From him, I learnt to look for musicality in the most unexpected of places, to keep an open mind and an open ear and not to take received opinion on trust.

At primary school, one teacher took an interest in me and took me and a couple of other musically inclined children to Robert Mayer concerts[1] on

---

[1] Sir Robert Mayer, a businessman and keen amateur musician, founded a series of public concerts for children in London in 1923. With the support of his wife, Dorothy, a professional soprano, the series expanded to be a national network of concerts, attracting the most prestigious performers of the time, including Sir Adrian Boult, who conducted the first concert (see Sadie, 1979).

Saturdays. I regret never being 'chosen' to sing in the choir at primary school. I think it was something to do with my being in a remedial class for extra arithmetic or something! Secondary school, a grammar school, was a different affair. You were conscripted into the choir if you could sing in tune! I remember going to the first rehearsal—we were doing Handel's *Messiah* and I remember the thrill of joining in 'And the glory of the Lord'—one of my most memorable experiences. I sang in the choir until I was 14 and my voice broke, after that I did not sing again until I went up to conservatoire.

In truth, apart from choral singing, music was not a strong aspect of my academic grammar school. The class music lessons were dull and, besides, pupils in the top two streams (I was in the 'B' stream) dropped music (as a timetabled subject) after what is now called Year 7. I did not do music O Level and did the A Level by myself, with minimal coaching. However, perhaps unusually for the late 1950s/early 1960s, self-taught jazz, skiffle and rock groups were 'allowed' (I think the word 'encouraged' is too strong) to rehearse and perform at the school. I led a jazz band in my final two years at the school and as result, basked in the glowing approval of my peers!

My first piano teacher taught me from the age of 7-14. She got me going, took an interest in me and also encouraged me to compose. At the age of 15 I went to a Saturday music school (the Guildhall School of Music Junior Scheme)[2] where I had a teacher who was a young postgraduate student who really took my technique apart and built it up again. I am probably more grateful to him than to any other instrumental teacher I had for his determined, rigorous approach; although I never felt that he really rated me [highly] as a player. He also knew that I liked composing and encouraged me to bring pieces along to his lessons. At conservatoire I had two piano teachers—one who was less concerned with technique but was musically inspirational. Sadly, he left just before my final year and I switched to another who was, like my 'Junior Scheme' teacher, more concerned about technique. But by then, I knew I was never going to make it as a performer and decided to train as a teacher. I am grateful to all my instrumental teachers for the different approaches they brought to my musical learning.

Where learning about musical history and analysis was concerned, the chief lesson that I learnt about teaching was that the most inspirational teachers are those that convey their own passion and enjoyment of music. In

---

[2] The Guildhall School of Music and Drama (http://gsmd.ac.uk/) is a London conservatoire, which, in addition to training performers, composers and actors at degree level, offers specialist tuition to young people, chosen by competitive audition.

education, nothing succeeds more powerfully than commitment. Curiously, it has been mine and other people's experience that the PGCE[3] year was not simply a training in how to teach, but also a continuation of my musical education. One of the PGCE lecturers was interested in World Music, another in the Beatles. They chimed in with my own attitude of openness to musicality of all kinds that I had got from my father. My first Head of Music when I was a young teacher—a brilliant conductor (although a poor class music teacher)—taught me (by his example) how to rehearse a group.

My own pupils and students were a major influence, especially when I was a teacher working in schools. I started teaching in 1967, at the height of the progressive rock era. My pupils introduced me to groups such as Pink Floyd, Soft Machine and the Mothers of Invention. Later in the 1970s, working in an inner London school, my pupils introduced me to reggae. A highlight of my career was my success (against the odds) as a class music teacher—this is an area which seems little valued by parents or school authorities, but I feel that I made headway in giving children more interesting things to do in day-to-day class music lessons than I myself experienced as a pupil. I also enjoyed writing small works for the school choir in the early years of my teaching career, including a stage musical. I regret that I stopped composing. I bitterly regret this now. I could blame the lack of guidance that was available in those days, but mostly I blame myself, my indolence, my lack of self-belief and inability to listen to myself and where my natural creative impulses lay.

I have been professionally involved in music education throughout my adult life, as a teacher, as a teacher trainer and as a researcher. I am also a pianist who has played classical music and jazz and worked as an accompanist. Among my many interests is improvisation. Besides jazz, I have also improvised accompaniments to silent movies. Other highlights have included getting my ARCM[4], in 1965, a piano recital diploma for which I worked very hard. Also working for my PhD and my small batch of research publications, which, I feel, have had a positive influence on the development of musical education since the 1980s. Now I am retired, a lot of my time is spent on catching up with listening that I did not have time to do during a busy 40-year career as a teacher and as a lecturer. At the age of 62 I find my enjoyment of music of all kinds both as a listener and performer is undimmed.

---

[3] Postgraduate Certificate of Education: a one-year teacher training course undertaken after an undergraduate degree
[4] Associate of the Royal College of Music: an advanced performing diploma qualification

2 | Learning across Generations
MUSICAL CHILDHOODS IN 20TH-CENTURY BRITAIN

2.1 Lifelong Learning: A Reasonable Aim for Music Education?

P REPARING CHILDREN FOR a lifelong interest in music was once an explicit and central aim of music in British schools, undertaken for the
good of the individual pupil and wider society: "If by our manner of education we can cultivate and develop the inner nature of our citizens, we
will be raising up a nation full of vitality, striving after ideals [. . .] for the
art of music will give the means for self expression, and will provide a new
interest in life" (Yorke Trotter, 1914, p. 136). When the music educator and
writer Thomas Henry Yorke Trotter expressed these ideals in the first
decades of the 20th century, the expectations for musical involvement
beyond school were clearly defined: adults might become regular concert-
goers, discerning listeners to the increasingly available recordings of "great"
and "light" classical music, or perhaps members of the amateur choral
societies that flourished in the UK at this time. Music in schools held an
undisputed role as an arbiter of musical taste, and the predominant classroom activities of singing folksongs, learning "sol-fa" or staff notation,
and "appreciation" of the classical canon all assisted in preparing pupils to
respect and enjoy the musical opportunities available to them in the future
(Pitts, 2000).

Percy Scholes, an influential figure in the music appreciation movement,
reported the views of a London school head teacher of the 1930s, who aimed
to have his pupils "hum, whistle, and sing lovely tunes of their own accord

and to persuade mother to buy a gramophone record other than a jazz tune" (Scholes, 1935, p. 234). On into the 1950s, the view held that music teachers should "direct the child away from the lurid music and the banal lyrics to the better types of musical composition" (Niblett, 1955, p. 13), and it took several more decades before the active musical lives of teenagers outside schools were acknowledged as a positive influence on their musical development rather than one that needed to be countered or resisted in the classroom.

The certainty of early-20th-century educational intentions could not last, as definitions of music, education, and childhood were broadened and contested, and the dominant role claimed for school music in shaping musical taste and behaviour became increasingly illusory. The focus of music education turned to students' present experience, and writers emphasised the need to capture children's musical imagination through involvement in lively and expressive activities. Young people were to be engaged in music immediately, rather than trained for the promise of future enjoyment: as one report memorably stated, "Children do not hatch into adults after a secluded incubation at school. They are living their lives now" (Calouste Gulbenkian Foundation, 1982, p. 4). Music education in the closing decades of the 20th century can be seen as a struggle between those two goals of offering immediate engagement with music while laying foundations for continued development and interest after compulsory education. Such dual aims place enormous responsibility on teachers, who, as the life history accounts in this book will demonstrate, communicate as much to their students through their attitudes and priorities as through their curriculum choices.

Whether it is reasonable to judge the success of music education by its long-term impact is a question rarely addressed directly in the research literature: debate tends to focus mainly on identifying the skills and opportunities that are seen as essential to a comprehensive musical education, and discovering through practice and research how these can best be fostered. Least attention, at both research and policy level, is given to the formation of students' attitudes in relation to music, and yet it is perhaps in this respect that music education (indeed, education of all kinds) has its most lasting and significant influence, as teachers "seek to transmit to the young the personal and social attitudes, beliefs, practices, skills, expectations and dispositions to enable them to survive and flourish in the particular group of which they are a part" (Jorgensen, 2003b, p. 19). The acquisition of musical skills and the opportunities to use and develop them are closely intertwined with the formation of musical values and identity, these latter having arguably the most lasting effect on whether young people choose to continue their musical development beyond formal education. Such effects are not always predictable, however: a retrospective study of attitudes to singing in school found "more adults who sing now despite bad experiences at school than those who had good experiences at school and who now do not sing" (Turton & Durrant, 2002, p. 40). Recovery from an inadequate music education is clearly possible, given a high degree of self-motivation or a nurturing environment in the home or community, but regrets about lost years of musical learning can be retained into adulthood, limiting potential and ambition.

Encounters with music in school shape children's attitudes and belief systems as much as their skills, placing a heavy responsibility on teachers to enthuse and enable their pupils at all levels. Disinterested music students may, after all, occupy powerful positions later in life, as Wayne Bowman points out: "Where our most influential decision and policy makers have had no musical experience—or worse still, where experience in mediocre programmes has 'turned them off' rather than 'on' to musical experience—we can reasonably expect to reap only what we have permitted to be sown" (Bowman, 2001, p. 14). Even when such attitudes are not made visible through influential policy roles, the choices that adults make about supporting arts events, investing in their own children's musical education, or pursuing musical interests in adulthood all have an effect on the cultural fabric of society. Social attitudes to the arts—as manifest in aging audiences for classical music concerts, for example—are transformed for a variety of reasons, and changes in music education cannot be held solely responsible for generational shifts in musical consumption and behaviour. But the curriculum content and opportunities to which young people are exposed in school have a lasting effect on the extent to which music seems accessible, relevant, and desirable to them— and while a simple causality cannot be determined, the long-term impact of music education is worthy of more research attention than is customary.

The dual goals of immediate engagement in music and acquisition of sustainable skills and interest are of course highly compatible, and musical education at its best achieves both, laying secure foundations for lifelong interest and involvement. The chronological analysis of life history data that follows later in this chapter illustrates many moments of musical enlightenment and opportunity, as well as the disappointments of school years and their impact on later learning and engagement. The analysis enables a close evaluation of the long-term effects and outcomes of school music education, and of its place within the multiple influences of home, family, out-of-school music-making, and other locations for learning. Comparisons of the life stories across generations illustrate the slow change of aims and practices in British music education over the 20th century, resulting in widely varying experiences for respondents within and across generations. Although general trends in classroom practice are evident, the overlap of family culture and attitudes—changing at a similarly variable rate across the decades—results in a formative musical period that is nurturing and supportive for some young people but bewildering and discouraging for others.

2.2 Life Histories in Context: British Music Education in the 20th Century

To place the life histories that feature in this book in their broader historical context, a brief outline of British music education in the 20th century will be useful here, especially to international readers (for whom a glossary of terms is also provided at the end of the book). The life history accounts cover a period of immense educational change in relation to examination systems, school leaving ages, and approaches to teaching and learning, as well as wider social evolution in family life, conceptions of childhood, cultural diversity, and media technology. The values and aims for music education outlined in the previous section were situated within a school curriculum in which music was relatively marginalised: despite the persuasive rhetoric of prominent writers, throughout the 20th century music has typically occupied one hour a week in the compulsory timetable and has been pursued to school leavers' examination level by only a small minority of pupils. This fragile status has perhaps contributed to the impassioned defences of music in the curriculum that run throughout the 20th-century research literature, encouraging a vigorous debate of the value and purpose of music education that might perversely have risked highlighting the uncertainties about its universal relevance for children's aesthetic, emotional, and skill development.

Alongside this rhetoric, the content of the music curriculum has expanded throughout the 20th century as each generation has added to the priorities of its predecessors rather than re-evaluating more selectively: thus, the focus on singing and notation that was dominant in the 1920s broadened into "musical appreciation," involving the study of Western art music, initially through a growth in schools concerts, and then through the classroom use of gramophones and radios (Cox, 2002). The 1940s and 1950s saw an expansion in the provision of instrumental lessons and the flourishing of extracurricular music, so that directing school choirs and orchestras became a prominent feature of the secondary school music teacher's role (Rainbow & Cox, 2006). A period of greater uncertainty followed, as the 1960s and 1970s saw the introduction of experimental methods of teaching composing, fiercely opposed by some traditionalists who sought to defend the place of the classical canon in the classroom (Finney, 2011, p. 12). The resolution of these two positions was enforced in the 1980s by a new examination system, the General Certificate of Secondary Education (GCSE), which introduced a tripartite model of music education in which listening, performing, and composing played equal parts (Pitts, 2000). This was followed in the 1990s by the National Curriculum, which maintained the threefold content whilst prompting heated debate about the relative weight given to classical music, felt by some commentators to have been subsumed within a more pluralistic definition of music that focused on skills and processes as experienced through a wide range of repertoire (Cox, 2002). Music in contemporary classrooms might now include any or all of the elements of preceding decades: a review of provision carried out for the government in 2011 recommended that "for children to achieve their best, they need to gain an understanding of music as an academic subject from learning in the classroom; they need to develop practical skills in singing and playing instruments; and they need to have their eyes and ears opened to the widest musical possibilities by being given the opportunity to see and hear professional musicians at work" (Henley, 2011, p. 14).

The changing content of the English school curriculum was for many years determined implicitly by exam syllabuses, delivered according to the professionalism and particular musical interests of teachers, and monitored by the national system of school inspectors. The introduction of the National Curriculum in the 1990s was a significant departure, prompted by the Conservative government's desire to standardise provision across England and Wales and to measure attainment in the "core" subjects of literacy, numeracy, and science. The arts, including music, were somewhat peripheral to this agenda and became optional subjects for students after the age of 14 as the compulsory curriculum became increasingly overloaded (Rainbow & Cox, 2006, p. 363). In other ways, this marginal status left the curriculum designers (the "Music Working Group") free to pursue more radical debate, although their attempts to strengthen provision for teaching performing within the classroom were overturned by the politicians, and objections to the ambiguous status of classical music in the curriculum resulted in a rather bland statement on choice of repertoire (Pratt & Stephens, 1995). Teachers and academics alike subsequently judged the National Curriculum to have been less influential on music education than the demands of the GCSE syllabus and the increasing authority of the school inspection system (Pitts, 2000, p. 165). Debates about the purpose and effectiveness of music in schools have continued largely uninterrupted, and initiatives into the 21st century to increase the prominence of singing, popular music, and creativity in music learning show that the curriculum is still contested in practice, if not in policy documents.

2.3 Generational Trends in Formative Musical Experiences

The analysis in this chapter aims to provide a context for the rest of the book, offering an initial exploration of the generations and themes that will be discussed in the chapters that follow. This chapter focuses on the Phase 1 UK data, comprising 72 respondents of a largely classical background (coded UK1–72), ranging in age from 19 to 86 years; the data from popular musicians, collected later in the study, will be addressed in subsequent chapters. To discern generational trends, the coded responses have been grouped according to six main themes: (1) music in the classroom, (2) music outside the classroom, (3) teacher attitudes, (4) music in the home, (5) parent attitudes, and (6) lifelong learning and involvement. Events and memories that ranked most highly amongst participants from each age group were categorised within these six themes, generating an overview of the changing priorities and locations for musical learning throughout the 20th century. The coded results are given in full online, and the rank ordering of data is summarised in Table 2.1.

The growing importance of music outside the classroom is evident from this thematic coding and is supported by qualitative accounts of involvement in extracurricular ensembles, musical productions, and concerts, which for many respondents were some of the most fondly remembered and significant aspects of school musical experience (see Chapter 3). For the other thematic categories, upward or declining trends are not so obvious: there is an understandable gap between the importance of lifelong learning for the oldest and youngest groups, but also a surge in the 1970s that demands further explanation. Teacher and parent attitudes fluctuate in the significance they are afforded, and although a recency effect might account for their stronger presence amongst the 19- to 25-year age group, the preceding decades confound this. Music at home is a constant presence, while music in the classroom is absent from two decades and has low status in several others.

To explore some of these trends and anomalies in detail, this chapter will present first a closer examination of each of the generations in the sample, followed by a thematic analysis that identifies emergent topics for discussion in the rest of the book.

AGE GROUP	DECADE OF SCHOOLING	NUMBER OF RESPONDENTS	RANK ORDERING OF MUSICAL INFLUENCES
76+	1930s	5	1 Lifelong learning = 2 Classroom music lessons / Music at home / Music outside the classroom 5 Teacher attitudes
66–75	1940s	8	1 Music at home 2 Lifelong learning 3 Music outside the classroom
56–65	1950s	21	1 Music at home 2 Music outside the classroom 3 Lifelong learning = 4 Parent attitudes / Teacher attitudes
46–55	1960s	15	1 Music at home = 2 Lifelong learning / Music outside the classroom 4 Classroom music lessons 5 Teacher attitudes 6 Parent attitudes
36–45	1970s	8	1 Music at home 2 Music outside the classroom = 3 Classroom music lessons / Teacher attitudes 5 Lifelong learning
26–35	1980s	9	1 Music outside the classroom 2 Music at home = 3 Classroom music lessons / Lifelong learning / Parent attitudes
19–25	1990s	6	1 Music outside the classroom = 2 Music at home / Parent attitudes / Teacher attitudes 5 Classroom music lessons 6 Lifelong learning

2.3.1 1930s–1950s: Gramophones, Piano Lessons, and School Assemblies

With childhoods spanning the years of World War II and its subsequent impact on families and wider society, it is not surprising that respondents in the three older age groups recall a somewhat constrained musical education, often centred upon privately funded instrumental lessons, supported by church hymn-singing and family concert-going. Parents playing instruments in the home, and listening increasingly to broadcast and recorded music,

"My parents: father, tone deaf (!); mother played piano (popular classical), had scarce resources with six children to care for, but chose wisely—and sacrificially—to engage two of us in music lessons from a highly qualified teacher. My sister 'fell by the wayside' but I was 'hooked', and was forever on the piano at home. (I learnt sight reading simply through hours and hours at my music)." [UK39, aged 81]

were role models for their children, illustrating the pleasures of amateur musical involvement. Music was an accepted part of family life, and there was an expectation that young people would absorb its civilising in-fluence through home, school, and cultural activities. Disruption to ed-ucation and family life during the 1940s meant that the resources to support musical learning were not always readily available: the experi-ence of one of the oldest respon-dents (Box 2.3.1) captures many of the unpredictable variables in early musical experiences, showing how one child emerged as the only accomplished pianist amongst his siblings, first by being given the opportunity for lessons and then by persisting in practice and self-directed learning to a greater extent than his sister. Parents' and siblings' instrumental playing was often mentioned amongst this genera-tion, particularly by the 56- to 65-year age group, and the piano featured prominently, reflecting the fact that most middle-class homes of the time were furnished with this cross between "an expensive piece of furniture, a lavish plant stand and an unmanageable sculpture" (Hildebrandt, 1985, p. 1).

Once an interest in making music had emerged from a home environment in which this was accepted or even expected, inspiring instrumental teachers had a strong role to play in ensuring that musical skills were developed more systematically. Such teachers were often locally respected performers, some-times replaced after a few years by a more conventionally qualified teacher, a change that could cause a sudden adjustment in style and expectations for their young pupils: "From the age of six I studied piano with a lady 'down the road' who told me how wonderfully well I played and it was some years later after leaving her and going to a 'real teacher' that I realised how wrong she was. My technique was terrible and my knowledge of things necessary to pass exams left much to be desired" [UK46, aged 72]. The influence of a first, en-couraging teacher followed by a more demanding professional role model has been shown to be a widely successful pattern (Howe & Sloboda, 1991), but this pianist was not alone in expressing regret at lost time with a poor teacher, or with a disinclination to practise, that had limited future progress. Many others, though, appreciated the musical versatility that their eclectic combination of self-directed learning and private lessons had afforded and recalled an early appetite for music that had remained important throughout their lives: "I

"My father was a postman [mailman]—so we lived frugally—but when I was about 11 or 12 he bought a Dinette record player and we started with one LP [long-playing record], of Rimsky Korsakov's *Scheherazade*. It was some time before we added to that one disc, so we got to know that piece pretty well! But as constant radio listeners we enjoyed the 'usual' classics—Dvorak's *New World*, Rachmaninov's Piano Concertos, etc. I would say without question that my early home life contributed to my strong if passive love of music." [UK70, aged 67]

spent hours at the piano as a child at home and relatives' houses. I would rummage through their music stools and spend the time playing in their cold sitting rooms. As a result, I have always found sight-reading very easy!" [UK57, aged 64].

This generation was resourceful, too, in making use of public libraries to borrow scores and recordings, as well as drawing on their parents' tastes in recorded music and radio listening. For respondents aged 66 to 75, the radio and gramophone ranked alongside family concert-going as the strongest influence on their early musical enthusiasms, creating an appetite for hearing new and familiar music that had remained with them into adulthood. These recollections include detailed memories of specific repertoire, consistent with psychological studies of musical "imprinting", in which adolescence has been shown to be a time of heightened sensitivity to musical tastes, later reinforced by nostalgia and "the associations that form between particular songs and the many 'rites of passage' that occur at this stage of life" (North & Hargreaves, 2008, p. 110). Family bonds were also formed through shared experiences of listening, and since British radio broadcasting was confined to three stations at this time, and an expensive, newly acquired gramophone would be shared by the whole family, children's musical tastes were closely influenced by those of their parents rather than being independently pursued, as is the case with today's more musically diverse and technologically accessible listening (Box 2.3.2).

Home listening habits were often reinforced in school through schools broadcasts in which "the presenter would explain how pieces were put together and play the main themes, sometimes we'd be asked to join in and sing things—it was a treasure trove of information and I loved it" [UK8, aged 68]. Hearing music in assembly was also commonplace, and again there were detailed memories of the classical repertoire heard on the piano in this context: Robert [Interlude L] "often sought the teacher out to ask what she had played, writing the titles down in a little book so that I could watch out for the piece on a future occasion. I think I filled two pages before I left" [UK19, aged 74]. Communicating with adults about musical repertoire was a clear source of both learning and pleasure amongst this generation:

musical enthusiasms were shared within the home rather than being a source of teenage independence or rebellion as in later decades. As one respondent recalled of her Advanced Level (A Level) Music studies, "The course was entirely focused on Western classical music—pop music didn't really exist in the way that it does today. That suited me perfectly" [UK53, aged 69].

While music in the 1930s to 1950s home was characterised by respondents as a shared, valued activity, its presence in school appeared to have been rather more marginal and in many cases to have added relatively little to the resources provided by parents and instrumental teachers: "whilst my primary school made a passable attempt to stimulate musical awareness most of it failed to light my fire, particularly when compared to music that I was enjoying elsewhere" [UK16, aged 60]. Classroom music was rarely mentioned favourably by respondents aged 56 to 75, although belonging to the secondary school choir was a source of some prestige and enjoyment for many (discussed in more detail in Chapter 3). Older respondents recalled a curriculum centred around notation, sight-singing, and ear-training, often acknowledging that this provided a useful although somewhat rigid training for the choral singing that was to become an important part of both their school and adult musical participation: "We sang numerous national and foreign songs, which taught us voice production, breathing and clear enunciation of words" [UK 31, aged 86]. Writers on music education at the time promoted this approach as being fit for training the "audiences of the future" (Hale, 1947, p. 151), an aim that was successful for the majority of these life history respondents. However, provision was not consistent, and a lack of music in school was explicitly mentioned by several in the 56- to 65-year age group, sometimes attributed to a general failing in their school education but more often to the unimaginative teaching of a subject with low curriculum status: "class music lessons were dull and, besides, pupils in the top two streams (I was in the 'B' stream) dropped music (as a timetabled subject) after what is now called Year 7 [first year of secondary school]" [UK47, aged 62; see Interlude B].

Music teachers, likely at this time to have had a music degree but no formal teacher training (Rainbow & Cox, 2006, p. 296), were mostly remembered as eccentric organists who rarely offered the encouragement or identification of musical potential that would be a striking feature of school life in later decades. Their influence was likely to be greatest outside the classroom, where extracurricular activities nurtured musical interests and strong peer and teacher relationships: "I don't remember a great deal about what happened in class but it seemed like every evening there was something

"Being born at the end of World War II, most opportunities for learning music of any kind were scarce. This was the downside, the reverse was rather more interesting in that there were countless small string ensembles playing in city tea rooms and nearly every theatre had a resident orchestra of between fifteen and twenty players. Even cinemas had live music in the form of the cheerful theatre organ." [UK16, aged 60]

happening after school and I was hooked" [UK20, aged 62]. These years can be characterised as a time of resourcefulness and opportunity for those with supportive families but with a limited guarantee of access to a school musical education (Box 2.3.3). The relatively narrow scope of musical taste and knowledge, largely confined to classical and "light" music and sometimes including systematic training for choral singing, meant that there was a strong congruence between home and school music (see Chapter 3) and emerging enthusiasms were often founded on parents' and teachers' tastes.

2.3.2 1960s–1970s: Encouragement and Independence

Respondents aged between 36 and 55 offer a rich and diverse picture of formative musical experiences, with performing opportunities in secondary school assuming a dominant position that would remain constant for the rest of the 20th century. Parents' support and own playing and listening habits were still significant for this age group, but music teachers also assumed a stronger role, either as enthusiastic role models or, sadly, as sources of doubt and discouragement. Opportunities for singing and performing in primary school laid strong foundations for musical interests: Nikki in Interlude K was amongst those who recalled specific performing experiences that had encouraged her to view herself as a "musical person", an attitude shown repeatedly in the life histories to be self-fulfilling in causing young people to seek out and relish musical opportunities (see Chapter 4). Primary school music also typically included playing the recorder, singing in choirs, and performing in assembly—a programme that offered much more involvement in music than had been available to previous generations, but which was viewed retrospectively as an obvious stepping stone to later activities: "I played recorder in junior school in class like everybody else" [UK69, aged 53]. However commonplace such practical involvement seemed to those who were offered it, this marked a significant shift in thinking about how music should be taught in schools, away from an emphasis on repertoire and knowledge towards the creative, exploratory approaches that had already emerged in post-war English, drama, and art teaching (Marshall, 1963; Richardson, 1948).

It would take a little longer for such attitudes to filter into secondary schools and to embrace composing music as well as recreating it through performance. John Paynter, highly influential in bringing composing to the heart of school music teaching, writes of the confusion experienced during this transitional phase, when some teachers introduced new creative methods "without a clear picture of what [their] musical objectives were, and without much conviction that the activities would really lead to musical understanding" (Paynter, 1982, p. 52). Some of the resulting inconsistencies of secondary school provision are evident in respondents' descriptions of having successive music teachers with quite different approaches: Graham [Interlude F] experienced the transition from an "old music master [who] could be rather stiff" to an "ex-Cambridge choral scholar only just out of college (so only about 4 years older than us)", the latter using his choral training to "rejuvenate" the school's music, in and out of the classroom [UK64, aged 55]. Several respondents also had their first encounters with contemporary music in school, often through teacher-led listening clubs targeted at older students: "in the sixth form a wonderful teacher played us some music that's remained with me—Bartók, Schoenberg and others, and was truly inspiring" [UK67, aged 49].

Enterprise on the students' part was also encouraged, and instances of "trying out instruments in the lunch break" [UK64, aged 55] or setting up student-led music societies "to give recitals ourselves at lunchtimes" [UK21, aged 55] helped students gain recognition from their teachers and to begin to acquire what would now be thought of as a musical identity (MacDonald, Hargreaves, & Miell, 2002). Encouragement from teachers was important to this age group, perhaps marking a cultural growth in the concept of individuality: whereas doing well in class was sufficient for a previous generation, these young people sought recognition and opportunity in school and enjoyed the sense of distinctiveness that came with being well known for having musical abilities. The provision of instrumental lessons within schools—free of charge until the 1980s (see Chapter 4)—also helped bring pupils' playing to the attention of their teachers, and the life histories include reports of ambitious school orchestra concerts, supplemented for the most able performers by participation in county ensembles, where strong friendships were also forged.

With music recordings and playback equipment now much more affordable, children of this generation had greater independence in their listening in the home and pursued their own musical discoveries as well as continuing to be influenced by parents: "I can clearly remember being given a record of *Peter and the Wolf* and *The Young Person's Guide to the*

Orchestra when I was about 7 or 8—I liked both, but preferred my father's recording of Oistrakh playing the Prokofiev and Bruch 1st violin concertos" [UK64, aged 55]. Access to popular music also shifted the family listening dynamic as older siblings shared their interests in the latest record releases: "we only listened to the 'Top 100' pop songs because of my older sister" [UK61, aged 50]. In families where musical tastes had been classically based until this point, the exploration of new styles had an appealing sense of rebellion, even when it took place alongside the continuation of parentally encouraged classical music learning: "Although I only played classical music, I became interested in various kinds of rock, partly under the influence of my elder brother. My hero was Rick Wakeman, who had both classical skills and rebel credibility, having been kicked out of the RNCM [Royal Northern College of Music] for playing too many sessions" [UK40, aged 44]. For other respondents, the gap between their expanding listening tastes and their own musical learning proved more problematic: one gave up piano lessons on the grounds that "in those days (mid-sixties) there was no piano music available that you would want to buy; for example, had there been piano music of Beatles songs then it might have been another matter" [UK29, aged 54].

Respondents aged 36 to 55 were the last group to mention instruments in the home as a significant influence on their emerging musical interests, marking the end of an era in which playing music with family members was as readily accessible as listening to it. One respondent recalled her family acquiring a piano when she was ten years old, after an early childhood in which "if we ever visited a house with a piano, I used to gravitate to it and mess around on it until forcibly removed" [UK26, aged 52]. For another, this self-directed exploration of the piano continued through adolescence: "When my voice broke in my mid teens, and I started reading bass clef in the school choir, I would often sit down at the piano and play through classical pieces very slowly, chord by chord, enjoying the harmony, despite having virtually no technical facility on the instrument" [UK72, aged 45; see Box 2.3.4 for the continuation of this story]. For many of this age group, access to instruments and lessons was accepted as "normal—people like us learned music and played music at home" [UK69, aged 53], but the days of free instrumental lessons in schools were numbered, and some of this generation reflected with gratitude on the privileged early start that they were offered: "there's no doubt that without the enormous encouragement I received at my primary school, I would never have taken the path I did" [UK21, aged 55].

The most fortunate amongst this generation had arguably the strongest musical beginnings of the 20th century: they benefited from the overlap

Box 2.3.4

"Although I didn't have formal piano lessons until the age of 17, I remember often sitting down at the piano during my childhood and playing melodies both by ear and from the treble clef stave of my sister's piano music. [. . .] I have one particular memory of sitting at the piano one winter's evening and starting to work my way through some pieces in a book of Beethoven Sonatas. The piano was situated in a study/music room which at that stage had no heating, but I became so completely engrossed in what I was doing that I was oblivious to the cold. At the end of the session I couldn't believe how blue and stiff my fingers had become! Ultimately this enjoyment of harmony led me to ask my parents in my late teens if I could have piano lessons and my mother arranged for me to have lessons with a teacher who lived in our village who guided me to Grade 4 level during my two years in the sixth form." [UK72, aged 45]

between supportive parental attitudes, through which musical resources and lessons were readily offered, and a growing emphasis on practical music-making in schools, with creative approaches in primary schools and extracurricular opportunities for older adolescents. In addition, greater independence in listening caused this generation to question and expand their musical horizons, drawing on the tastes of siblings and peers and absorbing the new media influences and pop culture that were beginning to have widespread social impact. This richness of opportunity helps to explain the trends evident in Table 2.1, where those at school in the 1960s are the only group (apart from the most recent school-leavers) to mention all six home- and school-based factors as being influential in their musical upbringing. The individual narratives show that these strong foundations were not always so idealistic, and that off-putting teachers could have as lasting an effect as those who were encouraging (see Chapter 4), but nonetheless this generation shares an open-minded passion for music and a determination to overcome any initial obstacles and pursue their enthusiasms later in life. There are no doubt many others of this age group not represented in the life history responses who found the school music provision of this time to be patchy and inadequate: even amongst these musically active adults, there were some who "wrote off institutional [music] education as a sensible option fairly early on" [UK52, aged 49]. As the offering of musical support became less of a standard parental role, so schools became more influential, while all the time the musical dominance of both was increasingly challenged by teenagers' direct access to a wider range of musical tastes and values. The educational reforms of the coming decades took place in a rapidly shifting musical climate, perhaps not noticed at the time, but with direct implications for the next generation in this study.

2.3.3 1980s–1990s: Musical Pluralism and Exploration

The youngest respondents, those who received most of their schooling in the 1980s and 1990s, had the least distance on their experiences, and so it is unsurprising that most musical factors in their upbringing were judged to have been influential. Some of their early disappointments were also keenly felt, since these respondents lacked the experience and perspective of intervening years that had allowed their older counterparts to come to terms with or remedy lost opportunities, often by taking up or resuming instruments in adulthood. For 19- to 25-year-olds especially, the impact of influential classroom and instrumental teachers was still fresh, performing opportunities in primary and secondary school were relatively recent memories, and the attitudes of parents and teachers were frequently cited in explaining an ongoing interest in music. Most had only recently made the decision whether to continue their musical education or pursue other degree subjects or career opportunities, and so it could be said that their musical identities were in flux. These respondents were still weighing up the relative importance of music in their lives, not yet having established a secure career identity or life role that would bring relative certainty about whether music would remain a valued hobby or a professional pursuit—or perhaps be left behind as something that was important in childhood but would later be surpassed by other priorities and commitments.

Although school music lessons were frequently mentioned by this group, their impact was attributed more to the nurturing qualities of individual teachers than to the skills and knowledge imparted in their lessons. Classroom music was remembered by one of the youngest respondents as being "generally quite noisy, with something vaguely recognisable by the end" [UK1, aged 19], and the post-1970s incarnation of creativity in the classroom appeared to have been somewhat lost in translation in some cases: one respondent recalled "being sent into practice rooms in small groups with a xylophone and a broken piano to 'compose'. Obviously we did no work until five minutes before we were called back in, and then hastily decided who would hit what how many times ready for the 'performance' to the rest of the class" [UK9, aged 28]. This description captures all the dilemmas of mixed-ability music teaching in a culturally pluralistic age in which teachers were faced with introducing music of all kinds to children with diverse levels of skill and experience. Some respondents were sympathetic to the implicitly inclusive values of classroom music at this time, with Steph in Interlude H recalling supporting a friend by "helping her out with compositions, her performance on the keyboard or anything else she struggled with" while pursuing her own musical goals in circumstances where "sometimes we got away without doing anything but I was well aware of what standard I needed to be" [UK51, aged 29]. Others judged their teachers' efforts more harshly, stating that lessons were "unimaginatively taught, and seemed to cater to the lowest common denominator" [UK59, aged 33].

These varied experiences of a music curriculum that was in transition from formal, knowledge-based teaching to a more practical, exploratory approach show how the musical experiences and insight that children bring into the classroom have a powerful effect on how their teaching is received. This generation seemed more critical of their education than those older respondents who recalled an arguably more limited focus on notation, singing, and repertoire. The lack of congruence between the musical aspirations of instrumental lessons, classroom practice, and home listening had perhaps brought an inherent dissatisfaction that not all of these routes could be pursued to the full. Younger respondents also seemed to know their own minds in respect to educational and musical choices—a byproduct of social shifts including changing attitudes to childhood, an increase in child-centred learning, and a decline in the status of the teaching profession. As one respondent explained, "I listened to almost every teacher I had for music but still reserved my own judgement on what I would like to do" [UK2, aged 19].

The teachers who continued to command the greatest influence for this generation were instrumental tutors, often credited with maintaining an interest in music that would otherwise have floundered in secondary school years. Students felt challenged in their instrumental lessons, being "motivated to practise" [UK9, aged 28] or feeling that "we got on really well, I loved playing and she really pushed me" [UK12, aged 24]. Close relationships were formed that allowed these young people to feel sympathetically understood as musicians, with one appreciating her cello teacher's "understanding of the pressures of academic studies and that sometimes they or my instrumental practice had to give way to the other" [UK45, aged 20]. Learning several instruments was common amongst these younger respondents, though like their 1970s predecessors they sometimes regretted the resulting lack of focus in their skills, even while recognising the breadth of opportunity this had afforded: "I kind of regret not getting to a fantastically high standard and I feel like I could improve loads still but I wouldn't change it, I really enjoy what I'm doing now" [UK12, aged 24].

Most of this age group were still active as performers, although some had turned relatively quickly away from their school-based interests to pursue new musical avenues: "I get so much more satisfaction from playing badly in an amateur [brass] band than I ever have from orchestral playing in a university orchestra. It's probably because the audiences seem so much more appreciative of the music and seem to enjoy it much more (or maybe they just show it more . . .)" [UK9, aged 28]. This viola player had taught herself the tenor horn in order to join a brass band and was one of the few who had already rectified the perceived gaps in her musical experience after formal education had ceased. For others, the possibility of future musical learning remained, one stating that "there's nothing stopping me doing something new, that I want to do, now" [UK50, aged 25]. But those who had not received a high level of tuition in childhood were more pessimistic: "I regularly wish I could have learnt a musical instrument, especially the piano, but at the age of 31 I do not have the time or inclination to learn" [UK15, aged 31].

Music education for this generation seems to have been strong on offering possibilities but sometimes lacking in focus or direction, particularly in the classroom. Finding a nurturing instrumental teacher or having the right kind of parental support—"never pushy, but really encouraging" [UK12, aged 24]— was critical to ensuring that musical interest was recognised and developed. School music, it seems, had assumed a contested role in young people's development, aiming to fulfil a wide variety of roles, and dependent for its success on multiple factors, including teacher personality, school resources, parental support, and the receptiveness of students who were now bringing an increasingly broad range of musical values and references into the classroom.

2.4 Historical Trends, Current Debates

The experiences reported by the life history respondents illustrate how some of the most significant contemporary challenges for music education have strong historical roots. Debates on the purposes of musical learning, questions of elitism versus accessibility, and the implicit long-term goals of a school music curriculum have been resolved—or sometimes just ignored—in different ways across the decades. These rich, retrospective data raise many questions about the purposes and consequences of music education, and before leaving the historical analysis to pursue more thematic discussion in subsequent chapters, it is worth revisiting the six categories of influence outlined earlier and identifying the challenges that they pose in understanding past and current music education practice.

2.4.1 Classroom Music

As Table 2.1 illustrated, the presence of classroom music as an influential source of musical development and encouragement was by no means consistent in the life history accounts. Decades go by in which the classroom was hardly mentioned, crowded out of respondents' narratives by the greater influence of extracurricular music, parental support, or influential instrumental teachers. Although the classroom lessons of the 1960s end a two-decade absence of this factor, closer inspection of the data offers another reminder that negative experiences can be as lasting as positive recollections. One respondent in the 46- to 55-year age group describes her teacher as "an unpleasant and unimaginative woman, who ran the music department with cold efficiency, but no love or inspiration" [UK35, aged 52]. While others in this age group were more fortunate in their teachers, they were limited by the place of music within the curriculum: "the music teachers were great and I was the only student to do the O Level [16+ examination]. My regret was not being able to take A Level Music [18+ examination] as it wasn't offered on the syllabus" [UK61, aged 50]. Another respondent, who was able to pursue musical qualifications in school, stated that "we had good classroom music in those days" [UK63, aged 57]—perhaps hinting at a perceived decline in subsequent years, and an assumption that others of her generation had similar experiences. As will already have become apparent, however, the life history responses reveal the idiosyncrasy of music education provision, in which teachers' personalities, school resources, and the presence of like-minded peers all played a role in shaping young people's experiences of the music classroom. The impact of classroom music will be an underlying theme to this book, and its contested role in nurturing young people's musical skills and values will be re-evaluated in Chapter 6 in a discussion of the changing purposes of music education in different historical and cultural contexts.

2.4.2 Music Outside the Classroom

Extracurricular music was far more consistently represented across the generations, showing a broadly upward trend across the 20th century and prompting some of the most vivid recollections amongst the life history accounts. Outside the classroom, respondents seemed to have found the recognition from their teachers that was sometimes lacking in the formal teaching context, valuing the opportunity to display and develop their musical skills and coming to know their teachers as energetic role models and animateurs. Becoming involved in musical activities could change attitudes to school and self, as for one respondent who "loved the last three years at school because I spent as much of my time as possible in the music department where I felt truly at home" [UK26, aged 52]. The power of extracurricular music to nurture enthusiasm and confidence emerges as a striking feature of UK music education (see Pitts, 2008): Chapter 3 of this book will explore the different sources of performing opportunities in other countries' educational provision and will consider the extent to which the strength of musical involvement in schools lies in its ambiguous institutional status—within the formal setting of the school yet closer to the collective musical experiences of the wider world.

2.4.3 Teacher and Parent Attitudes

The role of significant adults in shaping musical attitudes and identity was evident across the generations: the youngest respondents were understandably most aware of their parents' and teachers' formative influences, and those in middle years often re-evaluated those sources of guidance as they took on similar roles for the young people in their own classrooms, instrumental studios, or families. Just as these respondents had been influenced by significant role models and mentors throughout their lives, their subsequent influence on friends, families, pupils, and children was shaped by their notions of what it means to be a musician, parent, or teacher. Chapter 4 will address these roles and responsibilities in more detail, considering the ways in which parents and teachers act as musical role models and gatekeepers, providing (or sometimes denying) the opportunities needed for young people to flourish musically.

2.4.4 Music in the Home

Educational research has been slow to acknowledge the influence of music in the home on children's learning, but the life history responses show that its presence has always been strong, with a peak in the 1950s that coincided with the increasing availability and variety of broadcast and recorded music, and the consequent independence of musical listening afforded to teenagers. Music in the home had meant different things across the generations: older respondents were most likely to hear their parents playing and singing, so encouraging their children to view music as an accessible and worthwhile use of leisure time. The vast majority of respondents mention listening to music in the home as part of their childhood memories: fathers appear to be more prominent than mothers in this respect, though mothers are more likely to have sung to and with their children, and to have been role models through their own musical activities: "My mother sang in a choir and did shows, and I quickly learnt all the songs" [UK42, aged 62]. Attending concerts as a family was also an activity more prominent in earlier decades but equally memorable and valuable to all generations, encompassing everything from "a weekly orchestra stalls reservation at the Palace, a number one touring theatre with a first class orchestra of twenty players" [UK16, aged 60] to "home-grown concerts [. . .] in the small Methodist chapel which was the focal point of the village" [UK55, aged 70]. In more recent decades, music in the home continued to involve the sharing of listening tastes, and siblings playing were more often mentioned than parents, shifting the generational balance of music-making in the home. Chapter 3 will consider music in the home as one of several locations for musical learning, exploring ways in which family musical influences extend to church, community, and concert life and provide new contexts for school music.

2.4.5 Lifelong Learning and Involvement

As would be expected in autobiographical accounts, the oldest respondents showed the greatest influence of lifelong learning, recounting the lessons they had resumed or begun in later life, the many concerts they had attended, and the experiences of making music in community, church, and family contexts. Amongst the older age groups, music had become embedded in social and personal life, and for some had also been the foundation of a career, now ended through retirement: "I took two diplomas on piano and did a great deal of music and singing until two years ago, including the experience of a small choir, a light orchestra, directed by myself, and finally 20 years at the church organ and as choirmaster before I reached 84 years!" [UK31, aged 86]. Lifelong learning, enjoyment, and participation were seen as closely related in ways that the youngest respondents—understandably least likely to mention lifelong learning as a significant influence in their musical life history—had yet to discover.

The extent to which adult learning was regarded as possible and desirable varied between participants, and while some had pursued new challenges, stating that "my only real regret is that I started singing lessons four years ago instead of forty" [UK69, aged 53], others were more resigned to missed learning opportunities: "I never did learn how to enjoy playing an instrument. I never will now, and on the whole I don't mind, but I envy those who can do it, whether they're classically trained or not" [UK67, aged 49]. Chapter 5 will consider the foundations for these differing levels of openness to learning later in life by taking the present musical lives of the respondents as a starting point and tracing their journeys back to identify predictors of involvement and the shaping of attitudes.

Interlude C: Sue Blaby [UK13]
Aged 58, left school 1966

Encouraging music teacher at primary school, discouragement at secondary school, followed by adult enjoyment of singing

I am the third child of six (the last two being twins). My eldest sister (twelve years older than me) learned to play the piano that we had at home. I can recall her playing songs for me to sing along. These were often songs that cropped up at Sunday School[1] and one of my favourite pastimes as a very young child was to play 'Sunday School teacher'—singing to the various toys sitting around in a circle. This later developed into singing along to the 'top twenty' on my transistor radio on a Sunday afternoon!

I was very fortunate that in my junior school we had a very enthusiastic and encouraging music teacher. He taught us to play the recorder and we also had a school choir. I think we reached quite a high level in recorder playing because I recall learning quite a complicated recorder sonata which we performed at a concert. The school choir also participated in borough events from time to time. This was a part of my education that I greatly enjoyed.

Sadly, when I moved into grammar school, my experience was quite different. The first music teacher I encountered there was a rather forbidding character and at 11 years old I felt rather nervous of him. The whole class was auditioned for the school choir, taking pupils two at a time. I was not accepted, much to my great disappointment. This must have had quite a negative

---

[1] Religious education for children, typically provided by voluntary teachers during church services

impact on me because I did not try again through all the years I was at the school. When I was in the sixth form and quite near to the end of my time there, the then music teacher arranged for an inter-house music competition. I am not quite sure how, but I ended up singing a folk song with a group of guitarists and I also entered into the solo competition. I can't remember if I won, but I clearly remember the music teacher's remark: "You have a lovely voice; why on earth are you not in the school choir?"! Fortunately, I had during this time joined a church choir and as time went on and I gained in confidence, I took the step of joining other choirs.

I am now involved in music at church: singing in the church choir, and sometimes singing soprano in a quartet of singers for Sunday services and at weddings. I also belong to a choral society. I feel 'made' to sing and feel quite unhappy when I am not involved in some sort of singing activity. My musical highlights include singing at a joint choir event at St Paul's Cathedral as a teenager; singing with Imperial College choir at various concerts (sometimes at the Royal College of Music); singing at the Royal Albert Hall in a multi-choir event a few years ago; participating in Verdi's *Requiem* at St Alban's Cathedral.[2]

I often wonder why my parents did not recognise my musical potential. I was always singing around the house and I can remember stating to my father that I wanted to study music—but he apparently felt it was not a good career choice. I can only assume that my parents could not afford for me to learn to play the piano; indeed my eldest sister was the only person ever to play the instrument we had at home. Had I only persisted in trying to get into the school choir, perhaps a subsequent music teacher would have encouraged me to take musical training at a higher level.

---

[2] All prestigious public venues in and around London

Interlude D: Tim Robinson [UKP73]
Aged 48, left school 1978

Independent learning as a drummer, extracurricular
participation at school, followed by performing and
teaching in popular music

There was lots of music in the family. I grew up aware that my parents
both used to play when younger, and that my grandma had been a fantastic pianist who had won big competitions and taught piano all her life. My
three elder brothers listened to records constantly (as did I), and they all
played instruments as I was growing up; my first formal lessons (aged 10)
were on the trumpet, a hand-me-down from a brother who had moved on to
trombone. By then however I was already playing the drums, having saved
up and bought first a snare drum and hi-hat, and then a couple of years later
a full kit. This was what I really wanted to do!

I wouldn't say that all this music and playing had a direct influence on me.
My choice of instrument was very much my own—I remember being offered the chance to take up the guitar (which two of my brothers played) but
I wasn't interested; it had to be drums. Equally, the music that I wanted to
learn and practised along to in my bedroom was what I liked, not what my
brothers or parents listened to. However, I think the most important thing
about having music around the house was that it was considered normal and
'a good thing' to be interested in music and to be playing an instrument.

I was aware that my parents were not so keen on the drums, as they were
noisy and involved music (at that time mostly rock and pop) that they didn't
like. Much more acceptable was the trumpet; they paid for lessons in school
and came to the school concerts I was in. But I never had to fight to play

drums; in fact, by the time I was 16 or so it was clear I was not going to stop, and my dad offered to pay for some lessons. So I would say, indirectly, the musical culture I grew up in was very supportive of involvement in and enjoyment of music generally, though my brothers and I all found our own individual paths according to taste.

The opportunity to rehearse and perform in the school band and orchestra was great experience and really worthwhile, even though I was playing the trumpet (not my first choice) and most of the music didn't really engage me. Singing in the choir (at least until my voice broke) was also good fun, and looking back was probably valuable ear-training. The first rock band I joined was also in school, and the first gig I did on the drums (aged 13) was at a sixth form dance in the school dining room. So school was certainly the setting for some really important, formative experiences. However, these were all extracurricular—classroom music lessons were utterly tedious, and consisted, as I remember it, of listening to extracts of classical music, and having the music teacher ramble on about how great they were. There may well have been some music theory, and perhaps some 'lives of the great composers' or whatever, but these have left no impression on my memory at all. There didn't seem to be any connection between classroom music lessons and the active music-making which went on after school or at lunch-time.

I guess my three elder brothers, the fact that they were all into music, and their choice of music that I grew up hearing, had a big influence. I had a series of fixations with a string of drummers who really interested me—their style, their sound, their musical choices, how come they can play so well? etc. A brief sample would include Ringo Starr, Phil Collins from Genesis, Billy Cobham, Dave Mattacks from Fairport Convention, Billy Ficca from Television and many more. And another major influence has been other musicians I've been in bands with—I think the experience of rehearsing and performing together, collectively getting a set of material to sound as good as possible and going out gigging it, has a profound influence on how musicians play and think about music, though often in ways that are hard to define.

Many, many highlights! Going into a posh recording studio and recording a track that made the hairs stand up on the back of my neck. Seeing myself on the telly. Hearing myself on the radio. Seeing my name on a list of credits at the end of a telly programme. Going to the premiere of a film whose soundtrack I was playing on. Seeing—over the years—thousands and thousands of people dancing to music I was playing. Touring regularly in the USA and Canada has been fantastic—loads of great gigs and hilarious/memorable experiences. When I was a kid I always wanted to do 'an American tour', whatever that was—the phrase seemed to me to sum up the ultimate success. Well I've done 12 so far, and counting. Playing at festivals alongside some awesome musicians and having to pinch myself that I'm actually there. Best of all, being in a great band, doing really good gigs with an audience going nuts. Some of the big gigs I've done have been very satisfying too—e.g. playing to 20,000 people in Canada was fun. Playing at certain festivals has a particular resonance for me too, as in a former life I used to run a catering stall and would be—literally—slaving over a hot stove while thinking: 'why aren't I playing here instead?' To come back to those festivals e.g. Cropredy and Glastonbury[1] as a performer rather than a caterer is profoundly satisfying!

I could wish I'd practised more, or learned more, or been more determined when I was younger, but I am who I am, and what happened, happened. I consider myself to have been almost unbelievably lucky to have had the opportunities I've had—fine, I never got to number one in the charts, or played with anyone really famous (yet!) but it's been a blast—no complaints. Though of course, like all musicians, I actually complain all the time!

Talking to people who don't have a passion in life, as I have had for music, has made me realise how lucky I have been simply to have this driving force, always interesting, usually entertaining, often frustrating, sometimes deeply satisfying. It's not always been easy to make a 'career' out of this, but it's always there, and that's a blessing.

---

[1] Large-scale UK music festivals: see Cropredy (also known as the Fairport Convention) http://www.fairportconvention.com/cropredy.php and Glastonbury http://www.glastonburyfestivals.co.uk/

3| Locations for Musical Learning

3.1 Where Musical Learning Happens

THIS PROJECT ORIGINALLY SET out to examine the long-term impact of music education, but it quickly became apparent that the effects of formal education were almost inseparable from the cultural context, specific to each respondent, in which they occurred. As the generational analysis in the previous chapter has illustrated, resources and attitudes in the home can vary widely and can influence in turn a young person's receptiveness and exposure to music. To examine these factors more closely, an analysis of the coded data from all 81 UK respondents (including the Phase 2 popular musicians) was undertaken, in which the people, events, and other factors most often mentioned were collated into a rank ordering of strongest influences.

Table 3.1 (updated from Pitts, 2009) shows the home- and school-based factors that were mentioned by more than 20% of respondents, listed in columns to provide a graphical representation of the balance of influence from the two locations. Factors that ranked equally (shown as =) are listed alphabetically to avoid bias in the ordering of home and school influences, and influences spanning both contexts, such as self-taught instrumental learning, appear in both columns. The percentage figures shown in Table 3.1 should be understood as indicating widespread or common influences rather than being a measure of depth of influence: for this, the qualitative data are necessary and are integrated in the discussion that follows in this chapter. Nonetheless, this rank ordering offers some clear signals about the relative influence of school, home, and self-directed learning and shows the strength

TABLE 3.1 Rank Ordering of Home and School Influences (% of 81 UK Responses)

HOME INFLUENCES	RANK ORDER	EDUCATION INFLUENCES
	1	Secondary school performing opportunities (52%)
Father listening (42%)	2	
	3	Belonging to secondary school choir (38%)
	4	Belonging to school orchestra or band (37%)
Radio/gramophone (35%)	5	
Parental support for lessons (32%)	6	
Inspiring instrumental teachers (31%)	7	Inspiring instrumental teachers (31%)
	= 8	Inspiring secondary school teachers (30%)
	= 8	Singing at primary school (30%)
Instruments in the home (27%)	10	
Mother listening (26%)	11	
Church attendance/hymn singing (23%)	= 12	
Developing own listening tastes (23%)	= 12	
Father playing (23%)	= 12	
Mother playing (22%)	= 15	
Self-taught instrumental playing (22%)	= 15	Self-taught instrumental playing (22%)
Siblings playing (22%)	= 15	
	= 18	Secondary school class lessons (21%)
	= 18	Studying for exams in school (21%)

of attitudes, as much as opportunities, in providing inspiration and support for young musicians.

In school, practical music-making was dominant in respondents' memories: performance opportunities (52%) were more than twice as influential as classroom lessons (21%), and the memories relating to those lessons were not always positive, as discussion in Section 3.2 will show. Parental support (32%), inspiring instrumental teachers (31%), and inspiring secondary school teachers

(30%) ranked closely together, showing the value of an influential adult in shaping and nurturing young people's musical intentions. Closer analysis reveals that only two respondents had experienced all three of these influences [UK71, aged 51; UK66, aged 40—see Interlude J]: both were educated during the 1960s–70s, which the previous chapter illustrated to have been one of the most fertile periods for encouraging musical development, and both came from homes where siblings, parents, and other family members were active as players or had a strong musical interest. Another 21 respondents experienced two significant adult influences, the most common combination being an inspiring instrumental teacher and a supportive parent (or two).

The financial implications of having instrumental lessons suggest a level of parental support for any respondent taking this route, but those particularly mentioning this influence were also grateful for their parents' praise, encouragement, and uncomplaining attendance at concerts: "My parents were always supportive and always came to listen to us, not to mention transporting bass drums around in the boot of the car. It must have been pretty unbearable for them some times, but they stuck with it and did admit that over the years the music did get better!" [UK29, aged 54; see also Box 3.1.1]. In total, 49 of the 81 respondents (60%) had experienced the support or inspiration of an influential adult; this figure dwarfs that of off-putting instrumental teachers (mentioned by 16%) and classroom teachers (15%) but still leaves a substantial proportion of respondents who do not directly report the presence of a significant mentor or role model in their formative years. With this proportion likely to be much higher amongst the general population, the varied experiences of these musically active adults offer valuable evidence of the effects of musical mentors—or their absence—on lifelong involvement, which will be discussed further in this chapter and the next.

This emphasis on the influence of people was balanced by a similar prevalence of opportunities and resources, whether directly provided by parents and teachers or sought out by young people forging their

---

Box 3.1.1

"It was my parents who suggested that I take piano and oboe lessons as a child, and who purchased first a keyboard and then a piano and oboe so that I could engage in these studies. They also supported me by attending every recital, sitting through annual exams in piano performance and solfège, and later finding and enabling me to attend a music camp for two summers. They believed that their kids should pursue what they loved, and thus never questioned my interest in music. On the contrary, my father especially told me repeatedly that he wished he could have done more with music as a youth." [OUK4, aged 30]

own musical direction. Opportunities for acquiring and demonstrating performing skill were prominent, both in the concerts, choirs, and orchestras that provided the strongest memories of school and the instruments that were explored in the home, either independently or with the help of a teacher. The presence of a radio or gramophone and its use by both parents, but particularly fathers, was strong across the generations, helping to shape musical tastes and provide the sense that music was a valuable part of daily life. Musical knowledge, rarely spoken of as a desirable attribute for its own sake, was strongly embedded in action, and respondents recalled the particular tastes and listening habits of their parents and siblings in detail, often feeling that these had established patterns for their own exploration and extension of the family record collection (see Interludes B, F, and I). Similarly, a teacher with a particular passion for music was likely to make the strongest impression when these enthusiasms were carried into performance opportunities: Britten's *Noye's Fludde* featured in several responses, alongside Handel's *Messiah*, hymns in four-part harmony, and "lusty unison singing" [UK19, aged 74] of English folk songs.

The life history responses show that the separation of home and school influences is difficult to achieve, even with hindsight: influential teachers need the support of parents, while opportunities within the home require recognition and nurturing by other significant adults. The responsibility for musical learning is held jointly, and achieving compatibility between home and school musical lives had been important to many respondents: "the combination of encouragement at home and at school more or less determined that I would do music in some form or another later on" [UK53, aged 69]. Where influence was attributed mainly to one or other source, this was often accompanied by a sense of blame or struggle: "My parents had the best of intentions, and would have done just about anything for me, but had no idea how talented I was and also had no idea that music colleges had junior departments. I now know I could have gone. The school knew though, and didn't do anything about it, and I feel slightly resentful about that" [UK37, aged 42]. This example shows how teachers can (or should) offer the necessary expertise and recognition that, even if parents' musical skills mean that it is available in the home, perhaps has the greatest impact when it comes from an adult outside the family. But parents do much more than provide funding and facilities: they were also recognised in many narratives as a stimulus for musical interest and a source of patient encouragement, particularly when motivation for practice or lessons was temporarily waning. The next section looks more closely at the home and school contexts, exploring the similarities and overlap between them and investigating what happens where there is a conflict between the musical ambitions and intentions of the two settings.

3.2 The Characteristics of Supportive Musical Environments

In both home and school settings, the critical factors in nurturing musical involvement centred around resources, attitudes, and opportunities. Respondents who were most strongly influenced by their home environment described well-resourced households in which musical instruments, the radio, and the gramophone featured prominently in daily life. Parents acted as role models through their own enjoyment of listening and playing and provided financial and moral support for the child's instrumental lessons and practice (Pitts, 2009). Wider family interactions might also involve music, with older relatives sharing their listening tastes—"the influence of parents and grandparents who lived together meant that I was also exposed to a wide range of music including dance and traditional music, classical and organ music" [UK10, aged 57]—or acting as teachers or accompanists for young people starting instrumental lessons: Matthew in Interlude I recalls how his grandmother "visited regularly and when I was a young cornet player she would often accompany me, very competently, playing popular melodies from the classical repertoire and musicals" [UK72, aged 45]. These older relatives sometimes also provided instruments—"My grandmother had a piano and she lived with us; she would play things like 'The Bluebells of Scotland'. Without this piano in the house, I may never have had much musical involvement in my life. (Horrors!)" [UK24, aged 65]—just one of a number of serendipitous routes to acquiring access to musical resources (Box 3.2.1). Grandparents, aunts, and uncles who played also helped to create a sense of musical culture within the family, unearthing stories of parents' lapsed instrumental playing and so strengthening the idea that musical learning was an integral part of childhood: "My father had also played the cello when he was a young teenager and so there was one in the house when I was young but I had never heard him play" [UK45, aged 20].

Other aspects of family culture also had musical implications, most

---

Box 3.2.1

"My parents bought a house that had a grand piano in it, which was not included in the original sale of the property. However, my father was determined to have the piano as well and only agreed to complete the transaction if the owners would agree to sell the piano, which they did. At this time I was not even born and nobody in our immediate family played the piano or any other musical instrument." [UK71, aged 51]

notably church attendance, through which some respondents came to "love the sung liturgy" [UK57, aged 64] and relish "the four-part harmony of congregational hymn singing, especially when my mother sang alto next to me" [UK28, aged 45]. One respondent described how her "family were active church goers, and hymn-singing, both congregationally and up the front as a family ensemble, were an incredibly important part of my musical background" [UK59, aged 33]. Several others had become more fully involved in church music-making during adolescence (see Interlude I), so taking their place in a musical world beyond home and school and gaining "the confidence to use music in a more professional context" [UK1, aged 19].

Although life history respondents were predominantly grateful to their parents for providing opportunities and support for musical exploration, there were a few reported clashes between parents' good intentions and the interests and ambitions of their young offspring: "My mother made me have violin lessons when I was four and I hated it! I liked music, just not the violin!" [UK2, aged 19]. The popular musicians, in particular, had experienced a disjunction between the family musical culture and their own emerging interests: describing his first forays into songwriting, one recalled how "family and friends were quite unsupportive of my new creative bent—I was quite awful and they had no vocabulary or concept of being able to tell me what I was doing wrong" [UKP41, aged 35]. Tim in Interlude D describes saving up to buy his own drum kit, rebelling against the trumpet and guitar lessons offered by his parents, and becoming more determined to pursue his own musical pathway: "I remember being offered the chance to take up the guitar (which two of my brothers played) but I wasn't interested—it had to be drums" [UKP73, aged 48]. While Tim's story includes an element of rebellion, he acknowledges that his was nonetheless a supportive musical background, with his parents eventually conceding his preference for "music that they didn't like" and paying for drum lessons. The violinist [UK2] and drummer [UKP73] in these examples share the experience of forging their own musical identities against the backdrop of a family in which music is supported and opportunities exist to pursue new directions; the songwriter [UKP41] was less fortunate in the reception of his emerging musical preferences.

These experiences illustrate that the musical resources, attitudes, and opportunities in a supportive home need to be guided but flexible, offering a positive role model for musical involvement but granting young people the freedom to pursue new interests and acquire intrinsic motivation for learning and engagement. The same might be said of the most effective school environments, which were remembered as offering a wide range of performing opportunities, alongside encouragement or inspiration from teachers who were receptive to their students' emerging needs and enthusiasms. In the most positive accounts of school experience, teachers were described as "patient and influential" [UK2, aged 19], "a role model for my musical aspirations" [UK62, aged 50], and a "key influence" [UK63, aged 57], showing how personality and guidance were closely intertwined in respondents' recollections (see Section 4.1 for further discussion). The attitudes of other teachers in the school could be important too, with head teachers setting the tone for the status of music in and out of the curriculum, and teachers of other subjects reinforcing or undermining the value of music: "there was a brilliant lady who taught at the school who used to give us lots of extra input. Somehow we had four lessons a week—I'm pretty sure she used to leave her class unattended for half an hour at a time while she rehearsed with us in the next door music room. The head teacher was also a keen musician so maybe that's how she got away with it" [UK38, aged 42].

For many of the most musically active respondents, classroom lessons were a relatively minor influence on their musical development, overshadowed by the insight and skills gained from instrumental teachers (see Section 4.2) and the performing confidence that came from enthusiastic involvement in extracurricular musical activities (see Section 3.3): "Performing as Pish Tush in *The Mikado* was the most enjoyable thing I ever did during my two years in the sixth form and I remember not being nervous at all as the curtain went up on the first night, but just being thrilled at the opportunity to take part in some music-making" [UK72, aged 45]. Opportunities for music-making within the classroom tended to be more circumscribed, limited by the challenges of managing a large group of mixed-ability students and causing frustration for some students who wanted to progress more quickly: "Music was the only lesson that I ever got sent out of to the headmistress, a serious disgrace, but it was probably because I was bored" [UK17, aged 65].

Lessons that were more successful often revealed something of the teacher's own musical passions—"my third year music class teacher was obsessed with John Cage" [UK2, aged 19]—or offered a glimpse of wider musical worlds than those encountered in the home. Across the generations, respondents remembered "the regular BBC wireless programmes *Singing Together*, which introduced us to such a wide repertoire that one would encounter years later in, say, youth orchestra, male voice choir or on record" [UK54, aged 54]. This long-running radio series began in September 1939, a few days after the start of World War II, and "school music teachers working in extremely difficult wartime circumstances were grateful for the programme's unaffected cheerfulness" (Cox, 2002, p. 46). By 1941 over 4,000 schools were tuning in, listening to programmes that were criticised by the music press as replicating too closely the model of a classroom lesson rather than providing additional and distinctive resources (ibid., p. 48); nonetheless, the programmes seem to have been of lasting value to some of the life history respondents in raising their awareness of repertoire and enjoyment of singing.

Infant school lessons that included recorder playing and singing folk songs were affectionately recalled as having laid foundations for later interest in learning an instrument: "Age 6, they started us off on the recorder—and I put that down as having perhaps the greatest influence on me becoming a musician" [UK43, aged 38]. Such activities held less immediate appeal for those of secondary school age, and here singing was remembered most favourably when it had been of a high standard and so provided a valuable training: "At senior school we had singing lessons with [. . .] a demanding and inspiring teacher and I consider myself lucky to have been taught by him at a state school. Otherwise class music was easy and I did well" [UK66, aged 40; see Interlude J]. Less fortunate respondents recalled that "we would have to listen to 'classical music' and didn't really know what to listen for or why we were listening to it" [UKP30, aged 58] or judged that they were "never pushed to learn—music lessons were taken as a joke" [UK15, aged 31]. While music teachers themselves could be inspirational (see Section 4.1), this occurred only rarely in the classroom, although it occasionally affected students who were more marginally involved in music and admired their teacher's knowledge from a distance: one lifelong listener recalled his secondary school teacher as "a short stout humourless fellow (who kept his sticks of chalk in a silver cigarette case), he introduced us to musical notation by working in detail through Beethoven's 5th Symphony, writing melody lines up on the blackboard and playing them on the piano in the classroom. I found it fascinating" [UK70, aged 67]. Experiences such as this showed a congruence of values between home and school: this man's parents were "keen radio listeners and fond of music as background" [UK70, aged 67], and the supplementary knowledge he gained at school helped to affirm his family culture of appreciative listening to classical music.

With supportive homes and schools sharing the same characteristics of encouraging musical involvement and allowing young people to find and explore their own enthusiasms, it is logical that the most influential factors for many respondents were those that bridged the gap between these two worlds: instrumental lessons, in which a teacher gave close attention to the nurturing of specific musical skills within the context of broader mentoring (see Section 4.2), and extracurricular activity, where teachers and pupils were able to work together in pursuit of a shared musical goal that transcended the limitations of the classroom. The final chapter will return to a consideration of the relative absence of memories of fulfilling classroom lessons and will evaluate the resulting arguments about the role of music in and out of the curriculum. Meanwhile, the next section analyses in more detail the evidence for extracurricular musical activity as a greater source of inspiration and involvement and identifies the distinctive qualities of this kind of musical learning.

3.3 Extracurricular Music-Making

In many of the UK life history responses, recollections of school music were centred not on classroom lessons but on the extracurricular musical activities that took place in lunch breaks and after school—participating in the orchestra, singing in the school choir, giving concerts, and putting on full-scale productions of music theatre works. Nowadays, these activities have broadened in many UK schools to include more student-led ensembles, incorporating music technology, improvisation, and a broader range of musical genres (Kaiserman et al., n.d.).

In the decades represented by the life history respondents, activities were more traditional and consistent with the predominance of classical music in the curriculum: around half of the respondents had belonged to a school choir at some time (30% in primary school, 38% in secondary school, and 17% in both), 37% to a school orchestra or band, and 19% to a county orchestra that drew exceptional players from across local schools. These latter figures, although substantial, were reduced by the prominence of pianists amongst the respondents and the absence of ensemble playing opportunities in schools for those educated before the 1950s. Participation in such ensembles and events was an affirmation of musical identity for many respondents, recalled decades later as a stimulus to seek further playing or singing opportunities in adulthood: "I can remember in the first week [at grammar school] the head teacher keeping me behind from assembly and asking me if I would like to join the orchestra. I was thrilled. There were no other [11-year-olds] in it" [UK33, aged 56]. Recollections of exclusion were also significant in memories of school music, even when overlaid with success as an adult, as Sue shows in Interlude C: positively or negatively, the extent to which respondents had been involved in the musical scene at their school had a lasting effect on the way they viewed themselves and the educational establishment (cf. Pitts, 2008).

Adults who had been members of their school choir or orchestra often cited specific repertoire, recalled many years later as an integral part of their school memories: a clarinettist recalled that he "had lots of encouragement to play at school—the orchestra had a repertoire that extended to things like Brahms' 1st symphony, Beethoven's 1st, 4th and 5th piano concertos and the Schumann (we had two star pianists, but there were good clarinet solos too!)" [UK21, aged 55]. Participation was shaped considerably by the character of the teacher (Box 3.3.1) and was not always entirely self-motivated: "opportunity amounting to compulsion to sing" [UK6, age 65] was mentioned by several of the older participants, recalling a time when music was stronger out of the classroom than within it (Rainbow & Cox, 2006, p. 303). Such forceful direction contributed to the "very strong musical ethos" [UK3, aged 52] of some schools, where the breadth and intensity of musical activity contributed to respondents' recollections of a busy and creative period in their musical lives: "choirs, orchestras, chamber music, recitals, you name it, we did it!" [UK25, aged 49].

A vibrant musical environment of this kind could generate further, self-directed opportunities, such as the founding of a music society to give concerts and play in assemblies: "we played chamber music (kids and staff together) after school, and I arrived early to practise for an hour before school started, as well as playing during free periods—I was up to something like four or five hours practice a day by about 14, the time I got my Grade 8" [UK21, aged 55]. Extracurricular participation benefited young people of varying temperaments, from the "shy boy [who] used performing music as a way of winning approval from others" [UK40, aged 44] to the confident older student who "led a jazz band in my final two years at the school and, as a result, basked in the glowing approval of my peers!" [UK47, aged 62]. A role in the school musical production could leave individuals feeling "specially chosen" [UK5, aged 37; see Interlude K] and so provide the affirmation of a fragile musical identity as well as the opportunity to gain familiarity with new skills and repertoire: "I think the development that comes from rehearsing regularly (weekly) in any ensemble, learning loads of new repertoire, giving concerts, accompanying soloists, and having to mix with others cannot be matched anywhere else" [UK51, aged 29].

The majority of the extracurricular activity recalled by participants had occurred during their teenage years, drawing on the specialist music staffing in secondary schools, and extending into auditioned county-level ensembles for pupils of a high performing standard. Membership of county ensembles was particularly prestigious, offering opportunities for ambitious music-making and providing like-minded company among which people "formed very close friends" [UK45, aged 20] or even met their future spouses [UK20, aged 62]. School ensembles, too, were a source of pride and pleasure, except on the rare occasions where participation was unwilling or unenjoyable: one respondent recalled being obliged to attend the school orchestra, "otherwise I wouldn't have been allowed to do A level music," and attributed the failings of this ensemble to lack of ambition—"rehearsing exactly one piece per term, over and over again"—and a "very boring" teacher [UK35, aged 52; see also Interlude I]. More fortunate respondents had memories of being inspired by their teachers and conductors, who often combined high levels of skill with a volatile personality: "a brilliant musician and composer who would sometimes throw a temper at us but we respected him and he got the most out of us as players" [UK20, aged 62]. Indeed, the emotional richness embedded in the descriptions of extracurricular music is striking: rehearsals, concerts, repertoire, and personalities are recalled much more vividly than classroom experiences of music, suggesting that the qualities of extracurricular participation contain some useful clues as to what makes musical education memorable.

The first of these qualities relates to sense of purpose: working with peers and teachers towards the common goal of a performance offers a focus to school life beyond the cycles of assessment that punctuate the academic year. The septuagenarian who "can still remember nearly all the set works in the examinations, and many of the works sung by the choir" [UK56, aged 73] illustrates how the intense learning most often associated with exams is also a feature of musical participation: another participant recalled similarly that "at school I only remember the works we studied for O Level and the pieces we played in the orchestra" [UK44, aged 64]. In rising to the challenge of a performance, respondents appear to have found in extracurricular school music an authenticity that might have been lacking in classroom tasks, now long forgotten. Working collectively for a public performance, young people involved in extracurricular music gain a model of musical engagement that is sustainable into adult life, beyond the institutional boundaries of teacher-directed assessment and into the negotiated world of voluntary community participation (cf. Pitts, 2005). Performances are judged by real musical criteria—solos successfully executed despite nerves, words to a song accurately remembered, ensembles playing together and in tune, and the audience sent home satisfied. This "real world" appraisal occurs simultaneously and transparently—participants know immediately when they have done well and are spurred on to achieve greater things next time. They know too when they have failed, of course (and those stories are admittedly under-represented in this group of respondents), but there are useful lessons in the risks of live performance, especially when carefully mediated by trusted adults. Even when teacher-directed, extracurricular music places greater responsibility on young people, presenting them with a clear challenge that should ideally be risky but achievable and giving them a taste for the immediacy of musical performance that might provide the foundation for future involvement.

Closely linked to this sense of collective purpose is the quality of self-discovery, whereby participants become aware of their own potential as musical contributors and have this potential validated by teachers, peers, and ultimately an appreciative audience. In his study of a school production of the musical *Godspell*, Peter Woods suggests that participation of this kind can change students' attitudes in far-reaching ways: "in giving people a sight of the ultimate, an indication of possibilities, some hitherto undreamt of, and new views of themselves, it established a platform for even greater endeavours" (Woods, 1993, p. 140). Some of the life history respondents traced a clear narrative line from their teenage involvement into adulthood (see Chapter 5), with the pride associated with a successful performance helping to cement their identities as performers (Box 3.3.2). While such self-discovery is certainly possible within the classroom, the regular, less formal teacher–student interactions that are intrinsic to extracurricular activity make this a more fertile ground for the "critical event" described again by Woods: "all became totally involved and committed as they created a life together, making new characters, language, voices, gestures, developing a culture peculiarly their own" (Woods, 1993, p. 117).

The third distinctive quality of extracurricular music is its sense of difference: part of its appeal lies in the fact that it is voluntary, taking place out of hours and slightly outside the regular rules of school interaction, inviting greater informality with teachers and a stronger sense of individuality, particularly for those with starring roles in a staged production (cf. Pitts, 2007). Participation in a school orchestra likewise

---

Box 3.3.2

"It was a chance whim on the part of the teacher that I was given a pair of timpani sticks and asked to play a short passage on the drums. By the end of my first year at the school I was timpanist in the school orchestra. Regular end-of-term concerts took place plus a concert during the spring which was our 'main event'. One year it was Britten's cantata *Saint Nicolas*, for string orchestra, piano, percussion, tenor and choir. The foreword in the score indicated that it should be tackled by a professional timpanist using chromatic instruments—we managed it using hand-tuned drums. I must confess to a certain smugness after the performance." [UK29, aged 54]

demands discipline and responsibility beyond the usual expectations of the classroom but, at its best, combines these with a sense of engagement and achievement that also surpass everyday school experience. There is a kind of institutionalised rebellion in the relaxing of school rules, combined with the increasing demands of performance, which invites students to reappraise their relationships with teachers, peers, and school. Extracurricular activity of all kinds, including music, sport, and drama, has been shown to increase school engagement among disaffected students (Cooper, Valentine, Nye, & Lindsay, 1999) and, more controversially, to increase teachers' expectations of students and their academic performance (Van Matre, Valentine, & Cooper, 2000). Participation in extracurricular music, therefore, has the potential to change students' views of themselves and the reinforcing responses of those around them.

The benefits of extracurricular music are uncomfortably accompanied by concerns and compromises, both for the teachers who have to balance their dual roles as classroom practitioner and after-school animateur and for the pupils who might find themselves excluded from musical activities that cannot (or will not) accommodate everyone who wishes to be involved. Both dilemmas have a long history in UK music education but have rightly become increasingly troubling as ideologies have moved away from an emphasis on identifying and supporting a musical élite (Fletcher, 1987) towards an ideal of accessibility and involvement (Paynter & Mills, 2008). William Salaman's reflections on life as a music teacher in the 1970–80s capture this growing realisation that music in schools had a problematic dual identity: "As the headmaster made an appropriate speech and shook my hand after a school concert, some awkward thoughts ran through my head: 'If you're so pleased by this event, why don't you employ me to mount concerts and make the classwork voluntary? I know why *I'm* pleased with this concert, but why are *you* pleased?'" (Salaman, 1983, p. 1). While a head teacher's satisfaction with a successful school concert might cynically be thought to focus on marketing the school's image and impressing parents, music teachers more often note the pleasures of sharing their own musical enthusiasms, making music as part of their daily work, and enabling students to grow in confidence and skills (Cox, 1999). Faced with multiple pressures to produce a performance of high quality, however, the resulting selection processes can leave some pupils excluded (see Interlude C), and the communities of music-making that are so beneficial to those within them can become inaccessible or unwelcoming to others.

David Bray cautions against the tendency to see extracurricular activity as "the barometer of the musicality of a school environment" (Bray, 2009, p. 10), and yet many of the life history respondents did exactly that, recalling an over-all impression of the music department being "extremely active" [UK50, aged 25], with "a wide range of musical activities" [UK3, aged 52]—or, conversely, noting that "in a sporting public school, the music staff had about as much kudos as the RE [religious education] staff" [UK7, aged 63]. Extracurricular activity could sustain an interest in music where class lessons had fallen short: "Music in my secondary school was readily available and I spent a lot of time on it, but the academic lessons themselves actually in the end put me off con-tinuing with it academically. The music teacher I had for GCSE was nearing retirement and I ended up relying on my mother's help for things such as composition" [UK45, aged 20].

Characterful music teachers were recalled by respondents for their pas-sionate commitment to music, more often demonstrated outside the curric-ulum than within it—and therefore echoing Salaman's (1983) questions about what the formal curriculum adds to the satisfaction gained through voluntary collective music-making. While the life history respondents wrote most favourably about their extracurricular activities, many of them noted with regret the absence of effective classroom teaching, implying that they sought other dimensions of musical learning within their lessons, and that a school experience consisting only of singing in the choir would have been insufficient. Much more of a concern at a policy level would be the absence of classroom lessons for those who choose not to participate in extracurric-ular music, whether through preferences for other activities or lack of moti-vation for music. Classroom lessons secure the place of music in the school experience, providing a grounding in musical knowledge and skills that ensures that all students have at least the opportunity for further engage-ment, even if such engagement occurs much later in life.

Interesting comparisons can be made with the North American model of embedding performance activities within the curriculum, through struc-tured programmes of band and choir participation, often linked to perfor-mances at competitive festivals and sports events (Radocy, 2001). Students "opt in" to the instrumental programme, which is estimated to serve around one fifth of the population in a typical district school (Morrison, 2008, p. 166) but holds a prominence in the school music provision that appears (from a UK perspective) to be more systematic and acknowledged than the varied level of commitment to extracurricular performance in British schools. A Canadian study of students' retention in band programmes showed that students considering whether or not to participate in high school band were concerned about being branded "geeks" and characterised band mem-bers as being "smart, successful, and strong individuals who do not bow to pressure from their peers" (Gouzouasis, Henrey, & Belliveau, 2008, p. 86). Other studies have shown that academic achievement is a predictor of band enrolment and that socioeconomic status is linked to retention, such that lower-achieving or socially disadvantaged students are less likely to participate in band programmes (Kinney, 2010).

These trends are consistent with the UK life history responses, which while not always reporting a high level of parental income, reflected the aspirational tendencies of parents in supporting and financing musical participation in childhood. Middle-class parenting, across Westernised cultures, has been characterised as "'concerted cultivation'—[. . .] a process of experimentation of making and finding the child, ensuring that talents and abilities are located and made the most of" (Vincent & Ball, 2007, p. 1070). The placing of musical participation in or out of the curriculum appears not to make a difference to the likelihood that particular groups of students will participate, or to their experiences of doing so, which in US and UK cases similarly are dependent on teacher enthusiasm, the presence of like-minded friends, and the sense of developing personally and as a musician (Gouzouasis, Guhn, & Kishor, 2007; Pitts, 2007).

Where clear differences between the UK and US experience emerge is in the long-term impact of performance in schools. The UK life history responses illustrate strong connections between experiences of singing in the choir, for example, and seeking out a choral society to join in later adulthood; conversely, some younger respondents expressed anxiety that their university performing experiences might be their last opportunities to make music—a fear that older respondents mainly demonstrated to be unfounded. However, under the North American system of strongly teacher-directed ensemble performance, "many students put their instruments away for good on high school graduation, even after exclaiming repeatedly that they love band or that orchestra is their favorite class" (Morrison, 2008, p. 181). Rudolf Radocy agrees with this assertion, stating that "many 'graduates' of American music education do not continue their active music-making experiences into adult life" (Radocy, 2001, p. 123) and suggesting that this trend turns music into a "commodity", with "a few making most of the music for the many". Music education in the US undoubtedly has an effect on its adult population, making them more "omnivorous" or open-minded listeners (Graham, 2009) and so contributing to "values of cultural openness and cultural diversity in society" (p. 298). Nonetheless, for the benefits of band participation to be confined to the school years seems an unnecessary limitation, and researchers have recently begun to challenge the assumption that "ensemble membership may not be an experience that transcends time and place" (Morrison, 2008, p. 181) and to look for ways in which longer-term engagement in music can be fostered within the curriculum.

Roger Mantie and Lynne Tucker, investigating the sustaining of musical activity from school years into adult life, concur that "music teaching, as it presently occurs in many schools, is premised on the belief that the goal of the activity is to 'make it' to grade twelve, after which point one can safely pack the instrument away in a closet until it is time for one's own children to play an instrument in the school's band" (Mantie & Tucker, 2008, p. 218). The fault-lines, they suggest, lie in teachers' perceptions that this self-contained musical world is the one in which they should be operating, and in students' consequent lack of awareness of the connections between their school music-making and the community activities taking place beyond the school grounds. As with my life history project, Mantie and Tucker collected their data from "people who have made the volitional choice to continue participating with their instruments" (p. 225), judging these to represent a small minority of high school music graduates. The few American respondents in my sample confirm this picture: after "fantastic" experiences of being in a marching band at school, one flute and oboe player had mixed success in continuing with ensemble playing, stating that "after school I joined a chamber orchestra and I absolutely adored it. I tried to join a local band when I lived in Chicago but they were terrible at attendance and had concerts where only three or four members would attend" [OUK49, aged 29].

The life history responses suggest that the disjunction between school and adult music-making in the UK is not so great, although the preponderance of older respondents, satisfied with the smooth transition from school choirs to adult choral societies, represent a different experience from that of today's school leavers, entering a more diverse musical world in which the skills acquired in school are not so readily accommodated. The North American model therefore offers a useful illustration of the limitations of pursuing teacher-directed musical participation in schools without a clear sense of how students' skills and engagement can be sustained in the longer term. Whilst music-making in the school years has clear immediate benefits, it runs the risk of fixing musical identities in childhood, with participation valued as part of a person's past rather than his or her potential future. When teachers and school structures define music solely in terms of school goals, rather than within lifespan and community contexts, they contribute, however unintentionally, to the number of instruments "currently sitting in closets collecting dust" (Mantie & Tucker, 2008, p. 225). The many highly motivated individuals amongst the life history respondents show that personal determination and the continuing quest for musical engagement are also strong factors in lifelong participation, but it seems that across the continents schools could be doing much more to celebrate the later achievements of their music graduates and to present them as role models for current students.

3.4 Musical Self-Education

Beyond the curricular and extracurricular provision of schools and the encouragement of parents and the wider family, a substantial proportion of the life history respondents engaged in musical self-education and recalled this as a significant influence on their musical skills and attitudes. Seventeen (21%) of the UK respondents had learned instruments without the intervention of a teacher, extending their musical experiences beyond those they were gaining in formal education in ways that often exhibited a spirit of resourcefulness rather than rebellion. Those with instruments available in the home wrote of how they would "pick out tunes on the piano" [UK66, aged 40], "learn to play chords on the guitar" [UK61, aged 50], or teach themselves "to play the recorder from the Schott's Recorder Tutor" [UK53, aged 69]. These signs of musical interest were sometimes encouraged by parents, with lessons following later, and in other cases were an alternative to formal tuition when this was not available: "Piano lessons at age 8, but these were short-lived as it was during the war and my mother did not like me being out during air raids, so thereafter I was a self-taught pianist" [UK18, aged 76].

School break-times were another source of musical resources and exploration, with senior students particularly enjoying the freedom of such activities as "trying to teach myself bass clef and learning to make some noises on a cello"— an experience made "even more enjoyable as this was a permitted excuse for missing 'games'" [UK22, aged 60]. As Graham's experience in Interlude F shows, such chance encounters with new instruments could have far-reaching consequences, in his case drawing him into the school and county orchestras and ultimately to a thriving amateur playing life as an adult. Although lessons from inspiring teachers were also central to that journey, the sense of having discovered the French horn for himself seems important to Graham's story, which is full of enthusiasm and a sense of seizing opportunities—qualities that are found in many of the self-educators' narratives.

As might be expected (cf. Green, 2002), some of the popular musicians in the life history sample had initially pursued their interests through self-teaching, acquiring instruments by saving up for them, and learning alongside friends or by listening to recordings (Box 3.4.1). As with the respondents who discovered new orchestral instruments in cupboards at school, the direct contact with an instrument was important and provided access to new musical worlds, which in the pop musicians' cases were distinct from those inhabited by their parents and teachers. Transcending the formal provision of music education, students who sought out their own musical direc-

> **Box 3.4.1**
>
> "I began by singing together with a school friend and we learned to sing the harmonies of pop songs while accompanying ourselves rhythmically playing on any available surface with our hands. Often we would copy exact drum patterns that we heard on records especially 'Love Potion Number 9' by the Searchers (I think). Later, I taught myself to play bass guitar and Hammond organ by ear and played in several groups over the following twenty years." [UKP30, aged 58]

tions often did so with determination, comparable with recent studies of student-led "garage bands" (Fornäs, Lindberg, & Sernhede, 1995), which have revealed a gulf between the musical skills and interests of students outside school and the objectives and outcomes of the classroom. Life history respondents had little to say about the absence of teachers from their independent forays into pop music: often they inhabited both musical worlds, as in Tim's account (Interlude D) of having trumpet lessons even while acquiring the drum kit that represented "what [he] really wanted to do" [UKP73, aged 48].

It seems that the challenges in relating formal and informal learning are greater for teachers than for emerging popular musicians: "School can be a place where positive musical identities are established, but not if students believe that the musicians they are in school are different from the musicians they are in their garage" (Jaffurs, 2004, p. 198). Classical musicians were prone to expressing disappointment if their musicality was not recognised by teachers and years later would still "regret never being 'chosen' to sing in the choir at primary school" [UK47, aged 62]. For popular musicians, this concern was not so great, and it was accepted as the norm that their musical interests would be pursued amongst peer groups, though recognition was welcome when it was offered: "My music teacher at school was amazing— she really embraced my passion and musical ability and would encourage and empower me for in- and out-of-class activities" [UKP74, aged 18].

Five of the twelve popular musicians mentioned having been influenced by their listening, recalling particular artists "whose styles I tried to copy and combine to find my own playing style" [UKP30, aged 58]. Such influences were not confined to the pop musicians, as this organist recalls while looking back on her first encounters with the classical organ repertoire: "my brother bought an organ record to test out his new speakers—both the 'tweeters' and the bass—and this particular Bach record was a good one to use apparently. I was 'hooked' on it, though he didn't like it all that much. (I've still got it)" [UK24, aged 65]. Even when their listening did not lead directly towards a choice of instrument, the development of individual tastes and independent listening was an important strand of musical self-education, recalled by 19 (23%) of the UK respondents. Listening to iconic artists sometimes marked a departure from family tastes into musical independence: "Bob Dylan when I was 18 made me listen to music differently and got me into new styles. No one in my house liked him and I bought a CD just to see" [UKP14, aged 26]. As with the self-discovery of musical instruments, the excitement of finding new nourishment for growing musical appetites was evident amongst those who recalled listening to the radio (Box 3.4.2) and building up their own record collection (see Interlude F), making the most of all available resources: "big brother's increasing collection of records and, with pocket money and second-hand shops, acquiring records of my own too, most notable being a boxed set of Brahms songs on 78s" [UK22, aged 60].

Shared listening with family members was important to many of these respondents too, but self-directed listening could help to form a distinctive identity and sometimes filled the gaps in parents' tastes: "my parents were a huge influence on my musical development though no help at all with the world of rock/pop" [UK67, aged 49]. Research on the formation of young people's listening tastes (e.g., North, Hargreaves, & O'Neill, 2000) shows that this process of discovery and exploration is a strong factor in establishing a musical identity, as is the talk about music that reinforces friendships and allows young people to negotiate and display their musical and social values (MacDonald, Niell, & Wilson, 2005). As the life history respondents demonstrate, these developing tastes can have lifelong effects on musical outlook and preferences, setting up attitudes to listening that continue into early adulthood (Lamont & Webb, 2010) and later life (Hays & Minichiello, 2005).

3.5 An Italian Perspective: Music as Specialist Education

The experiences reported so far in this chapter illustrate the ideals and pitfalls of musical education in Britain. At its best it offers a solid foundation for learning, with diverse opportunities for performance and self-discovery, and a coherent bridge to the musical worlds occupied by supportive and interested parents; but when this fails, it is a source of alienation or discouragement through lack of opportunity or support in the home or school. In this section, the data from Italian respondents will be presented as a case study of a distinctive music education system that has historically prioritised specialist training rather than the generalist approaches of the British curriculum (Guardabasso, 1989). A first overview of the data reveals clear differences between the home and school influences prevalent in UK responses (Table 3.1) and those from Italy (Table 3.2), showing an absence in the Italian responses of school influence beyond elementary level and a greater dominance of parental attitudes and family culture.

Once again, caution is needed in interpreting the percentages in Table 3.2: the numbers of responses are small, and the quantitative analysis offers only a rank ordering with no claims to wider generalisation. Nonetheless, the stronger influence of home over school for Italian respondents is immediately apparent, and all the more striking when the negative associations of the educational memories are noted: lack of music is the main memory for 42% of respondents, and experiences of recorder playing and learning of notation are not often fondly remembered (Box 3.5.1).

One older respondent stated categorically that "In my day we did not do music in school" [IA18, aged 67], whilst a younger musicology student described the current situation as follows: "In Italy music is not very present in the school system. Although it is included up to the age of thirteen and

---

Box 3.5.1

"I have never received a specific music education, although in middle school I played the recorder for three years, but not out of passion, it was part of the music education curriculum. During the third (and last) year, thanks to my mother's push, I also tried to learn how to play the guitar. However, after six months of arpeggios (the teacher did not let us do anything else because she said that we had to practise), I gave it up because of the boredom that made me lose motivation. However I am now very envious of a friend of mine who plays it, because when we meet with our group of friends, for example at the gardens, and we do not know what to do, his guitar is the focal point among us and we spend beautiful moments. Who knows, maybe one day I will start to play it again—I would still like to." [IA12, aged 24]

TABLE 3.2 Rank Ordering of Home and School Influences from Italian Adults (% of 25 Responses)

HOME INFLUENCES	RANK ORDER	EDUCATION INFLUENCES
	1	Singing in elementary school (48%)
	2	High school: lack of music in school (42%)
Parental support for lessons (40%)	3	
	4	High school: recorder playing (36%)
Mother listening (32%)	5	
Instrumental lessons (28%)	= 6	Instrumental lessons (28%)
Singing in choirs as an adult (28%)	= 6	
Developing own listening tastes (24%)	= 8	
Father listening (24%)	= 8	
Friends' influence (24%)	= 8	
	= 8	Learning theory and notation (24%)
Lack of listening in the home (20%)	= 12	
	= 12	Performing opportunities (20%)
Siblings listening (20%)	= 12	
Singing in the home (20%)	= 12	

Box 3.5.2

"As for music in school, I have good memories only for middle school (11–13 years): I had a blind teacher who loved music and transmitted this love to us; we used to play the recorder and he made us sing in harmony (po-lyphony). My experience in secondary school was horrible: the teacher was lazy and less than competent. No experience in primary school: the teacher did not carry out the lessons of music education." [IA11, aged 28]

in pilot high-schools, it is taught in an amateur fashion, very little practice, no musical ensemble" [IA15, aged 28]. Memories of school music were therefore often patchy (Box 3.5.2), focusing on the singing of national songs in nursery and elementary schools, and beyond that being dependent on the enthusiasm of individual teachers: education was limited to "the weekly singing lesson hour" [IA8, no age given], and sometimes "the hour of music was not [included] in the curriculum" [IA12, aged 24]. School-aged and adult respondents alike appear to have absorbed the message that music in Italian schools is enjoyable at its best but has low status in the curriculum. Janet Hoskyns has suggested that underlying educational values contribute to the "commonly-held view that an academic curriculum needs moments of leisure and recuperation; music, visual art and physical education have often been required to fill this slot in European education systems" (Hoskyns, 2002, p. 56).

Those adult Italian respondents who had acquired high levels of performance skill had done so through the optional conservatoire system, encouraged by their parents to seek a more rigorous musical training, which was sometimes criticised as being "too rigid with little attention to our interests" [IA5, aged 27] and which created a divide in schools where the conservatoire-educated children "already knew more than I was taught" [IA22, aged 43]. The absence of a structured musical education within mainstream schools appears to have created a void of opportunity for the Italian respondents, which some filled through the intervention of supportive parents and inspiring instrumental teachers, while others were left regretting in adulthood that they had not received sufficient encouragement to persist with instrumental tuition: "had I followed the advice of my brother, who wanted to convince my parents to make me study the piano, maybe my life would have been different" [IA9, aged 46].

The most memorable aspects of school music were consistent across the adult and student responses, showing limited evidence of the generational change that was a feature of the UK sample (see Chapter 2). Younger respondents generally spoke more positively of their experiences, either having enjoyed their class lessons in recorder playing or singing or feeling that the minimal provision was appropriate to their level of interest: "in primary school we sometimes sang some songs, and I liked it very much, although this subject was never very present and developed during the school year. In middle school I played the recorder" [IS5, aged 17]. End-of-term concerts were recalled as highlights, with changes in repertoire marking the passing years: in the 2000s "I remember singing 'The Lion King' and in middle school I played 'We are the World' on the recorder at the end of school concert" [IS11, aged 18], while in the 1970s "we often sang patriotic songs while our teacher played the harmonium" [IA9, aged 46]. For most current students, music in school was inconsequential: they could recall no specific highlights and had "no regrets, because I am not particularly interested" [IS8, aged 17].

The exclusive focus on performance and theory within the curriculum meant that those adult respondents with an interest in composing, most often

"After the end of the school, I went on holiday to the seaside and many of the boys in the group I associated with there could *play*! Actually almost all had started to play a few months before, but they said they could get away with it quite well, and among them there was someone who even considered himself a genius [. . .] I remember that all the boys who began to play the guitar at that time learnt the first chords through Nirvana songs. Following the steps of Nirvana, I got to know punk music by the Sex Pistols, the Ramones and other groups; I, however, still preferred The Doors. I decided that I absolutely *had* to learn to play an instrument!" [IA14, aged 29]

expressed through songwriting, had pursued this independently: one story of a guitarist who had "written songs since I learnt the first chords" [IA14, aged 29] was close to those of the UK pop musicians in recalling specific artists—Michael Jackson, Guns N' Roses, the Beatles—whose music he had discovered in adolescence and learned to copy in bands with his friends (Box 3.5.3). His experience illustrates the clash between the classical music education that was supported by his parents and the pop music that was motivating his interest in music: lessons with a classical guitarist involved "a year of little waltzes and mazurkas" before finding in later adolescence "a private tutor who introduced me to different music genres: blues, jazz, bossa nova" [IA14, aged 29]. Like this man's parents and first teacher, some respondents dismissed their playing of popular music as not constituting part of a recognised musical pathway: one mentioned playing "only guitar at parties" [IA9, aged 46] during adolescence, and another characterised her guitar playing by saying "I only play rock music, that is to say rock intended as pop music for the young" [IA13, aged 22]. The clear distinction made by respondents between having attended the conservatoire or not seems to lead to a closely bounded definition of musical education, whereby other aspects of musical learning are tacitly accepted as being less significant or worthy of recognition.

The conservatoire system in Italy—as in other central European countries—inevitably reduces the status of generalist music teachers while at the same time increasing the influence of parents, who have the responsibility of deciding whether or not to encourage their child into instrumental learning. Such a choice exists under the UK system too, of course, but there is a greater fluidity between classroom music, private instrumental tuition, and extracurricular activities, meaning that decisions can be made later in a child's life and after greater exposure to musical opportunities in school. The Italian respondents were consistent in attributing the decision to learn, and sometimes also the choice of instrument, to their parents: typical stories included "my mother enrolled me in a music school, I began to play the flute but I stopped at 13" [IA8, no age given] and "my father, who had been a violin player and had studied at the music school for a few years, insisted (too much) that I carried on with the instrument, sending me to the music school" [IA24, aged 23]. Like the UK respondents, some of those who began lessons in childhood had continued learning to a high level, whilst others had stopped after a few years. However, there was more limited evidence of the Italian respondents returning to learning in adulthood, and they were more likely to express a sense of regret at having given up their lessons: "when I hear somebody playing the flute, I regret not having carried on, and that nobody ever explained to me the beauty of jazz" [IA8, no age given].

One Italian respondent's father was a musical enthusiast who brought guitars, harmonicas, and an accordion into the home, but access to these instruments without the guidance of a teacher was a mixed blessing for his daughter: "The chance that I had to play the musical instruments that I had on hand at home, has certainly affected my playing experience, my desire for discovery, knowledge, my fantasy. Sometimes, however, I think it has created a sense of defeat, or inadequacy—being surrounded by a number of instruments, without being able to play one seriously" [IA16, aged 24]. Once again the need for the validation of the conservatoire is in evidence, and learning that has been acquired less formally is presented modestly. It seems that a system geared towards training élite instrumentalists has unforeseen long-term effects, narrowing the definition of what it means to be a musician and leaving those outside that system with only limited routes into musical participation. Writing about the state of Italian music education in the 1980s, when some of these respondents were students, Giovanna Guardabasso confirmed that "There are no state-run music schools available to anyone wishing to learn to play a musical instrument at the amateur level," stating that "this gap is filled by private initiative or by local organizations which promote courses and music schools at various levels, too often, however, conceived on the conservatory model" (Guardabasso, 1989, p. 36). The life history respondents offer some evidence of the social implications of this national system, which relate not just to the restricting of musical training to a small proportion of the population but also to the attitudes and expectations of the wider majority.

Another implication of a divided music education system is its effects on future teachers in creating a separation between musically trained adults, more likely to become secondary school music teachers, and untrained adults, more likely to go into primary school teaching. A study of Italian pre-service teachers' beliefs about music found that trainee primary school teachers saw music as a specialist discipline or talent, with fixed skills that they could not expect to acquire themselves; by contrast, "factors such as study ability, performance skills and music interpretation were considered more subject to improvement by trainee secondary teachers probably because they are musicians and they know already how study can lead to progress" (Biasutti, 2010, p. 62). These beliefs are comparable with those of English primary school teachers, who are also reported to be low in confidence for teaching music despite their adaptability for all other curriculum subjects (Hennessy, 2000). Teachers' fixed beliefs about their own capacity for music can lead to a "cycle of low expectation in the development of musical skills" (Biasutti, 2010, p. 64) whereby generalist teachers not only lack confidence to teach music but also assume that musical potential will be the exception rather than the norm amongst their pupils. However, some encouraging signs of the potential for these attitudes to change were evident in the life history responses from those who had trained as teachers, including one who was learning guitar "because I would like to develop activities with children" [IA1, aged 33]. Another reflected that "at university my musical memories are linked to the two classes in which for the first time I explored music of the environment and using recycled materials" and reported now being "happy to be able to use my musical abilities working with children" [IA6, aged 27].

Outside school, Italian parents and the wider family were also influential in shaping the musical environment of the home, and details of specific repertoire and parental listening enthusiasms were comparable with those of the UK respondents (Box 3.5.4). There were stories of mothers singing around the house, grandmothers teaching national and folk songs to young children, and older siblings bringing modern pop into the house for the first time: "My brother, who was always very fond of good rock music, criticised me if I happened to listen to poor music and made me discover the quality music of our time; my father made me discover the quality rock music of the 60s and 70s (we got from him the "old" cassettes); and my mother introduced me to classical music (from her we got many CDs and the chance to go to see operas)" [IA13, aged 22]. This ambient musical learning was seen as having

Box 3.5.4

"When I was little I listened to the commercial music that my family liked (Madonna, Duran Duran, Michael Jackson), the music of the 1980s that my sister loved. My mother always listened to Italian singer-songwriters like Fabrizio De Andrè and Paolo Conte, and to opera, especially Verdi, whilst my father preferred blues and soul, particularly Joe Cocker. I'm sure that listening to Italian songs influenced my decision to learn the guitar, whilst I liked and still like blues for singing." [IA6, aged 27]

shaped tastes and interests into adult life: a grandmother who listened constantly to opera on the radio left her grandchild knowing "the words of operas without knowing when I learnt them" [IA8, no age given], and several respondents recalled that as children they "always sang the signature tune of cartoons" [IA19, aged 29]. Another recalled singing in the car with her mother on the way to school, saying that "I have always loved that sense of relaxed sharing that was there in those moments" [IA23, aged 34; see Interlude E].

Friends, too, were influential, particularly from teenage years into young adulthood—from the woman who had "had three fiancés, all musicians!" [IA19, aged 29] to the trainee teacher influenced by "my friends and listening to the radio a lot" [IA11, aged 28]. And while a relatively small proportion of the Italian respondents had experienced the influence of an inspiring teacher, those who had done so valued teachers with character, such as "an extremely playful (but not superficial) approach to the subject" [IA24, aged 23]. Italian respondents therefore show themselves to be open to positive musical role models in the same way as the UK respondents, but to be encountering these less reliably in school, and therefore being perhaps more aware of the influences of parents, friends, and others.

While some of the life history respondents were willing to assert that their education system "results in a very high lack of music knowledge in the average Italian" [IA13, aged 22], there is too little evidence here for me to make any such judgement as an outsider. Certainly, the 25 adults and 28 school students were consistent in their portrayal of minimal music provision in mainstream schools, and their stories illustrate some of the consequences of the high status of conservatoire music education, which is of clear benefit to those with ambitions as classical performers but largely disenfranchising to those who have other interests or who lack the parental support or intrinsic motivation to learn within a traditional system. The life history reports also suggest that music in mainstream schools is defined rather narrowly, focusing mainly on singing, recorder playing, and listening and lacking relevance to the wider musical interests of many students. These problems are not, of course, unique to Italy: Mikko Anttila (2010) expresses similar concerns about music education in Finland, asserting that "most music cultures of today and ways of enjoying music are left outside the curriculum" (p. 251). Like the Italian respondents, Anttila attributes Finnish pupils' lack of engagement with music to its minimal provision in the curriculum, explaining that "pupils at the upper level of the comprehensive school (aged 13–16) usually have only one lesson per week, and music is a compulsory subject during only the first year" (p. 242). This level of provision is not so different from that in Britain, where music becomes optional after the age of 14 and is usually allocated only one timetabled hour per week.

The difference across these European countries seems therefore to be in attitude as much as in access, and in expectations as well as experiences.

3.6 Summary: Situated Learning for Music

The experiences of the life history respondents show how musical learning takes place across a range of locations: in school classrooms and in school halls after hours, through singing at church, by attending concert venues, at friends' houses, in instrumental teaching studios, in practice rooms or in a corner of the dining room at home, round the radio in the kitchen at a mealtime, at rehearsals of the county youth orchestra, and in unexpected conversations with adults and peers who share an enthusiasm for music. They also illustrate how it is the connection between these locations that help to nurture a coherent sense of musical learning and identity. Musical messages can be reinforced through hearing the same kinds of music at school and at home, or by acquiring skills in an instrumental lesson that are then recognised and affirmed through extracurricular participation. Gaining musical confidence in a church setting, for example, can help open the possibility of a musical career, for which parental encouragement and teacher guidance can provide a supportive pathway. The task of making these connections, however, can be a bewildering one for emerging musicians and is often thwarted by apparent conflicts between the musical values of home and school, parents and teachers, creating a disjunction between the formal education being provided in school and the informal learning acquired in a range of other contexts.

The theory of "situated learning" proposed by Jean Lave and Etienne Wenger (1991) sheds further light on the translation of values and attitudes that occurs across different locations for learning. By viewing learning as a process of apprenticeship, or "legitimate peripheral participation" (p. 29), Lave and Wenger show how learners of all ages not only acquire skills and competence by working alongside established experts in their field of learning but are also enculturated in the social norms and cultural values of their new community—whether this is a workplace, a support group, or a school. Applying these concepts to music in schools highlights the need for musical education to connect with the wider art world (cf. Becker, 1982), and the responsibility of teachers to make young people aware of the longer-term goals of their rehearsing, performing, creating, and listening. Without this, school music is self-contained and becomes a threat to future musical identities rather than their foundation: young musicians whose focus is entirely on exam results and competition success "simply do not envision what they do as leading towards an in-the-world social practice" (Mantie & Tucker, 2008, p. 221).

Outside school, children are situated learners in their parents' musical worlds, acquiring and appraising their musical preferences, understanding the prominence given to music in their home life, and perhaps witnessing the satisfaction that their parents, siblings, and wider family gain from musical activity and participation. Through media influences in the home and beyond, young people learn about the music of their time and how this relates to the musical teaching they are offered in school (Lum, 2008). There are clear dangers in having too great a gulf between the musical worlds of home and school, but the life history respondents show conversely that finding new musical interests through their teachers' enthusiasms and expertise could have life-changing effects. While the informal expertise acquired in music should not therefore dictate the curriculum, music in schools needs to take its place alongside the multiple musical influences of a child's world, acting as a model of musical engagement that is sustainable beyond the limited hours of timetabled teaching.

Patricia Shehan Campbell's (1998) ethnographic study of young children's musical experiences, *Songs in Their Heads*, provides a child's-eye perspective on the bridges between musical learning in all aspects of life, from the musical toys in a children's store to the rhythmic sweeping of the dining hall floor undertaken by volunteers at the end of a school lunch break. Sympathetically but alarmingly, Campbell observes a school music lesson and finds that "Mrs Bedford's music class" engage in more musically sophisticated play as they enter and leave the classroom than they are permitted to display in the teacher-directed activities of the lesson (p. 55). Teachers, it seems, do not always know their students musically, as demonstrated by the stories of missed opportunities and lack of recognition in the life histories. However, when that recognition of shared enthusiasm and interest is made between a child and a significant adult, it is a powerful impetus to lifelong musical engagement, as reported many times in descriptions of influential teachers and supportive parents. Chapter 4 will now explore more closely the effects of the people within the locations for learning that have been considered here, showing how personal interactions and situated musical opportunities combine to leave a lasting impression on formative musical identities.

Interlude E: Valeria Benvenuti [IA23] Aged 34, left school 1993

Italian singer with memories of influential mother and primary school music

At home my mother sang a lot. I remember that singing was a daily activity, at the point that every morning, during the long car journey to school, we used to sing all together a choice of songs that we all loved. I think that this influenced my musical development a lot. I have always loved that sense of relaxed sharing that was there in those moments. I believe that her strong musical interest left me with a legacy of passion for music and singing in particular.

During primary school I had a teacher who made us sing a lot. Compared to my brother and sister's teachers, I did many more 'musical activities' than they did, although it was only limited to the songs of the folk repertoire or to the creation of songs regarding specific events (such as the change of seasons, or people of our class), composed by our teacher for us. I have very boring memories of musical activities at school from 11 to 13. Our teacher just made us study history of music and at times we did a bit of musical analysis. The fact that there was a disabled girl in the class made the teacher decide not to make us play any instruments so that this girl did not feel uneasy. This, however, put the girl in an even more difficult position, because she was made to feel guilty in front of all of us for having prevented the class from playing the recorder or the diamonica, the typical instruments that students play at that age. We were all sympathetic towards our school friend and I remember that we carried out campaigns so that we could start to play and the girl herself could experiment too with some instruments, but it never happened.

My mother remained one of my strongest musical influences, from many points of view. Her singing and playing fascinated me and I liked the fact that I could share with her this passion for music. For this reason, since I was little, my mother always insisted, ever arguing with my father, that I studied an instrument. I don't know what she saw in me, but I know that when I was 5 she bought me a piano for my birthday. I remember that I liked singing but I had no desire to study any instrument. My mother's insistence to make me study led me to not particularly love the piano, which I studied nonetheless for seven years (starting again later on for my teaching job). Every year I begged her to let me start to play the guitar, an instrument that seemed more familiar to me because my mother and uncle played it. The usual answer was that she knew that I didn't particularly enjoy studying the piano, but it was only an exercise and that when I was older I could choose to play whatever I wanted. When I was 12 I finally started to play the guitar and at 15 to take singing lessons. A particular singing teacher was very important for me when I was a teenager. She passed on to me the passion for the repertoire and she was always a very positive person, letting me acquire a confidence in my abilities that I believe determined many of my following choices. My teachers were essential. Even those from whom I did not learn anything in the music field had a positive influence, because they did not undermine my desire to progress, but helped me to understand my boundaries (what I like and what I don't like).

Maybe at 16 I would have said that I wanted to become a professional singer. For the last few years I have said that if I was born again I would like to play the cello. I am however extremely satisfied with what I have done and I am doing, therefore I don't think I have any regrets.

(*Translation: Anna Ferrarese & Stephanie Pitts*)

Interlude F: Graham Stroud [UK64]
Aged 55, left school 1970

Childhood playing and listening encouraged at school and home; now an enthusiastic horn player, conductor, singer, and listener

There was always music at home, but not to any very great degree. My father was (and still is) a lover of classical music. He had played clarinet and piano, but no longer did so when I was born. We had a piano, which I started to learn at the age of about 4 or 5 and my father had a very small collection of classical LPs (they were very expensive) and some sets of 78s. I was given an old wind-up 78 rpm gramophone when I was about 4 and had a few (mostly non-classical) favourite records. My mother preferred lighter music, including Elvis. My parents are not religious, so I did not know hymns until I went to school. I can remember being taken to two Robert Mayer children's concerts in the Festival Hall[1] and hearing the Mozart 4th horn concerto, which I loved. Afterwards, I can recall doing drawings at school of a symphony orchestra stage layout.

I went to four different schools in total, as we moved house several times and music was very different in all of them. At my first preparatory school, music was limited to the morning hymn—we sang only two hymns, on alternate days! I also attended the Crusaders (Sunday school at a local church) because a friend of mine went—they had various songs, some of which I can still recall. We then moved to Surrey, and at the local County Primary was a teacher who played the piano well and had sung with the

---

[1] See Interlude B for details of Robert Mayer concerts.

D'Oyly Carte[2] company; she produced a Gilbert and Sullivan operetta every two years with the top two forms. Although I was still having piano lessons and moving up through the ABRSM grades, I didn't greatly enjoy them (not a very inspiring teacher), but the G&S was a big watershed, as I got a leading part and enjoyed singing and acting hugely. Another teacher also started a music appreciation club after school, where we were encouraged to bring along some favourite records to play to the others. I remember taking along Offenbach's *Bouffes Parisiennes*, which was a big hit. I got a scholarship to a private school in London where music was a huge part of the curriculum. The whole ethos of the school was very competitive and I auditioned for the choirs. I first got into the Concert Choir (the middle choir), but didn't stop trying until I got into the Anthem Choir (the élite). Apart from the kudos of being in the top choir, there was the added attraction of missing assembly for rehearsals each morning. I remember the teachers being good choral trainers, but not their music lessons in general.

Perhaps one of the most important influences on my musical life came about because the school allowed pupils to try out instruments in the lunch break. I booked a horn (as I still remembered the concert I'd been to) and immediately took to it. I subsequently taught myself a scale of C major in lunch breaks. When the music master heard, he immediately invited me to join the junior orchestra and I was allowed to take the horn home to practise. The first 'proper' concerts I ever took part in were at school (Britten *Ceremony of Carols*, Haydn *Creation*). My father's job moved, so after less than two years there, I was moved to a grammar school in Huntingdonshire, where music was present, but less active than at my scholarship school. I had to give up the horn (the school had no instruments), but was an enthusiastic choir member. The music master was close to retirement and a pretty strict disciplinarian, which put off people who were not interested, but he had such a profound love and enthusiasm for music that this rubbed off on those who were already inclined in that direction. He fostered a profound respect for the 'greats' (particularly Haydn, Beethoven, Brahms) and also for some lesser lights (particularly Franck—he was an organist by training). I had been getting progressively more and more enthusiastic about classical music during my secondary school years, particularly through having a close friend who was equally enthusiastic, having a good and kind piano teacher and the fact that our lessons were very good fun.

---

[2] D'Oyly Carte was a professional light opera company founded in the 1880s to perform the works of librettist W. S. Gilbert and composer Arthur Sullivan, collectively known as the "Savoy Operas" and including *The Mikado*, *Pirates of Penzance*, and other works still popular with amateur opera groups in the UK today (see Eden & Saremba, 2009).

A decisive moment came when Huntingdonshire county music service decided to create a county youth orchestra. My friend and I volunteered to learn percussion, receiving free lessons from a local maths teacher who had played with the Concertgebouw and the New York Philharmonic when he was younger. Of course, this meant a lot of hassle for my father, who had to transport us and our instruments around to rehearsals and concerts. After a couple of years, we both fancied an easier life, so my friend went to the county music office to see if he could borrow another orchestral instrument to learn. He came back with a bassoon and a horn, as that was all that was available, and I took up the horn again at age 17. This time, I had lessons (arranged through the county music service). Although my teacher was not a horn player, he was a very fine musician (a former champion cornet of the UK) and taught the basics very soundly. As a result, I progressed rapidly and was soon 1st horn of the county youth orchestra (and my friend was 1st bassoon). As a school-leaving present, the new music master wrote a mini-concerto for the two of us to play with the school orchestra.

I went to university to study chemical engineering, but immediately took up with the music undergraduates (where I met my wife). I took part in all that I could at the university (chamber choir, orchestra, opera society) and had lessons with the 3rd horn of the City of Birmingham Symphony Orchestra.[3] He was a truly inspirational teacher and I worked very hard at the instrument. As a result, I was asked by him to play with the CBSO in my final year when they needed extra players—I actually ended up sight-reading the 1st horn part in a concert on one occasion. This was probably one of the high points of my horn playing career, although I am actually a much better player now, after years of experience. My greatest regret is that I did not continue with the piano once my horn playing took off. I reached Grade 7+, but failed to keep it up and often regret not being able to read accompaniments more easily. I have plans to re-start the piano when I retire. I now also regret that my horn teachers did not insist on diligent scale and arpeggio practice when I was younger—although I can play at sight most parts I meet, I realise that certain passages would be much easier and 'automatic' had I been forced to 'hard-wire' the fingering patterns when I was young. When I was younger, I regretted not doing music as a career choice, but I now realise that it is a very difficult profession and that it takes huge perseverance and tenacity to have anything approaching a comfortable life.

---

[3] A professional orchestra based in Birmingham, in the English Midlands: see http://www.cbso.co.uk

4 | Inspiring, Affirming, Challenging
SIGNIFICANT PEOPLE IN MUSICAL LEARNING

4.1 What Makes a Memorable Classroom Music Teacher?

T HERE ARE MANY WAYS IN which teachers can be memorable: through their eccentricities, their personality, the ethos of their lessons, their attitudes to students, their disciplinary style, and perhaps above all through the individual interactions that are imprinted on a child's memory and taken into adulthood as being representative of that person and, by association, that subject. Those among the life history respondents who remembered their music teachers fondly told stories of larger-than-life characters whose own musical activities shaped their teaching and spilled out into life outside school through attending and giving concerts with their students (Box 4.1.1).

Inspiring music teachers were associated with "tireless support" [UK62, aged 50] in their work, providing extracurricular opportunities, offering additional tuition and coaching, and making links with performing groups and societies outside school. High levels of musical skill were admired in teachers—one had "just casually played Chopin's black key study. That I still remember tells you that it influenced me" [UK36, aged 81]—but so too was a willingness to embrace new challenges, as Steph in Interlude H recalled of her infant teacher: "The teacher there was very enthusiastic and started a small group of us on the treble [recorder] so I felt quite privileged. That was a new thing for her as well and I remember she learnt with us" [UK51, aged 29]. One respondent recalled "the archetypical inspirational teacher, totally devoted to her subject and her pupils" [UK29, aged 54], and these blurred boundaries between educational and musical enthusiasm perhaps explain the strong associations between subject and personality that are embedded in many memories of music teachers.

"The second music master, a mad (well, mad to us) Eastern European gentleman had big ideas for the school's music and decided to work up and put on a public performance of Handel's *Messiah*. However he needed a much bigger school choir to achieve it. Volunteers were few and he had to resort to a less orthodox recruitment method. He would walk around the school in search of the slightest misdemeanour from a pupil. Instead of giving the luckless lad a detention, he would pounce and say 'Boy! You are in ze kvayor!!' In fairness he rehearsed us well and the performance was of a high standard." [UK70, aged 67]

While music teachers who are passionate about their subject have a powerful effect on those who are drawn into their ambitious plans for school music-making, the impression they make on pupils who are less involved in music—often the majority of the school population—might not be so favourable. Some of the life history respondents considered this dilemma, setting their own memories of school music in the context of their peer group: Graham (Interlude F) recalled a teacher who "was close to retirement and a pretty strict disciplinarian, which put off people who were not interested, but he had such a profound love and enthusiasm for music that this rubbed off on those who were already inclined in that direction" [UK64, aged 55]. Another demonstrated how memories of school music were dependent on individual teachers, having experienced a change of teacher that stifled an emerging interest in music: "School music initially excellent (sang *Messiah* at age 11). Change of music teacher brought standard down" [UK68, aged 53].

The unpredictable influences of teachers on their pupils have been investigated in depth by Tom Barone (2001), who presents a longitudinal case study of Donald Forrister, a high school art teacher in North Carolina, using interviews with the teacher and his former pupils to gauge the lasting impact of Forrister's charismatic teaching approaches. Forrister is shown to be an inspiring teacher, credited with improving job prospects and artistic horizons amongst the socially deprived school community in which he worked. However, his championing of particularly responsive pupils is shown to have negative effects on those who had been excluded from that inner circle, and concern is expressed too about the extent to which the pupils were dependent on Forrister for their sense of self-worth. Forrister himself reflects with anxiety on his choices as a teacher: whom to encourage, how to share out insufficient resources, how to use his finite energy, how to shape his students' ambitions and attitudes? Barone holds that such concerns should be at the heart of the educational debate: "then what often is—narrow and shortsighted notions of educational outcomes—will indeed have become closer to what should be—teachers and schools dedicated to the endurance of the cognitive, the ethical, the aesthetic, and the useful, within lives that stretch out far beyond graduation day" (Barone, 2001, p. 180). Like Forrister's art students, some life history respondents had experienced a sense of exclusion even within a lively musical environment, recalling disappointment that "the head of music seemed only interested in children who learnt instruments in school and I was never allowed to play in assembly like them" [UK17, aged 65]. Having aesthetic opportunities within school is clearly only part of the picture: young people also need to feel invited, included, and affirmed in such activities if their involvement is to be lasting and meaningful.

Balancing the positive recollections of musical mentors, two negative characterisations of music teachers emerge from the life history data: the incompetent or negligent teacher, and the fearsome or dismissive one. These latter qualities were captured with heartfelt insight by one respondent, who wrote that her teacher "was an unpleasant and unimaginative woman, who ran the music department with cold efficiency, but no love or inspiration" [UK35, aged 52]. Such evidence illustrates again the close intertwining of teacher personality and pupil experience: "efficient" opportunities for learning are not sufficient if "love" and "inspiration" are perceived to be lacking. Likewise, students who felt that their own love of music "was never recognised at school" [UK46, aged 72] missed out on the encouragement and affirmation that was so important to their more fortunate peers in other schools: "[My] teacher saw an ability in me right from the start and always went out of her way to encourage and nurture that ability through introducing me to playing the violin and later the viola alongside my piano playing" [UK3, aged 52]. This need for personal recognition seems to be felt particularly strongly in relation to music—not just because there will often be only one or two teachers in a school to offer possible role models, but also because to take a creative risk in front of an adult and have it criticised or dismissed can be a lasting blow to musical confidence.

The life history respondents' varied experiences of teacher attitudes and their effects have implications for teacher training and development, illustrating how far the teacher's role goes beyond the demonstration or imparting of musical skills. In *The Art of Teaching Music* (2008), Estelle Jorgensen draws teachers' attention to the effects of their own values and temperament on their students, suggesting that desirable qualities of tact and compassion should be deliberately cultivated within the profession, using tools such as case study analysis, writing journals, and discussion with colleagues: "Learning to teach well is a life-long process and we improve as we gradually construct the beliefs, habits, dispositions, skills, and practices that together comprise our teaching selves" (p. 55). Although the life history respondents showed themselves to be highly adaptable to their teachers' eccentricities and styles of interaction, Jorgensen challenges teachers to be more self-reflective in observing the effects of their own behaviour—and so to generate the favourable memories that feature in many stories: "I believe I could not have received any more support in my musical education. The teachers were patient and very influential" [UK2, aged 19].

4.2 Instrumental Teachers as Mentors

The role of instrumental teachers in nurturing young people's skills and interest in music differs from classroom teaching in the level of attention it is possible to give to individual pupils: the sense of connection that was sometimes lacking in reports of classroom education ought therefore to be a stronger feature of successful instrumental tutor–student relationships. Instrumental teachers offer a more direct role model, demonstrating the specific skill that they aim to foster in their students, rather than the wide range of musical attributes expected of a classroom teacher. Through regular contact with a student, often over a number of formative years, the attention offered to emerging musicians by their instrumental teachers can be one of the strongest influences on musical development and, as the life history responses will demonstrate, a valuable source of personal confidence and guidance too.

Respondents' descriptions of their instrumental teachers often included all three aspects of their potential influence—personality, performing skill, and educational style: "My first piano teacher, who was a wonderful performer herself, was extremely patient with me as a pupil and when I was a teenager she became a friend and we used to talk about all sorts of things after the lessons were over. Many years later she said she had always thought I would do well with my music although she never said that at the time" [UK17, aged 65; see also Box 4.2.1]. Some teachers held

> **Box 4.2.1**
>
> "My first violin teacher had no experience of teaching, and did it very well. At grammar school I learnt from a retired London Symphony Orchestra player and just loved him. He was a huge inspiration to me. I don't think he had any training in teaching. He played beautifully and was very caring. He coached the county youth orchestra, of which I was a member." [UK33, aged 56]

highly significant roles in their young students' lives, described retrospectively as "a substitute parent" [OUK34, aged 58] or "the only adult, it felt to me, who was remotely interested in me" [UK38, aged 42], with the effect of "making me feel special" [UK26, aged 52]. Such depth of connection brings real responsibilities for instrumental teachers, who might find themselves in the role of counsellor as well as musical mentor, with the potential to have a profound impact on their students' lives. Occasionally, this could be stifling or result in "a rather unhealthy dependent relationship" [UK59, aged 33] of the kind cautioned against by Kim Burwell, who identified a need even at university level for greater development of "the student's contribution to the learning process so that it is more active, reflective and responsible" (Burwell, 2005, p. 214). Remoteness in teachers was, however, more commonly problematic (cf. Creech, 2010a, p. 301), and several respondents had given up lessons because of unsatisfactory student–teacher interactions: one could clearly recall years later "the feel of my first piano teacher's two-inch long varnished nails digging into my fingers as she tried to position my hands on the keyboard, and the frustration of being made to play two-system reductions of themes from famous orchestral works instead of the 'real' piano music that some of my friends were working on" [UK28, aged 45].

For a few students, the content and impact of lessons had been sufficient to overcome any personality clashes: one pianist recalled a teacher who was "very thorough and experienced. I'm not sure I ever liked her much, but that wasn't important" [UK33, aged 56]. Such ability to overcome the dislike of a teacher and still benefit from his or her lessons shows a maturity or self-determination that was not typical; other respondents had given up lessons because of personality clashes or lack of progress—"I played the violin at primary school but didn't like the teacher or lessons much so I packed it in" [UK12, aged 24]. On other occasions the ceasing of lessons was prompted by the teacher rather than the pupil: "I was desperate to learn an instrument, and started piano lessons at school with the organist of York Minster (poor man, earning an extra bob or two); who after a year or two of my complete non-coordination, suggested to my parents that they were wasting their money, so I stopped" [UK7, aged 63]. Another respondent had experienced the frustration of being an undiagnosed dyslexic struggling with notation, and described his lessons by saying, "Don't get me started . . . if I had had proper tuition and help in understanding the 'dots' or even if I had been exposed to alternative scoring at a young age, I could have written down some of the music I used to hear in my head" [UKP81, aged 44]. Both positive and negative experiences of lessons reported by respondents illustrate the many factors involved in securing a good relationship with an instrumental tutor, relating not just to musical and pedagogical skill but also to personality, sensitivity, and a willingness to engage with the musical goals and perspectives of pupils.

At its most successful, the interaction between instrumental teacher and student was shown to have been a genuine partnership in which the teacher provided motivation and guidance and the student was determined to work hard and make progress: "I had a new piano teacher when I was 17 and this changed my practice habits drastically—I was very self-motivated because I felt I was learning much more about technique and interpretation. She sharpened my sense of aural awareness towards my playing" [OUK60, aged 24]. Students like this one, who had encountered a new teacher in late adolescence, reported some of the qualities also experienced by those who resumed lessons in adulthood, when the link between challenge and confidence-building was most appreciated: "[my teacher's] insistence on technical work, rhythm and interpretation was extremely valuable and made me realise the huge gaps in my skills" [UK57, aged 64] (see Section 5.4 for further discussion of adult learners).

A mentoring or encouraging role was not, in itself, sufficient to secure students' lasting respect for their instrumental teacher, as even the kindest teachers were later evaluated for the contribution they had made to players' technique and abilities and their subsequent musical potential. The most highly valued teachers were those who provided solid technical tuition alongside a wide repertoire, taking students beyond "what needed to be learnt for grades" [UK45, aged 20]. Some respondents recognised that technical work that might have felt effortful at the time had provided a strong foundation for their subsequent playing; others attributed their later study or careers in music to their instrumental teachers—in one case, "not just due to skills she taught, but also to her passion for music" [OUK4, aged 30].

Like unpopular classroom teachers, instrumental teachers could lose their pupils' loyalty by failing to recognise or support an emerging interest in music, or through slow progress resulting from a downward spiral of low motivation and lack of practice. As the respondent in Box 4.2.3 had hoped, however, the caricature of a fierce knuckle-rapping piano teacher was uncommon—and even this respondent recovered from an unfortunate start and several changes of school and teacher, eventually being taught by a band conductor who "set about transforming my life" [UK37, aged 42]. Her story illustrates the choice

---

Box 4.2.3

"I went for piano lessons at the age of 6, but I had a really nasty teacher, the sort we hope doesn't exist anymore. She used to rap me over the knuckles with a ruler. Looking back, I now know I made good progress. I gave up after a year though, because the teacher was so horrid!" [UK37, aged 42]

---

and autonomy that is one of the advantages of the UK system of employing private instrumental tutors: where relationships are not working, or progress is not being made, pupils and their parents are free to cease lessons and find a different teacher. Such freedom to choose is of course dependent on having financial resources and supportive parents, and the greatest disadvantage in instrumental tuition lying outside state provision of education (as is currently the case in England) is its inaccessibility to children in less affluent family circumstances. Several respondents recognised with gratitude the sacrifices made by their parents to provide them with instrumental tuition, recalling the hire-purchase agreement that meant "paying the princely sum of 50p per week" for a violin [UK38, aged 42] or noting that their parents "could not afford any formal music lessons" [UK22, aged 60].

This inequality of access has not always been a feature of the UK education system, and some respondents in their forties and fifties were aware of their good fortune in having grown up at the time when instrumental lessons were "available free of charge, from a county peripatetic teacher" [UK54, aged 54]. These peripatetic tutors were employed by the local government to form county music services, which provided instrumental lessons, large-scale ensembles, and often a Saturday morning music school for local pupils. Substantial education funding cuts in the 1980s hit the county music services hard, and there was legal debate on whether charges could be made for instrumental tuition provided within the school day—the eventual outcome ruling that group musical activities should be offered free of charge, but individual tuition should be paid for by parents (Rainbow & Cox, 2006, p. 357). While arguments at the time focused on the collapse of the music services, the longer-term implications of charging for lessons included reducing access to the General Certificate of Secondary Education (GCSE, the national 16+ examination) in Music, whose performance component is theoretically available to those who had undertaken all their musical learning within the classroom, but in which a high level of attainment is only really possible with the support of additional instrumental lessons (Bray, 2000). Small numbers taking Advanced Level (A Level) Music at the age of 18 inevitably followed, and at degree level entry, at least in more traditional university music departments, the student population is overwhelmingly of a high socioeconomic status (Dibben, 2006)—a situation likely to be worsened by the political move to introduce higher student tuition fees from September 2012.

Recent years have seen new attempts to redress the balance and make instrumental learning more widely accessible, most notably through the Wider Opportunities scheme in which whole classes in junior schools (aged 7–11) receive instrumental tuition for a short period of time, sometimes followed by subsidised small-group lessons for those who hope to progress further (Ofsted, 2004; see Section 6.3). There has also been increasing recognition among researchers and practitioners that traditional models of private instrumental tuition are not the only way to acquire high-level musical skill: informal learning and self-tuition have a central role in the development of popular musicians particularly, leading to differences not just in skills but in conceptions of expertise and musical value (Papageorgi et al., 2010). Among the life history respondents, the popular musicians were almost unanimous in feeling that their childhood instrumental learning had not equipped them with the skills or strategies needed for their chosen musical route: several had rebelled against their parents' choices of classical instruments, developing their learning further once they had the financial independence to pursue their own interests (see Interlude D). Despite in some cases high levels of success as performers or singer-songwriters, several among this group had insecurities about their musical skills relating to the reading of notation, sight-reading, or ability to improvise: "I was taught formally with music and therefore find it very hard to improvise and play without music" [UKP78, aged 24]. Their adult experiences as musicians were mismatched with the expectations of their parents and teachers, who had followed a relatively traditional model of encouraging instrumental learning through notation, lessons, and practice—not least because, for the older respondents at least, the route into popular music was a remote and unfamiliar one for their families.

The pop musicians' experiences of feeling parental pressure to maintain sometimes unsatisfactory instrumental learning offers a reminder that the relationship between instrumental teachers and pupils is mediated by parents, who are influential in the decision to have lessons and in the sustaining of good learning habits in the years that follow. Andrea Creech describes the parent's role as a demanding and flexible one, which "may involve remaining resilient in the face of reluctant practising while remaining as the child's interested and supportive advocate long after practical help has ceased to be appropriate or welcomed by the teacher and pupil" (Creech, 2010b, p. 29). The next section considers the life history evidence for parental intervention in lessons and practice, and the many other ways in which parents' musical attitudes and activities are influential.

4.3 Parents as Role Models and Mentors

Across the life history accounts, parents were strongly represented as holding as much musical influence as teachers, if not more. Their most tangible contributions included sharing musical tastes through listening in the home, offering financial and practical support for instrumental lessons, taking their children to concerts, and sometimes teaching, particularly in the beginner stages. Beyond those practical influences, it was parents who set the musical ethos of a home, through their own behaviour and attitudes, the presence (or absence) of instruments, recordings, and sheet music, and the extent to which they encouraged, or even pushed, their children to take lessons and then to persevere with practice. Among the older generation of respondents especially, there was a sense of music being "normal", an accepted activity for the offspring of reasonably affluent or aspirational parents: piano lessons as a "badge of respectability" (Rainbow & Cox, 2006, p. 303) perhaps, but nonetheless one that was well intentioned by parents and generally appreciated by their children. This self-selecting sample of musically active adults therefore offers some insight on homes in which there were varying levels of support but reasonably consistent musical awareness. Many other homes not represented in this sample would lack the factors outlined above, and some respondents were aware of their good fortune in being born into families who valued music and sought to encourage skill and interest in this area.

In addition to reporting these environmental influences, there was a tendency among the life history respondents to reflect on the genetic contribution that their parents and extended family might have made to their own musical inclinations. While some respondents were proud to be "first-generation" musicians, saying "neither of my parents is particularly musical" [UK48, aged 26], others traced a musical heritage back to grandparents, in ways that often seemed to have been reinforced by family lore: "I grew up aware that my parents both used to play when younger, and that my grandma had been a fantastic pianist who had won big competitions and taught piano all her life" [UKP73, aged 48]. A few respondents referred directly to inheriting "musical genes" [UK47, aged 62; see Interludes A and B], sometimes observing the continuation of this legacy in their own children: "Something that has really warmed my heart recently is the realisation that both of my children have inherited my perfect pitch" [UK38, aged 42]. However, this last respondent—who describes her own family as one in which "neither of my parents played or sang and my three brothers showed no particular talent" [UK38, aged 42]—illustrates that a parent's receptiveness to signs of musical ability could be just as influential as any genetic component, if not more so. One respondent had challenged his mother's view of herself as "unmusical" for just this reason, describing the rich musical environment provided by his parents and grandfather (Box 4.3.1), and so endorsing one view of musical

Box 4.3.1

"Have you spotted what is missing? Parents, of course!!! Who encouraged me at our piano, accompanying me from Mrs Curwen's Piano Method? Who wound up the gramophone and played us their 78s, followed later by a continually developing collection of quality LPs? Who sang to us as he carried us gently around to comfort us? Who noticed my fascination with Scottish dance music and—at some expense—treated me to a piano-accordion with a complementary tutor book? (My grandfather—that's how I learned harmony.) Who swears to this day that she is totally unmusical, yet brought up a trombonist, an outstanding violinist, an equally brilliant cellist and a trombone-competent viola player and church chorister? I remember our Mother's bedtime singing." [UK54, aged 54]

heritability that suggests that differences in musical ability cannot reliably be attributed to genetic factors but are more likely the product of early musical exposure and encouragement: "it is generally impossible to conclude, from observing two children differing in musical behaviour, that they differ in musical talent, if by talent one means an inherited or inborn difference in capacity" (Sloboda, 2005, p. 299).

Other researchers maintain that there are innate differences in children's levels of musical aptitude that, coupled with variations in their predisposition to engage with persistent study, account for the exceptional performance of a small proportion of the population: "those who work at something for thousands of hours are a highly select breed to begin with. They are not simply ordinary individuals who have worked slavishly' (Torff & Winner, 1994, p. 362). Further support for a biological component in musical perception and cognition comes from the research into congenital amusia, a condition that renders around 4% of the population unable to process musical pitches and melodies: "People with amusia fail to recognize familiar tunes, cannot tell one tune from another (unless the tunes have lyrics) and often complain that music sounds like noise" (Stewart, 2006, p. 904). Studies of amusic families have shown a high likelihood of inheriting the condition, but where parents have compensated for the deficit by providing musical tuition and opportunities for their children, the risk is considerably reduced, suggesting that "music processing, like most complex cognitive systems, owes its ultimate functional properties both to the genetic prewiring and to experience-based plasticity" (Peretz, Cummings, & Dubé, 2007, p. 587).

The growing evidence for a biological component to musical ability is therefore illuminating not only the function of the brain in determining the capacity for musical perception, but also the much stronger influences of enculturation, tuition, encouragement, and practice in acquiring musical skills. In this sense, the attitudes and expectations for music that parents pass on to their offspring are more powerful than genetic inheritance—although the two are interlinked, since parents who have not acquired musical skills themselves are less likely to observe and encourage early signs of musical development in their children. Conversely, parents who recall music being a valuable part of their childhood are more likely to replicate such an environment in their own parenting style: a study of 2,250 parents in California, New York, and the American Midwest found that "experience matters—parents with specific music educational experiences as well as memories of being parented musically were much more likely to sing and play music with their infants than those without those experiences" (Custodero & Johnson-Green, 2003, p. 109).

Such differences in parenting are not usually discernible outside the family home, and so the myths of "natural talent" are retained, as the diverse musical environments experienced by young children produce differences in ability that are colloquially explained through reference to the parents' own musical skills rather than varying levels and types of musical stimulus. Regardless of the scientific evidence, strong cultural assumptions persist that musical performance is the preserve of a gifted élite: one singer-songwriter spoke of overcoming those beliefs years after school, when joining a "vibrant, welcoming and forgiving musical scene" encouraged him to "break down music industry myths that 'music just comes'—that you have it or you don't" [UKP41, aged 35]. The life histories provide many examples of individuals' attempts to make sense of their musical heritage, with or without reference to inherited ability: they variously recognise the presence of music in their early lives and often express gratitude for their parents' influence, whether provided deliberately through the financing of lessons or inclusion in family music-making, or informally through shared enthusiasm for listening and talking about music.

Where strong cultures of musical learning existed in the home, these were usually rooted in parents' own musical ambitions—whether realised or thwarted—and meant that the question of whether a child should take up lessons was at least present, in ways that it would not be where there was no family history of playing an instrument: "My Dad played violin and we had a piano—I just accepted that as normal—people like us learned music and played music at home" [UK69, aged 53]. Where children were "first-generation" instrumental learners, taking up an instrument when their parents had not had similar opportunities, an older sibling could pave the way for this "odd thing" of learning a musical instrument to begin to seem "normal" (see Interlude K). One respondent reported feeling envious of her siblings' playing until "my protestations were finally listened to and my own piano lessons began" [UK71, aged 51]; likewise an older brother purchasing a guitar was a "starting point for realising that I could be a part of music as well as an appreciator" [UKP41, aged 35]. In families with more of a history of music-making, the decision was not whether to play an instrument but which one to choose, and starting lessons often emerged from the many other influences that set the musical tone for the household, including parents' own playing and listening. Such variations in access to music create educational challenges and inequalities, since the experiences of children even by the time they start compulsory schooling will be enormously varied.

Comparisons can be made with parental attitudes to literacy, where the presence of books, parents' own enjoyment of reading, and their habit of reading to their children all have a positive effect, with an absence of these influences leading to lower literacy ability in the first years of schooling (Weigel, Martin, & Bennett, 2007). Parents for whom such activities are an automatic part of home life are surprised that others do not do them; likewise, the "ordinary" musical activities of playing musical games, singing at bedtime, and encouraging spontaneous play are easily overlooked as sources of musical learning (Sloboda, 2005, p. 298), although some recent studies have documented the prevalence of musical resources in the home (Young, 2008) or made deliberate attempts to introduce singing activities to families and monitor their effects (Baker & MacKinlay, 2006).

Whilst some of the disparity in access to musical learning is undoubtedly dependent on financial resources, without which the systematic learning of a Western classical instrument is much harder to achieve, parental attitudes and encouragement also play a strong role that is less easily predicted. The provision of instrumental lessons through means-testing, for instance, would therefore be a crude solution, since the introduction of musical learning to a family culture for the first time needs support and guidance as well as finance. As the life history responses show, some parents struggled to provide instrumental tuition for their offspring, and their efforts to do so were as important as their success: by investing limited family resources in paying for lessons, they showed a faith in the value of musical learning—and in this particular method of doing so.

Around a third of the life history respondents had significant memories of their parents' own music-making, and this generated one of the strongest impetuses for learning—to join in with the family culture of playing, and to make use of instruments, music, and recordings that were available in the home. A retired music lecturer recalled how his parents held "Brandenburg parties" in the home, as well as playing "sonata and trio repertoire involving violin, cello, piano, frequently after my own bedtime but still audible" [UK6, aged 65]. Parents' playing provided evidence not only of musical skill being attainable through practice, but also of the ways in which music could provide pleasure, relaxation, and a connection between friends or family members: "We had a piano in the home. My mother used to play (not so well) and liked Mozart, Beethoven, Granados, Debussy . . . My father loved to sing the old Viennese operettas" [UK65, aged 78]. Playing "not so well" or with "little theoretical knowledge to back it up" [UK37, aged 42] was no obstacle to enjoying music, which might also include membership of a local choir or chamber ensemble.

Most respondents recalled their parents' choral activities fondly, recalling how they, too, "quickly learnt all the songs" [UK42, aged 62] as their mothers sang around the house, though one acknowledged a less immediate appreciation of such commitments: "As I child I hated Monday evenings, when my mother went out to choir practice—but I was growing up in a household where singing in a choir was considered to be a normal thing to do, and there has never been a time when I did not follow suit. I did not realise how fortunate I was" [UK28, aged 45]. Setting aside any childhood jealousies of their parents' evening absences, these life history respondents were learning valuable early lessons about the contribution of music to a fulfilling life, which in turn provided a foundation for their parents' desire to encourage their offspring on that route. Offering role models for musical enjoyment, as well as skill, parents who played were a valuable source of inspiration for their children: "Both my parents played the piano for pleasure and sometimes played duets together; I think this is what initially sparked my interest" [UK40, aged 44].

Parents with some musical knowledge and, perhaps more importantly, a high level of interest in music could also be helpful in supporting children's practice, a factor recognised by research in instrumental teaching as being essential to successful progress (Creech, 2010b; McPherson, 2009). One respondent recalled that her mother "herself took up the recorder and later the violin in middle age" [UK44, aged 64], a process of learning alongside children of which Shinichi Suzuki, founder of the family-orientated method of instrumental learning, would have approved (Suzuki, 1970). More typically, parents sought to instil practice routines through encouragement rather than example, and the life history accounts show that getting the balance right in fostering diligent practice without turning it into a chore is a recurring challenge for the parents of young instrumentalists.

The respondents reported a variety of approaches, with approval for parents who were "never pushy—it was always up to me whether I practised or not, but they were really encouraging" [UK12, aged 24], and likewise for a mother who, in the face of a despairing teacher and a lack of practice, "did

Box 4.3.2

"One of the aunts [whom I lived with] was a good pianist and started piano lessons because, as she reported 'You used to stand by the piano as I played, transfixed, soaking it up.' I had to practise before breakfast every morning. The piano-playing aunt listened to me while she had breakfast in bed. Any mistakes were answered by she banging her stick on the floor above me." [UK8, aged 68]

not give up on me and allowed me to continue lessons for which I am very grateful" [UK17, aged 65]. Given that the highest instance of regret in the life histories was lack of practice in childhood, however, some adults felt their parents should have been a little more forceful in their support, feeling that their progress had been limited by a "parental wish not to struggle against my natural laziness" [UK6, aged 65]. Stronger regimes of practice supervision were also reported, most often involving family members who were themselves professional or semi-professional performers or teachers (Box 4.3.2). Sometimes there were tensions between a young instrumentalist and a parent who "would always notice and comment upon any wrong notes or mistakes when I played the piano" [UK71, aged 51], a habit that was perhaps revealing of general approaches to parenting rather than specifically to music, as was the case for the violinist who "lived in a house where praise and encouragement were in very short supply" [UK38, aged 42].

These varied experiences show how the home environment is critical to effective practising: children in all environments sought their parents' approval and response for their playing, and were encouraged most when this support was readily offered but not heavily imposed. Research on motivation provides some explanation for this, since the extrinsic reward of parental approval is a good first step in building practice habits but needs to be replaced by intrinsic satisfaction in playing if progress is to be sustained (Chaffin & Lemieux, 2004, p. 30). Susan Hallam (1998) suggests that for young children, practice supervision helps to build habits and strategies to enhance learning, whilst teenagers need to become more responsible for their own practice routine and might resent parental reminders so much that they cease learning (p. 81). The life history data do not provide this level of detail on changing parental roles in adolescence, but they certainly illustrate the sensitivities around practice support and the lifelong appreciation felt by children who experienced encouragement without excessive interference. They contrast with Amy Chua's (2011) autobiographical account of being a "Tiger Mother", demanding discipline, excellence, and obedience from her children in a style of parenting associated predominantly, though not exclusively, with Chinese culture and intended to generate a "virtuous circle of confidence, hard work, and more success" (p. 146). Chua contrasts stereotypically Chinese and Western styles of parenting in ways that highlight the flaws of both, not least in her fierce arguments with her half-American children, and admits that "when I see the piano- and violin-induced calluses on my daughters' fingertips, or the teeth marks on the piano, I'm sometimes seized with doubt" (p. 101).

Chua's approach might seem extreme to more liberal parents, but the phenomenon of the Asian or Asian-American "music mom" is a familiar and influential one at the highest levels of musical excellence in the US, interpreted by Grace Wang (2009) as the attempt by immigrant parents to "assert their own cultural and personal agency in the face of racialized discourses imposed upon them" (p. 900). Perhaps all parents seek some measure of "cultural capital . . . through classical music" (p. 899) when they invest in instrumental lessons for their children, but the life history accounts suggest that the majority of them do so less blatantly or forcefully, encouraging the exploration of classical music as one of a range of experiences. This might be a less certain route to musical excellence, but for many of the life history respondents this relaxed attitude had led to an open-mindedness and warmth towards music that had sustained them throughout their lives, resulting in the commonly expressed view that "There is absolutely no doubt that all this musical activity at home over many years shaped my life and formed the basis of where I am today" [UK63, aged 57].

When parents were not themselves musicians, they often shared their musical interests in other ways, most notably through listening. Specific musical preferences and pieces were recalled decades later as having formed the soundtrack to childhood: memories included "father's brass band records (to which I marched vigorously round the room!)" [UK32, aged 57], "a radiogram and a selection of records from Eartha Kitt to Swan Lake" [UK42, aged 62], and "a diet of Jelly Roll Morton and Fats Waller" [UK29, aged 54]. In addition to being exposed to particular repertoire, these young listeners had learned from their parents a sense of the value of music and noted that being "a classical music fanatic" [UK57, aged 64] or "a keen hi-fi enthusiast" [UK63, aged 57] was a central part of their parents' lives, and one they were eager to share with their children. Some respondents had absorbed particular musical preferences, whilst others valued the breadth and variety of a parent's appetite for listening: one recalled how his mother's tastes "span from classical to hard rock and this openness to different genres helped broaden my mind to new things" [OUK49, aged 29].

Those respondents with a parent who was a keen listener but did not necessarily have any skill as a player had learnt the complexities of what it means to be "musical", rejecting simple definitions of musicianship as they noted the influence of a non-playing parent's attitudes and enthusiasms on their own musical development. Piers in Interlude B describes learning from his non-playing father to "look for musicality in the most unexpected of places, to keep an open mind and an open ear and not to take received opinion on trust" [UK47, aged 62]. In a parallel with parental support for instrumental practice, the deliberate sharing of music listening appears to have been most memorable and effective, whether achieved through sheer quantity of exposure or through specific recommendations and discussions of musical tastes. The recollection that "there was always music on the radio or record player" [UK3, aged 52] was sufficient to give many life history respondents a sense of having had a musical childhood, and to make the connection between their parents' pleasure in listening and the desire this generated to encourage their children into active music-making.

Memories of attending concerts with parents further reinforced the sense of music having value in the home (Box 4.3.3) and often had a lasting impact on lifelong listening and live arts attendance habits (see Section 5.5). Likewise, parents' religion and church attendance habits were influential in exposing their children to sacred music and communal singing, and while one dismissed the musical standard as "not that good probably" [UK52, aged 49], others became more involved through their family circumstances: "My father was a village clergyman so my mother, brother and I used to lead the singing in church every Sunday. I well remember the first time I tried the church organ and was fascinated by all the different sounds" [UK8, aged 68]. Another clergyman's daughter recalled that "church music was an important part of my background—my earliest musical memories are of singing hymns in church!" [UK53, aged 69], while a Jewish respondent had been told by her family that "at the age of three I sung my cousin's 'Bar Mitzvah' in my own type of Hebrew language. I could understand what they meant and how I did this when my own son did similarly some thirty years later" [UK71, aged 51]. Singing in church and listening at concerts, as much as exploring parents' record collections and hearing instruments being played in the home, helped

---

Box 4.3.3

"I was taken, from a young age, to hear oratorios at other local chapels. It seemed at the time that every chapel had a large choir. Every November the Temple Street Methodist Chapel gave *The Messiah* and for the evening performance people had to queue for up to two hours to be sure of getting a seat—I can remember queuing in all weathers and not minding having to do so. Not only did we have to queue but we did not have a car and there were no buses from the village so we also had a long walk to get to the chapel." [UK55, aged 70]

to provide musical connections between parents and their children, reinforcing respondents' memories of having had a musically enriched childhood.

4.4 Siblings, Extended Family, and Friendships as Sources of Musical Learning

The role of siblings in shaping musical lives has been observed in previous research to hold the potential for rivalry as well as solidarity (Borthwick & Davidson, 2002), and whilst the life history questions did not ask specifically about sibling relationships, many accounts included descriptions of this kind in their reporting of both childhood and adult musical experiences. Several respondents mentioned sibling order and age gaps as having had an effect on their exposure to musical tastes and activities (see Nikki's reflections on this in Interlude K). Older siblings were often reported to have expanded the parental record collection, leading to a typical pattern of listening that reflected the varied tastes of the household: "Classical music, 60s–70s rock with my parents, 80s rock with my sisters" [OUK49, aged 29]. Younger siblings could discover musical tastes outside those of their peer group, as recalled by one of the pop musician respondents whose "brother and sister were twins and seven years older than me. They played pop records all the time in our house and I was introduced to music that people who were older than me listened to" [UKP30, aged 58]. These effects were mostly reported in relation to pop music, although a few respondents had been drawn to classical music through the enthusiasms of an older sibling: "My brother is almost 8 years older than me, and had been introduced to 'classical' music at a fairly early age by a friendly neighbour, so I grew up with some 78s being played in the house" [UK22, aged 60].

Siblings also contributed to early musical memories through their playing, and in many cases appeared to have paved the way for learning an instrument, opening up the possibility of having lessons by making this an accepted part of family life, and providing a realistic musical role model to raise a younger sibling's aspirations (Box 4.4.1). Being the second or third child to learn an instrument within a family meant that a realistic sense of the practice needed and the progress that would therefore result had

---

Box 4.4.1

"There happened to be a woman in the village who had learned the violin and my brother started lessons. I can remember him getting the violin when I was 4 or 5. He was four years older. He had seen an orchestra on television somewhere (we didn't have one) and wanted to play. I wanted to play because he did. He still plays the guitar professionally (he's 60)." [UK33, aged 56]

"My brother asked [my piano teacher] if there was any way that he could stop me with my music practising. However, by this time I was unstoppable! My brother's reaction was not surprising given that I used to wake the house up at 6am to practise the piano [. . .] I guess it was not that easy for my brother to revise for his school exams under these circumstances. The banging on the floor to attempt to stop my efforts was not uncommon. Interestingly, although he was thrown out of the class for not singing in tune, now my brother loves music and attends many concerts and operas. He has even recently passed his Grade 1 saxophone exam, with my husband as his teacher." [UK71, aged 51]

already been acquired, not just by the child but by his or her parents, too. Consistency in parenting was evident in stories of being "preceded into the church choir" [OUK34, aged 58] by older brothers, or of equal access to instrumental lessons being provided by well-intentioned parents: "They were very encouraging and supportive, and started all three of their children on the piano at age 7. We all began other instruments later, my sister played the clarinet, my brother the cello, and I started the flute at age 13. All three of us later regretted not starting the orchestral instruments earlier" [UK35, aged 52]. Parental efforts towards musical equality were sometimes resisted, as with the pianist whose "two elder sisters dutifully started piano lessons aged 7 but I rebelled and did it my own way" [UK63, aged 57]—this rebellious route involving self-taught recorder playing, clarinet lessons from the age of 12, and piano lessons two years later. Other respondents had used their siblings' lessons as leverage for their own desire to start playing, with the pianist in Box 4.4.2 remembering "collecting my sisters from their piano lessons" for some time before her "protestations were finally listened to and my own piano lessons began" [UK71, aged 51].

These adult respondents are of course interpreting their parents' decisions in retrospect and have no reliable means of disentangling the influences of their siblings' experiences on the intentions that parents may already have had for their younger children's musical tuition. Nonetheless, just as a musically active school could leave a lasting impression of being surrounded by opportunities, so the presence of siblings learning instruments contributed to a feeling of being from "a musical family" [UK53, aged 69] in ways that reinforced expectations and engagement with music. Only one respondent mentioned being an only child, reporting the advantage of this as being "able to listen exactly as I liked" [UK42, aged 62], and recalling a close relationship with her father that included listening to music together and attempting to teach him to play the piano from notation instead of by ear: "I used to check his Moonlight Sonata slow movement for mistakes—there never were any—by following the music as he played" [UK42, aged 62].

Siblings were sometimes recalled as being an obstacle to musical ambitions, in one case through their protests at excessive practising (see Box 4.4.2), but more often because the decisions made by siblings (or by parents on their behalf) appeared to limit the choices available to other children in the family. One frustrated pianist had remedied this situation as an adult learner: "I took up the double bass at the age of 40, having always wanted to play it but been prevented when at school because my little brother was learning it and I might have been better than him" [UK26, aged 52]. Another respondent appeared to feel resentful of the privileging of a sibling's musical efforts: "My younger sister was made to learn the piano, practising two hours daily. As a sideline I was given a trumpet so I didn't feel left out" [UKP77, aged 49]. A study using family script theory to explore parents' distribution of musical resources noted a tendency in two-child families to label the first child as "talented", so inhibiting the progress of the second even while pressuring him or her "to follow the same musical path as the first-born in a bid to preserve sibling equality and success" (Borthwick & Davidson, 2002, p. 71). Balancing the musical aspirations and potential of their children is a delicate task for parents, and respondents seemed most appreciative of approaches that had been open-minded and allowed children to find their own direction. Tim describes a situation of this kind in Interlude D, recalling that "the musical culture I grew up in was very supportive of involvement in and enjoyment of music generally, though my brothers and I all found our own individual paths according to taste" [UKP73, aged 48].

It is difficult to determine from the life history responses the extent to which musical relationships between siblings were mediated by other rivalry or harmony within the household. Clearest evidence is provided in the accounts of making music together, which was often encouraged by parents, though not always running

---

Box 4.4.3

"My sister who is almost 4 years older than me is also quite musical. She learned the flute (up to Grade 8) and piano (up to Grade 7). This meant that I did many musical activities with her; we went to the same school playing in the school orchestra, music festival and singing in the choir, we also attended the same youth orchestra. My sister and I have also worked together in the Music for Youth National Festival. My sister, myself and my mother also did a couple of festivals playing as a piano trio. However, practising often ended in tears or fights so that didn't last!"
[UK45, aged 20]

smoothly in practice (Box 4.4.3). The inclusion of wider family and friendship groups seemed to have a moderating effect on sibling ensembles, as for the young violinist who with a clarinet-playing brother and pianist sister "did a lot of playing of chamber music together at home in various combinations, often with friends of my father" [UK53, aged 69]. Grandparents, aunts, and uncles were also a presence in these family ensembles, especially those who lived in or near the family home and so were available as accompanists for young instrumentalists (see Matthew in Interlude I), or to contribute to "family get-togethers ending with musical entertainment, with my aunt playing piano and my cousin singing" [UK71, aged 51].

As with the listening tastes of older siblings, contact with extended family members could provide access to the musical enthusiasms and skills of another generation: "the influence of parents and grandparents who lived together meant that I was also exposed to a wide range of music including dance and traditional music, classical and organ music" [UK10, aged 57]. One pop musician recalled a great-grandfather who was "an old time music hall singer and also played the accordion, so I remember hearing all the old songs, and when he passed away I was left his suitcase full of sheet music" [UKP80, aged 42]. A sense of musical heritability and family lineage was reinforced by knowing that "grandma had been a fantastic pianist who had won big competitions and taught piano all her life" [UKP73, aged 48], and some respondents had found encouragement for their musical interests from their extended family: one case involved a grandfather who "noticed my fascination with Scottish dance music and—at some expense—treated me to a piano-accordion with a complementary tutor book" [UK54, aged 54]. While the life history respondents recalled their own pleasure in these relationships, musical connections across the generations can be mutually beneficial (Frego, 1995), as demonstrated by those respondents who now have their own grandchildren (see MW in Interlude A). The retired organist who sings in church "to support my daughter and two of her sons who sing in the choir" [UK18, aged 76] echoes research with an intergenerational choir in Michigan, which reported on the satisfaction of musical interactions that transcended anticipated barriers of age by uniting participants in shared musical activity (Conway & Hodgman, 2008).

A further source of musical influence proposed in the existing research literature is that of peer and friendship groups, widely held to contribute to musical tastes and engagement, particularly through the social affiliations of shared musical preferences in adolescence (Tarrant, North, & Hargreaves, 2002). When I returned a summary of initial research findings to my life history respondents in July 2007, I commented on the relative absence of data

"In secondary school I had a very good friend who played cello and we teamed up quite a bit to explore the cello-piano repertoire and occasionally the piano trio repertoire when we were joined by the leader of the county youth orchestra. Some of this was beyond our technical ability at the time, of course, but it was an invaluable experience—we weren't really rivals, just friends who enjoyed making music together and had the encouragement from teachers to do so." [UK27, aged 64]

on "peer pressure" and friendship influences, given their prominence in previous research as contributing to young people's tendencies to continue with or withdraw from musical activities (e.g., Austin, Renwick, & McPherson, 2006). One respondent [UK27, aged 64] got in touch to correct that impression in his own life history account, describing a close friendship through which he had shared musical enthusiasms and expanded his playing opportunities (Box 4.4.4). This observation highlighted the specific nature of the peer influences across the sample, which tended to feature significant friendships built around music but a relative absence of a wider peer-group context, suggesting that a strong bond with a few like-minded people was more important than achieving popularity in a larger group. This pattern of behaviour is consistent with high-achieving musicians in other studies, whereby "the teenagers who were more successful in music and more motivated to participate were those who surrounded themselves with other teenagers engaging in similar musical activities" (Davidson & Burland, 2006, p. 477).

Among the close friendships recalled by respondents, MW in Interlude A describes attending lunchtime concerts accompanied by a mathematics teacher, while another keen listener came to an arrangement with a friend "whereby we would agree on record sets we wanted to buy and then each of us would save up and buy alternate sets and keep them to listen to in turn, thus sharing the costs" [UK63, aged 57]. A young pianist formed lifelong friendships with the two girls with whom (unusually for the 1940s) she shared her piano lessons: "It was a social occasion and we played duets and helped each other with our work. We have remained friends and are still in touch with each other" [UK55, aged 70]. Friendships formed in adolescent pop groups and youth orchestras were also prominent among the responses, and one person summed up this tendency by stating that "I have always found I have made better, more lasting friendships through music than any other activity" [UK35, aged 52]. Even when these close relationships included an element of competition, they appear to have been of lasting value: "Every year I used to get

100% in the school end of year music exam, and to this day my very good friend, now co-principal viola in the BBC SO [British Broadcasting Corporation Symphony Orchestra], tells of how she came second in aural for seven years!" [UK37, aged 42]. Whilst it is perhaps inevitable that these lifelong friendships would be the ones most frequently mentioned in telling a musical life history, their lasting positive influence is an optimistic counterbalance to concerns over peer pressure in adolescence; if such pressure was experienced by these respondents, it no longer has prominence in their musical recollections.

4.5 Learning from Learning: Becoming Teachers and Parents

This chapter has already shown how the influence of teachers and parents can extend beyond the direct, practical provision of opportunities for music-making into the attitudes and level of encouragement they offer to the young people in their charge. Casual conversations, probably forgotten almost immediately by the adult, could have a lasting impact on a child's determination to become a musician or his or her confidence to continue with lessons in the face of apparent lack of progress.

Disenchantment with teachers was felt particularly strongly by those who were already substantially involved in music: "At school I was told I was tone deaf (many years after completing the AB theory exams and at about the time of my Grade 7 classical guitar) so wrote off institutional education as a sensible option fairly early" [UK52, aged 49]. One respondent recalled a teacher who "used to rant and rave at me during my piano lessons because he said I didn't work hard enough. I think he may well have been right but because of that, I never became a very good pianist— competent but not really good" [UK8, aged 68]. Subsequently becoming a teacher himself, this respondent explicitly avoided the replication of his own experiences, favouring instead a stance of "praise at all costs with the worst of pupils but then saying 'but look how we can make it even better!'" [UK8, aged 68]. His is a clear "redemption" story (Pillemer, 2001, p. 130), in which a negative experience became an impetus to seek out other avenues of musical progress, and goals were achieved in spite of external discouraging factors. Other respondents told stories of "contamination", where similar events were viewed more negatively and blamed for long-term failures to reach full musical potential (McAdams et al., 2001, p. 484). David Pillemer uses a helpfully musical example to explain further the unpredictable influences of a teacher's evaluation, a parent's counselling, and the child's response:

A child who is sharply criticized by a music teacher or sports coach can attach several possible beliefs to this event. Subsequent discussions with a sympathetic parent (or therapist) will help to frame the child's perspective. The offending adult may be cast as villain. The child may be encouraged to pursue other activities in which success is more likely. Or the parent may offer an interpretation that reframes the painful interaction as beneficial and even inspirational: criticism actually demonstrates the coach's or teacher's attention, interest, and a belief that the child has strong potential for improvement. (Pillemer, 2001, p. 131)

This range of possible responses is evident in the life history accounts and is referred to most explicitly when respondents reflect on their own intentions and behaviour as parents and teachers. Experiencing discouragement or lack of opportunity in childhood had given some respondents a heightened sensitivity towards this aspect of their own parenting or teaching practice, making them keen to offer the support that they perceived to have been denied to them. Those who had experienced more positive role models also acknowledged these, such that characterisations of their own teaching practice could be framed as a tribute to their teachers—"I hope that I bring music to life for my charges as it was brought to life for me" [UK16, aged 60]—or as compensation for an impoverished musical education: "I feel that I have made headway in that I certainly give children more interesting things to do in day-to-day class music lessons than I myself experienced as a pupil" [UK47, aged 62].

Comparisons between self-as-pupil and self-as-teacher also included reflection on particular teaching styles, as respondents sought to avoid their own teachers' tendencies to push students towards assessment or competitive festivals or to dominate the lesson: "One piano teacher I had when I was about 11 used to spend a lot of time playing in the lesson, ostensibly to demonstrate to me but I felt cheated that I hardly played at all; this has made me conscious of the fact that though I need to demonstrate in lessons, I must not 'take over' and make the students frustrated as I so often was" [UK24, aged 65]. The desire expressed here to take note of students' responses and modify teaching strategies accordingly would not have been so commonplace in the teacher-directed ethos of the 1950s, when this respondent was taking piano lessons. Major social changes in the understanding of childhood and adolescence have made contemporary education practitioners both more accountable and more reflective, their professional status now earned through good practice rather than automatically bestowed.

Much more is also known now about motivation, learning styles, the effects of assessment, and teacher–student interactions, and so it is perhaps to be expected that today's teachers should show greater awareness of their students' learning and seek to engage them through a variety of approaches (e.g., Hallam, 1998). As one older respondent reflected, however (with his own emphatic underlining), an instinctive understanding of such matters has always made for good teachers: "There are people who are <u>very naturally</u> good with children; '<u>bonding</u>' with them in the general sense, <u>inspiring</u> them, and <u>communicating</u> their skills in a clear, palatable way. All the 'paper' qualifications will not be of much avail without such innate gifts—and children, as naturally, pick up the 'vibes' of any situation of the kind—whether one to one in private tuition or class structured music" [UK39, aged 81]. This description highlights the empathy and sensitivity needed for effective teaching and avoids the pitfalls implicit in UK24's approach (above) of teaching in ways that would have been preferable to oneself as a learner but that might not work so well for a pupil of different character and inclination. In studying the teaching strategies of popular musicians who were largely self-taught, Tim Robinson (2010) observed this dilemma at its most perplexing: musicians who had found their own experiences of receiving formal tuition to be unsatisfactory often reverted to quite traditional methods in their teaching—using notation, for instance, when their own playing was much more reliant on aural methods of copying records and learning in a group (cf. Green, 2002). Robinson's popular musicians acknowledged that they were sometimes teaching their "ideal selves" rather than being fully responsive to their pupils' needs—assuming, for example, a similarly high level of the self-direction that had been a feature of their own musical development.

With a number of respondents having been fortunate enough to discover through experience that "the most inspirational teachers are those that convey their own passion and enjoyment of music" [UK47, aged 62], several expressed a general enthusiasm for providing musical opportunities and watching their students make the most of these. Having grown up playing in Salvation Army bands, one respondent aimed to provide group music-making opportunities that were "effective and encouraging" [UK43, aged 38], whilst Duncan (Interlude G) traced a similar inclination back to his "father's passion for being near music somehow and being glad that others are as well", stating (perhaps over-modestly, given the extent of his performing and teaching activities as an adult) that "my musicality comes across in enthusiasm not competence, in commitment, not example" [OUK34, aged 58]. For these teachers, the pleasure of sharing their musical involvement with students was at the heart of their educational practice (see also Chapter 5): this echoes the experience of teachers interviewed by Gordon Cox, for whom "the rewards of dealing with young people making music" were a necessary balance to the frustrations of the job, which included coping with noise, with discipline problems, and with the low status of the subject in schools (Cox, 1999, p. 43).

Summarising their musical life histories, several respondents concluded with statements about how supporting their own children and witnessing their musical achievements had been amongst the highlights of their musical journeys. One mother of twin teenagers in the prestigious National Youth Orchestra acknowledged that "I suppose you might think they are fulfilling my own frustrated dreams for me, which they are, but I emphasise that they are doing it willingly, and with their eyes open, as to how difficult the profession is" [UK35, aged 52]. She reflected also on how much her own musical skills had continued to develop as a result of her children's involvement, saying that "I have learnt so much while they have been learning [. . .] One twin started the violin aged 6, the other the horn aged 9, and I went to their lessons, taking notes, and helping them to practise. They were obviously keen and talented, but I was careful to encourage without over pushing" [UK35, aged 52]. Avoiding "pushy parenting" was a concern for several others, but there was nonetheless a widespread hope that children would come to share their parents' enjoyment and involvement in music, and early signs that they seemed "very musically inclined" [UK38, aged 42] were noted with pleasure.

Other parents reported a sense of disappointment when their children opted not to pursue music beyond childhood: "sadly, despite encouragement of our four children and early piano lessons by three of them on an instrument we bought at home, only one remains interested in playing occasionally" [UK70, aged 67]. Nonetheless, the life history responses as a whole illustrate the value of such opportunities, with even those lessons that were abandoned in later adolescence being a source of musical awareness and an impetus to later involvement: "although I did not particularly enjoy playing the violin, I recognise what a considerable amount of musicianship I acquired through those lessons" [UK54, aged 54].

The pianist Susan Tomes has reflected similarly on how "when families suffer through the early stages of a youngster learning to play the violin, for example, they should remember that the scratchy melodies are not the only product of the enterprise" (Tomes, 2010, p. 24); she suggests that the benefits of training, endurance, and "self-denial for a greater goal" are more readily recognised in sport—perhaps because the rewards of increased fitness and improvement in skills are more easily observed. By demonstrating the unpredictability of the outcomes of instrumental learning, the life history respondents show that all such tuition must hold the potential for long-term success as well as immediate satisfaction. As Estelle Jorgensen puts it, "the neophyte musician is simply in the process of becoming an accomplished musician", and if that distant goal is never reached, the journey will still have been worthwhile: "what is of greatest importance is that the student becomes a better person through the play and effort of becoming a musician" (Jorgensen, 2003a, p. 205).

4.6 Summary: Musical Supporters and Role Models

This chapter has focused on the people who provide the foundation for musical experiences: the parents whose alertness to musical opportunities is needed to guide and encourage their children; the school music teachers whose recognition of musical potential can nurture or stifle an emerging musical identity; the instrumental teachers whose individual attention can build musical confidence as well as skills; and the wider network of siblings, extended family, church music leaders, concert performers and organizers, and school head teachers who might act—often unintentionally—as musical role models and influences.

The life history respondents show an appreciation for the people who provided them not only with skills and opportunities but also with a sense of the value of music, whether demonstrated by adults through their own involvement or through their support for the respondents' own childhood activities. While only a few reported having had the "archetypical inspirational teacher" [UK29, aged 54] or "parents [who] were great" [UK12, aged 24], all had taken elements of their parents' and teachers' behaviour as a stimulus to their musical learning, whether flourishing in their encouragement and guidance or, in a few cases, defying their potentially devastating criticism or dismissal. These respondents had sometimes been resilient in their response to less-than-ideal circumstances, although in their comments about teachers who "put off people who were not interested" [UK64, aged 55] they acknowledged that others in their peer group were not so fortunate, so offering a reminder that musical identities are more fragile than some of these life histories might suggest.

These discussions support previous evidence (Sloboda & Howe, 1992) that finding a well-liked first instrumental teacher and supporting the early stages of learning through active parental participation are vital foundations for musical progress. As one respondent summarised it: "What matters for a child's music education? 1. Parents. 2. Being in the right school which happens to have the right teacher or other adult. (This applies to absolutely everything from science to minority sports. If there happens to be somebody on the staff with the enthusiasm and the time to share, the child is fortunate)" [UK54, aged 54]. The life history accounts also demonstrate, however, that the impact and outcomes of these early influences are not directly predictable: few of the respondents had clearly stated ambitions for lifelong music-making, and while many reportedly attained high levels of skill in adolescence, their later uses of music in careers and leisure would be diverse and sometimes surprising even to them, as Chapter 5 will demonstrate. In contrast with the professional musicians of other studies (e.g., Manturzewska, 1990; Smilde, 2009a), parents and teachers in these life stories appear to have promoted the immediate benefits of musical learning over the long-term goals of performing success, sometimes leaving the respondents unaware until later in life of the alternative musical pathways that might have been open to them. This suggests that those within the music profession, including instrumental and classroom teachers, have a responsibility to make parents and pupils more aware of the lifelong potential of musical learning; and conversely that researchers could do more to ensure that the multiple outcomes of learning are investigated and valued alongside the professional routes that have previously dominated the research field.

Chapter 5 will examine in more detail the life trajectories of the UK respondents, exploring the ways in which the foundations for musical learning discussed so far have had a long-term effect on respondents' lives. The answer to whether lifelong engagement is a legitimate aim for musical education becomes clearer through these discussions: musical teaching and parenting inevitably has an effect of some kind, and so warrants careful consideration as a previously underdeveloped aspect of music education discourse. In David Myers' call for school music to embrace lifelong learning as an explicit goal, he suggests that "those who have found avenues of meaningful musical pursuits in adulthood [. . .] may offer us the best clues as to how we can achieve coherence in music education across the lifespan" (Myers, 2005, p. 16). The life history respondents provide confirmation that this is the case: in their evaluation of their musical influences, role models, and opportunities, they show that their childhood musical experiences have lasting effects and tremendous potential—and a great deal to tell current music educators, parents, and researchers about their work and its impact.

Interlude G: Duncan Dwinell [OUK34]
Aged 58, left school (USA) in 1967

Piano lessons and church choir, followed by an unexpected shift from the study of history to music

My father was a great music enthusiast: fervent singer in both the church choir and in Glee clubs (American), he had played the banjo in a jazz group, tuba in his school band and hankered to be the next Tommy Dorsey.[1] Highly emotional with a taste for indulgent music both classical and theatrical: Mozart's Requiem to Show Boat. He had to have the latest stereo hi-fi equipment even in the early 60s. My mother could hardly carry a tune and played nothing. Both brothers preceded me in the church choir, neither playing an instrument. I started piano from the choir master at about the age of 9 and made modest progress. He left and I stopped. Within the next year I was itching to start again with my school music teacher. Further modest progress. It wasn't until the original choir master returned now as my secondary music teacher that I began to find the piano an outlet for expression, angst and much soul-searching. That teacher was a substitute parent in my life. My commitment tailed off in adolescence, but I continued to sing.

As a chorister I also took on the exalted position of organist's page-turner, as I could read music from my piano lessons. From this weekly experience of practice and performance I had an enormously wide range of styles, sounds, composers and drama offered me. I even had the chance to pull stops and play the organ during breaks! Fantastic! The organist used me as his 'key poker' when he did local tunings and I had further chance to experience the

---

[1] American jazz trombonist, trumpeter, and big band leader

differences in instruments. Never aspiring to become an organist, I did become a bit of an aficionado. I fear that my parents were dubious of 1) my increasing attachment to music in terms of appropriate gender activities ("What would your brothers say if you took up violin!") and 2) my choirmaster's increasing attachment to me. Neither issue ever came to anything at all, but on reflection, they were probably right about the second.

I had been introduced to the local youth wind band by a fellow choir member. I sat next to the euphonium and was interested, but watching the conductor was riveting. I had been conducting recordings of Beethoven's 5th in front of my father's hi-fi with a knitting needle for some time. The orchestra followed my beat reliably and obeyed every cue! I had attended several concerts in Boston (Mass., USA) but not regularly. I clearly remember coming out of Brahms' 2nd piano concerto on my own aged about 17 and not being aware of my surroundings or how I had got onto the public transport home. I immediately bought the record. University opened new experiences and I bought a tenor recorder. I amused myself with this, especially as the stairwells had amazing acoustics.

Upon leaving university to take up a Masters degree in the UK, I asked my parents for the hire charges of a French Horn, simply because I loved the sound. Nobody told me how difficult it was or that it was a transposing instrument. Using my recorder to work out the pitches, I taught myself to play at pitch. Wonderful. So I arrived in the UK to start a History MA carrying a French Horn. Stopped in the Quad[2] by the graduate music student in charge of the chamber orchestra, I was asked if I played the horn I was carrying. I said yes, but that I hadn't had any lessons. His reply may have turned my life: "You are better than the horn player we don't have—come to tonight's rehearsal!" First up was Beethoven's 1st symphony. I made quite a good job of it actually and was complimented, especially as I hadn't had any lessons. They all thought I was transposing the Horn in C part at sight and was a wizard! Being in C it was at pitch just as I had taught myself. Just dumb luck! Anyway I stayed. I clearly remember having to decide whether to go to final concert rehearsal or to finish an important history essay: I knew this was a miniature life choice. I chose in favour of the concert! Inside 6 months I had dropped the MA course, enlisted at the Guildhall[3] for lessons from a top performer, enrolled at King's College London for a post-grad certificate course and was away. Two years later, fed up with books and needing money, I taught at a rough school in South East London, then back to college to

---

[2] Short for quadrangle, the grassy square around which an archetypal Oxbridge college is built
[3] Guildhall School of Music and Drama, one of London's conservatoires

qualify as a teacher, and finally in 1976 my first proper job as an assistant music teacher. As time went on, I transferred my skills to being a peripatetic teacher[4] of brass and woodwind instruments. My wife and I started a local music school on Saturday mornings and all three of our children were very musically involved.

I gained no O Level or A Level equivalents or even a degree in Music. I never took any grades or even Grade 5 theory! My late start has not allowed me to be a 'real musician'. I don't think music; but I do think performance. Hence I have devoted my greatest energy to promote young performers. I continue to run a steel band, I conduct a local youth wind band, I organise all the school concerts, but I do very little performing myself. The horn is in the loft and I hardly ever play either the recorder or the piano for pleasure. I've stopped singing in choirs. As Head of Music at a grammar school, my musicality comes across in enthusiasm not competence, in commitment, not example. It's still just my father's passion for being near music somehow and being glad that others are as well.

I have no regrets that I gave up my History MA for music. I feel 'handicapped' that I have such basic keyboard skills, have such a shallow experience as a horn player (not much more than 3 years!) and that I am best known as a steel band player, never having been to the Caribbean! Watching and hearing all of my children perform at incredible standards makes me both very proud and envious. For all this and maybe more, I was awarded the regional Ted Wragg Teaching Commendation for Lifetime Achievement. I am left with no regrets for my role as middle-man between young players and their destinies in music.

---

[4] A teacher employed by a local education authority to visit schools giving instrumental lessons

Interlude H: Steph Reeve [UK51]
Aged 29, left school 1995

Supportive home and school experiences, now a clarinet teacher who performs regularly

Mum remembers we went to see a Salvation Army[1] band concert when I was about 7 or 8. Apparently I was really taken with it and keenly listened throughout. When the conductor asked if any of the children wanted to conduct my hand shot up and I was asked down. Mum said I loved it and beamed all the way home. I have vague recollections of going down the stairs and waving something in my hand at this band, then somebody politely grabbing my arms and moving them, presumably to make sure I was conducting in time (not sure if the grabbing of a child's arm would be allowed these days). I don't remember feeling particularly excited but I don't remember any negative feelings either.

I have very fond memories of school music. Started and loved the recorder at lower school (aged 6 or 7). Still remember lots of duets and trios that we did and the recorder group always took part in school productions. The teacher there was very enthusiastic and started a small group of us on the treble so I felt quite privileged. That was a new thing for her as well and I remember she learnt with us. There were opportunities to learn violin and guitar but these never interested me. Not sure why. Middle school[2] (aged 10 to 13) had an excellent classroom teacher who encouraged us all to learn something. I chose clarinet

---

[1] A Christian movement with a strong tradition of brass band training as part of worship, outreach, and education

[2] Lower, middle, and high schools, described here, are a less usual alternative to the primary and secondary school structures described in the Glossary.

and started in group lessons at school. Played in school band, wind ensemble and almost all other non-clarinet clubs (steel band, handchimes, choir, recorder). It took up most of my lunch breaks but I was never bothered about missing play time. The choir took part in a children's opera one summer which was a great experience. Middle school ensembles always went to music festivals doing well and school concerts were always very well prepared and good fun. There was an inter-form competition each year where each form had to put together a programme including a few solos and a whole form piece. All of this was run by one very energetic music teacher who sadly died last year. I had seen her the previous year and both she and her husband (my piano teacher) had always been keen to hear about my progress as well as that of almost all the other pupils she would have known. Over 300 attended the funeral and she will be greatly missed.

Upper school (aged 14 to 18) had a good music teacher. The one I attended had less music than many of the other schools I could have gone to but I was doing a lot of playing through the county music service. I was already one of the more advanced players in the school when I arrived and didn't have much other competition so school band (or rather chamber ensemble of between 5 and 12 depending on who turned up) was relaxed. There were a few other clarinets so I often helped them out showing them new notes or helping with difficult bits. Hardly anyone chose to do GCSE music so this class was small. One of the other girls chose music because she couldn't stand the alternatives (art or drama) so I often worked with her helping her out with compositions, her performance on the keyboard or anything else she struggled with. Again these classes were relaxed and sometimes we got away without doing anything but I was well aware of what standard I needed to be. A level was much tougher but the teachers we had knew their stuff and were all very experienced.

However, most of my musical activity during my school years and where I gained a massive part of my musical training was through Northamptonshire Music School (now a Service). I often wonder where I would be now without having progressed from Saturday music centre through the three youth orchestras and clarinet choir, wind dectet and various trips throughout the year. I think the development that comes from rehearsing regularly (weekly) in any ensemble, learning loads of new repertoire, giving concerts, accompanying soloists, and having to mix with others cannot be matched anywhere else. It was fun at the bottom end, always enjoyable with great music, although we still worked hard. Anyone misbehaving didn't last long and those who didn't enjoy it were free to leave. As we had to audition at youth level I always felt I had earned my place and worked hard. It got tougher at the top end but we were still made to feel special at times. One member of staff selected players to do unusual repertoire (*Carnival of the Animals, Rhapsody in Blue* for jazz ensemble) so I realised I was getting some good playing opportunities. Competition was also much greater here (which was why I enjoyed school activities). I was friends with all the clarinets but with some there was a sense of trying to 'go one better' than the others. In youth orchestra, one particular friend used to get to the rehearsal stupidly early after a concert to look through the music and find all the good solos! I probably would have done this but my lift was always late so I never got the chance. It all worked out fair in the end with the solos. This particular girl was and still is a great friend and we used to do a lot of duet work together. I have no regrets about any of my musical activities, although I was a little disappointed to have to give up tennis club and Young Ornithologists Club at school when rehearsals started to clash.

I went to Trinity Music College and had a great four years. Biggest influences were my clarinet teacher and chamber music coach (both were fantastic teachers) and my friends, many of whom I am still in contact with. I continued to develop musically, worked fairly hard and passed each year easily. The biggest developments I had (chamber music, forming my own orchestra, planning and programming concerts, developing coaching skills) were not assessed at all while I was at college. These days I am mostly working as a peripatetic woodwind teacher,[3] and I play a few concerts each month as a clarinettist. I coach regular adult woodwind ensembles, run day and weekend workshops for adults and arrange music for chamber ensembles and other small to medium sized groups. I'm currently on the MA Psychology for Musicians course at Sheffield. My dissertation research is looking at adult learners and comparing them with children.

---

[3] A teacher employed by a local education authority to visit schools giving instrumental lessons

5| Opportunities and Outcomes
in Lifelong Musical Engagement

5.1 Musical Routes and Roots

A S WAS NOTED IN CHAPTER 1, studies of musical life histories have tended to focus on the lifespan development of professional musicians, tracing their early signs of musical promise through to success in a performing career, and noting any deviation from this path as an implicitly inferior, though often understandable, outcome. Researchers and course directors in music colleges and conservatoires have attempted in recent years to overturn the assumption that all performing students should aspire to a solo career, proffering the alternative model of a "portfolio career", in which performance activities sit alongside teaching, outreach, and other forms of employment as equally valued aspects of a professional life in music (see, e.g., Burt & Mills, 2006; Bennett & Hannon, 2008). Music graduates who embark on such a career through deliberate choice have been found to be more satisfied in their working lives, the mark of success being "when their objective work and their aspirations coincide" (Mills & Smith, 2006, p. 137).

Preparation for such a career choice begins early: rather than undertaking the 10,000 hours of single-minded practice needed to become expert on one instrument (Ericsson, Krampe, & Tesch-Römer, 1993), those musicians who opt for portfolio careers are more likely to have learned a second instrument, "not in the first place to increase their employability, but [rather] out of intrinsic motivation" (Smilde, 2009a, p. 130). This suggests that the attitudes of those musicians aiming for a varied life in music are different from the outset: "for some portfolio musicians playing an instrument is perceived more as a means than an end" (p. 131). These different attitudes might, in turn, be shaped by circumstances: a child who is not aware of the possibilities of a professional career is unlikely to aspire to one, and parents who do not have the knowledge or experience to offer specialist guidance might unwittingly fail to lay secure foundations for exceptional musical achievement.

For very many of the life history respondents, their route into lifelong music-making appeared to have been serendipitous, with chance meetings and casually offered opportunities contributing to an increasing awareness that music was important. As Matthew in Interlude I describes, an audience member whispering "Blimey, he's here again" in a school concert might be enough to increase a young child's sense of self-as-musician—but would not in itself lead directly to the hours of determined practice needed to pursue a professional career. Very few of the life history respondents claimed to have considered a professional career in music (see Section 5.3), instead defining the term "musician" more widely, or judging it not to apply to them, despite a lifelong interest: as Robert says in Interlude L, "I am not a musician in the accepted sense; I cannot read music, I do not play an instrument, and I would not know a Neapolitan Sixth if it bit my leg. On the other hand, personal relationships apart, music is the passion of my life" [UK19, aged 74]. Respondents' perceptions of what it meant to be musically active were defined by the sense of priority given to music in their lives, sometimes stemming from a childhood realisation that their own skills were superior to those of their peers—"in the infant class we did a percussion band which I loved, but I got annoyed with people not playing in time" [UK33, aged 56]—or by having these skills recognised by teachers who "saw an ability in me right from the start" [UK3, aged 52].

Although respondents commonly recognised the value of music in childhood and adolescence, this rarely translated into a determined decision to pursue professional excellence: enjoyment, encouragement, and involvement were intrinsically rewarding, without necessarily being seen to have implications for future life choices. Decisions about musical careers were typically made later, linked to choice of degree subject for those respondents who went to university, and sometimes prompting a new focus on musical learning that was judged to have come too late: "After deciding I wanted to study music at university, I took up the violin, but I had left this too late (aged 16) to get any good at it, and that is probably my greatest regret when it comes to missed musical opportunities" [UK40, aged 44]. Respondents appear to have been working with limited information when making their musical career choices: one chose not to study music at university "as I didn't want to be a school music teacher at that time and that is what I saw of the future if I followed that path" [UK63, aged 57], while another was discouraged from doing so—"my cello teacher advised against it, based on her own and her husband's experience, so I studied engineering instead!" [UK58, aged 52].

Those aged 50 or more had often experienced a strong divide between arts and science subjects at school, and some had been guided away from music in their choice of A Level subjects: "I followed a broadly science-based course, with a view to further education in Geography. At no time did I ever consider music as a career; it was seen as a worthwhile leisure pursuit, and I continued my trombone lessons beyond taking Grade V" [UK54, aged 54]. Although schools and teachers were most often held responsible for giving insufficient guidance on musical career decisions, a few respondents blamed a lack of parental support—"I was so often on my own with my music and feel I could have gone further with a more supportive home situation" [UK38, aged 42]— whilst others took full responsibility themselves: "bitterly regretting" having stopped composing, Piers in Interlude B reflected that "I could blame the lack of guidance that was available in those days, but mostly I blame myself, my indolence, my lack of self-belief and inability to listen to myself and where my natural creative impulses lay" [UK47, aged 62].

A further phase of decision making occurred during higher education, sometimes through an accidental drifting back into music after an alternative career choice (see Interlude F), but more often through a reappraisal of musical skills and inclinations in light of the options available: "in my younger days I had a conflict initially between the practical and the academic sides of music, but eventually came to the conclusion that I didn't have the temperament necessary for the former and was extremely happy in concentrating on musicological activities while still being involved occasionally in playing" [UK27, aged 64]. Realising "I was never going to make it as a performer" [UK47, aged 62] was a common feature of post-university decisions, leading a few respondents to feel that they should have taken a different pathway in their educational choices: "I do think I took the wrong course at [music college]: I should have done the BMus [degree], which would have involved more brain power and less practising" [UK26, aged 52]. The respondents who remedied these decisions as adult learners (see Section 5.4) show that the potential for musical learning and development remains through the lifespan, but there is no denying that some of the earlier decisions made by these respondents—often with a lack of information or deliberate intent— closed down the option of a professional performing career in which they might have been successful.

Comparisons can be made with the presence of sport in schools—another compulsory aspect of education with the opportunity for extension through voluntary participation, and one that invites similarly divided reactions both within school cohorts and in adult retrospection. As with musical activities, adolescent dropout from sports participation is a source of concern, and factors in family and coaching behaviour have been examined to try and understand young people's motivation to continue or give up their sports activities. In a study of adolescents who gave up élite swimming training, "dropouts" were found to have achieved competitive success earlier than those who continued swimming, but were less likely to have a close friend who also swam, and were often the youngest children of parents who had been élite swimmers themselves (Fraser-Thomas, Côté, & Deakin, 2008). The competitive pressures implicit in those factors had clearly proved too much for some adolescents, and led the researchers to conclude that a less goal-driven approach was preferable: "children should be encouraged to participate in a diversity of playful sport and extra-curricular activities" (p. 330). It might seem logical that training a child for competitive success should entail focused practice in his or her chosen sport from an early age, and yet a number of studies have shown that more diverse and less pressured activity increases motivation and still allows for specialisation at a later stage (Fraser-Thomas & Côté, 2009).

Contrasting the musical emphasis on deliberate practice (Ericsson et al., 1993) with a recommendation for deliberate play (Côté, Baker, & Abernethy, 2007), sports psychologist Jean Côté has traced the life experiences and sporting successes of a range of participants, finding that those who "sampled" a range of sports rather than "specialising" from the outset were just as capable of reaching high levels of performance, and were often more intrinsically motivated to do so than those who had been pushed by parents or coaches in a predetermined direction (Strachan, Côté, & Deakin, 2009). This approach matches the motivational stages observed in studies of instrumental learning, whereby a nurturing first teacher is followed by a more demanding performance role model (Sloboda & Howe, 1991), but is less usual as a strategy for selecting an instrument, for which an early decision is generally made according to pragmatic reasons, including the parents' and child's preference and the availability of a teacher and instrument (McPherson & Davidson, 2006).

The life history responses show that while there is certainly tremendous value in musical sampling—exploring opportunities without a clear goal—the chance to make up lost time and specialise later is not so great as in sport, perhaps because the advantages of physical maturity provide increased strength and stamina for sports performance, but not the finer motor skills needed for playing an instrument. Several respondents regretted "lost years" [UK35, aged 52] of insufficient practice or progress, or were dissatisfied with the feeling that "although I have played various instruments at different times I never achieved a really high standard on any of them" [UK53, aged 69].

In his book *Outliers*, Malcolm Gladwell (2008) shows that success across a range of disciplines is often dependent on seemingly insignificant chances, which give selected individuals thousands of additional hours of practice—whether in music, sport, computer programming, or whatever else—and in turn cause them to become exceptional in relation to their peers. Gladwell points out that the time and commitment involved in attaining such high standards has implicit costs for the whole family: "You have to have parents who encourage and support you. You can't be poor, because if you have to hold down a part-time job on the side to help make ends meet, there won't be time left in the day to practice enough" (p. 42). Hardly surprising, then, that Maria Manturzewska's (1990) biographical study of Polish professional musicians found that the vast majority were from wealthy, educated families with a tradition of musical involvement. In the years of post-war rationing and unemployment experienced by many of the older respondents, levels of education were not a reliable predictor of income and socioeconomic status, and several of the respondents refer to well-educated, aspirational parents who nevertheless struggled to fund music lessons for their children. Adding to these difficult circumstances the challenges of knowing how to advise their offspring, it is understandable that the parents of "first-generation" musicians sometimes lacked the information and direction needed to help shape their children's musical futures (Box 5.1.1).

Since aspiring to a professional career was not a feature of most respondents' experience, their life histories offer evidence of a previously under-researched

---

Box 5.1.1

"Growing up as a serious musician in a family who were new to this way of life had its challenges: 'What do you want to do this for?' said one brother-in-law, and the other brother-in-law just sat and listened to my practice as he read his newspaper. My mother was very positive in her encouragement of my music-making and took me to concerts on a very regular basis, often weekly. My father, who had a very good ear for music, was very supportive as well. However, my father, who used to tell everyone I was a 'concert pianist', would always notice and comment upon any wrong notes or mistakes when I played the piano. [. . .] I was fortunate that he lived to 90, by which time he had become, for the last 10 years, my greatest fan!" [UK71, aged 51]

TABLE 5.1 Categories of Adult Involvement in Music [UK1–81]

CATEGORY	ACTIVITIES INCLUDED	NUMBER OF RESPONDENTS
A. Teaching music	Lecturing, instrumental teaching, classroom teaching	38
B. Making music	Playing, singing, conducting, composing	36
C. Learning music	Adult study of academic or practical music	21
D. Listening to music	Concert-going, frequent or concentrated listening	15

aspect of musical development—the routes taken by individuals who retain a lifelong interest in music, within amateur, educational, or community settings. From the 81 UK respondents, four categories of adult involvement emerge, as shown in Table 5.1. Some respondents occupied two of these categories, combining teaching music with playing, or adult learning with regular listening. These activities encompass a range of musical confidence and expertise, from imparting musical knowledge and nurturing the skills of others (A), through displaying existing performance skills (B), or acquiring or developing musical attributes (C), to appreciating and absorbing musical stimuli as a listener (D). They show the variety of potential outcomes to a musical upbringing, and highlight the satisfactions of participation in a nonprofessional capacity—even while raising difficult questions about the extent to which these respondents were made aware of their potential to pursue other routes and attain conventional markers of musical success.

5.2 Becoming Music Educators

The 38 UK respondents involved with music education were notably among the most active and passionate of the life history sample. Many of them were involved in multiple activities, combining their teaching with performing, studying, or writing music, and expressing a strong commitment to offering their pupils an inspiring introduction to music. Like the trainee music teachers in a study by Dimitra Kokotsaki (2010), they viewed the maintaining of their own musical involvement as being beneficial to both their educational practice and their own wellbeing and personal development. Their childhood influences were various—some wrote of

TABLE 5.2 Distribution of Teaching Activity Across Age Groups

	A: TEACHING MUSIC				
AGE GROUP	UNIVERSITY LECTURER	INSTRUMENTAL TEACHER	CLASS TEACHER	OTHER EDUCATIONAL ACTIVITY	NO. OF RESPONDENTS (TOTAL = 38)
18–25		[OUK60]	[UKP78]		2
26–35	[OUK4] [UK59]	[UK51]		[UK51]	3
36–45	[UK5] [UK40]	[UK37] [UK38] [UK43] [UK66] [UK72]		[UK43] [UK66]	7
46–55	[UK52]	[UK3] [UK21] [UK26] [UK35] [UK52] [UK54] [UK64] [UK71] [UKP73]	[UK 61] [UK71]	[UK54]	10
56–65	[UK6] [UK27] [UK47]	[UK16] [UK20] [UK32] [UK33] [UK44] [UK63]	[UK32] [OUK34] [UK47]	[UK20] [UK24]	11
66–75	[UK8]	[UK8] [UK46] [UK55]		[UK46]	3
75+		[UK39]		[UK39]	1
No.	9	27	6	8	

supportive parents, others of the affirming influence of an instrumental teacher; some experienced an abundance of performing opportunities in school, while others were unimpressed with their classroom music teaching. In a study with American music educators, Clifford Madsen and Steven Kelly found that decisions to teach made in adolescence, rather than during college years, were generally more positive, and that "observing exemplary music educators, getting compliments from others, an awareness of one's performance ability, realizing the powerful effect music has on one's life, and not wanting to give up music seem to be major factors in making the decision to become a teacher" (Madsen & Kelly, 2002, p. 330). The life history respondents also shared common factors of determination and a willingness to take on new challenges, with these qualities expressed both in their childhood learning and in their adult capacity for maintaining self-development alongside a varied portfolio of work.

The activities of the music educator respondents are divided across the age groups, as shown in Table 5.2, with some individuals falling into two categories, most often as instrumental teachers who also did some classroom teaching or directed other educational activities outside school. Two groups within this category offer particularly fruitful scope for discussion: the instrumental teachers, who are the largest sample and present a lifespan perspective on undertaking this role between the ages of 24 and 81, and the "other educational activity" group, whose work sheds light on the different contexts in which musicians engage in teaching-related work. Of the other two groups, the classroom teacher sample is rather small, and the university lecturers said relatively little about their career choices or experiences of teaching in higher education. Existing research on the career patterns of both groups is also limited, and yet an understanding of the musical life stories of teachers in schools and universities would provide a valuable context for their training and development (see Bernard, 2009).

Some years ago, Norton York (2001) suggested that the musical background of most classroom teachers was more classically oriented than that of their students—an understandable product of their training, but one that could potentially undermine attempts to make the school music curriculum broader and more widely accessible. As Chris Philpott puts it, "Music teachers who emerge from school music, a university music degree and teacher education are highly likely to have been socialized into understandings which are informed by the western classical aesthetic. It is tough to become a class music teacher without having been through this route of progression" (Philpott, 2010, p. 89). In universities, too, lecturers are likely to be amongst the most academically minded of their cohort, usually being appointed to their posts by virtue of their research profile rather than their teaching skills. The relative homogeneity of teaching staff, compared with the diverse aims of the curriculum, could be a limitation for music education at any level—although the receptiveness of these life history respondents to learning new musical skills suggests that this problem, once clearly identified, could be remedied through self-reflection and professional development.

Turning to the instrumental teachers, the more substantial sample size offers some potential for considering the trends and influences that bring people into that career, and the attitudes that they display towards music and education. Life history research with UK instrumental teachers has previously identified a point of career crisis around the age of 36 to 42, when greater experience of teaching and sometimes parenting, combined with an awareness of the limited prospects for career advancement, meant that teachers "reached, or at least perceived, an apex of professional energy and aspiration" (Baker, 2005, p. 142). In my sample, several of the respondents within this age group had only recently embarked upon instrumental teaching, and were enthusiastic about its opportunities to use and develop their own musical skills: after pursuing a career away from music, one clarinettist had "gradually drifted into some teaching. I started with one student, then two, and now I have sixty plus, and I feel I have come home" [UK37, aged 42].

Some of the older respondents reported a similar experience of being persuaded into teaching after sometimes lengthy non-musical careers: another clarinettist had undertaken "a second career as a music teacher and I have found great success and fulfilment over the last 11 years. I would have to say my regret is that I didn't do it sooner but only got myself organised to do it when redundancy from my business career came in 1995" [UK63, aged 57]. Adding that she intended to "carry on for as long as my pupils are happy to teach them!" this teacher illustrated the scope for extending an instrumental teaching career well past typical retirement age, as the oldest respondent in this group had done (Box 5.2.1). Like the local education authority employees in David Baker's study (Baker, 2005), work as an instrumental teacher was sometimes begun with a sense of "occupational impermanence" (Baker, 2006, p. 45), although this was no obstacle to the longevity of subsequent careers.

Instrumental teaching careers had often started gradually, especially for mothers whose children's schools became aware of their potential contribution (see Interlude J): 62% of the instrumental teachers were female, following national trends for this to be a domesticated form of musical employment, more readily accessible to women who also have childcare responsibilities (Rowe, 2008, p. 118). Opportunities sometimes grew from family interactions, most often supervising children's practice, but sometimes involving older relatives: "my mother started to learn the piano with me—she has recently passed her Grade 1 piano at 85 years old! My father was quickly abandoned as a piano pupil as he would not practise and wanted only to 'do it his way' and play by ear. This was the start of my teaching piano and later cello at home" [UK71, aged 51]. Whilst there might be some concerns about the unregulated nature of the instrumental teaching profession—addressed to some extent in recent years by the introduction of professional development courses by the Associated Board of the Royal Schools of Music (ABRSM) and other bodies—these respondents illustrate that the opportunities to start teaching without requiring specific qualifications or specialist premises bring many enthusiastic and skilled musicians into contact with young people in ways that are potentially highly positive. Several respondents expressed the view, like Christina (Interlude J), that "I never imagined I would become an instrumental teacher" [UK66, aged 40], suggesting that while this career direction was found to be enjoyable once it had begun, it was not an ambition held by young musicians—a view consistent with recent research in conservatoires where "working in education was perceived as a career trap for those students who desired to emerge chiefly as performers" (Miller & Baker, 2007, p. 13).

This self-selecting sample provides of course only a partial view of the profession: others who have tried teaching and been unsuccessful or unfulfilled are not represented here and would be a difficult population to locate and research. Like amateur musicians who can leave a performing group more easily than their salaried counterparts, these highly motivated teachers display the "value commitment" of people making a choice to continue in their activities, more strongly than the "continuance commitment" of workers who fear the penalties that would be incurred by a change of direction (Stebbins, 1992, p. 51). Little reference was made to the financial pressures of this career choice, though in reporting often high numbers of pupils within their teaching practice, respondents showed their awareness of the precariousness of their income, whereby teachers' "livelihoods are directly dependent on pupils choosing to continue learning" (Creech, 2010a, p. 306). For many of these respondents, instrumental teaching had brought a level of autonomy that enabled them to feel engaged and satisfied in their work, valuing the flexibility to pursue other musical interests alongside freelance or part-time teaching. One versatile teacher of violin, piano, recorder, and singing reflected on the fulfilling nature of her work with good humour: "I received an e-mail only this morning from a teacher at one of my schools saying that a pupil's grandparent had told her how I have changed his boy's life. That's good! (I assume I changed it for the better!)" [UK33, aged 56].

Those respondents who engaged in "other educational activity" tended to combine this with their work as instrumental teachers, gaining additional musical and career satisfaction through activities outside traditional educational settings, including running music groups for toddlers [UK66, aged 40], training bands for brass players [UK54, aged 54], and adult chamber ensembles [UK51, aged 29]. While a few of the respondents mentioned this aspect of their work only in passing, as part of the context they provided about their current musical involvement, others spoke passionately about the pleasure of working with young musicians in ensembles:

Box 5.2.2

"I never foresaw becoming an instrumental teacher, always believing firmly that children should be taught by musicians properly qualified for the job. Surprisingly, such an opportunity presented itself a few years ago. I was persuaded that I met my own strict criterion, so now I have a few brass pupils at a local independent school. The joy of working with child flautists, clarinettists, trumpeters, etc. as young as 7 is that they don't know what they're not supposed to be able to play yet! Their rising to and beyond expectations continues to amaze me. Perhaps my early recorder teacher noticed the same phenomenon—I am glad that he did! Our band has one rule: that nobody cares what you can't play yet, just join in and enjoy the notes that you can." [UK54, aged 54]

"the greatest enjoyment comes from training children's bands. Thanks to other people's instrumental teaching, one presents the concerts and receives much applause which is due to them!" [UK54, aged 54]. This brass teacher articulated a clear connection between his own experience of instrumental learning and playing in childhood (Box 5.2.2) and his current position of being "fortunate to be able to pass on something of what I received freely in my own schooldays" [UK54, aged 54]. His experience of learning had therefore given him strongly developed opinions about what was valuable in music education, and a desire to replicate the opportunities from which he had benefited himself. However, a few respondents obliquely referred to the lack of career opportunities for these non-institutional educational activities in music, which might limit the extent to which amateur players are able to offer their skills within the wider community.

Although education and outreach activities are increasingly part of the portfolio of professional orchestral musicians' work (Bennett, 2008, p. 101), the life history respondents were often working for limited financial reward in pursuing activities beyond their main teaching: "I have done some composition writing for school, church choir bands and amateur dramatic performances. All good fun but not remunerative, but I did have teacher's salary" [UK20, aged 62]. These observations suggest that there is real potential for increasing the involvement of highly skilled amateurs in supporting community music activities, so bridging the gap between home and school involvement and providing more opportunities for non-institutional musical learning. Examples of such collaborations are rarely documented in the research literature, although they certainly exist in the various forms, including recent university outreach initiatives in which music is well placed to address the "motivation to bridge the gap between privileged university students and underserved school populations, in that disadvantaged youth may be encouraged and motivated to learn by positive role models" (Soto, Lum, & Campbell, 2009, p. 339). In some traditions and contexts, the exchange of skills and encouragement between learners of all ages is an intrinsic part of the musical culture: brass bands have a long history of training younger players through participation (Herbert, 1998), and Irish traditional musicians, likewise, pass their skills to the next generation in a playing culture firmly embedded in family and community (McCarthy, 1999). This structured provision can create a disjunction for young people between their community music-making and "statutory music education [that] had minimal influence on their development as traditional musicians" (O'Flynn, 2011, p. 261), and shows once again the need for school musical experiences to offer clearly accessible pathways into adult and community musical participation.

Two of the oldest respondents also shared their passion for music through leading classes as part of the "University of the Third Age" (U3A), a movement founded in France in the 1970s as "a self-help organisation for people no longer in full time employment providing educational, creative and leisure opportunities in a friendly environment" (u3a.org.uk). Both still active as piano accompanists for exams and festivals, the running of a "Music Appreciation" class [UK39, aged 81] and a "Singing for Fun" group [UK46, aged 72] for their local U3A perhaps helped to cement the lifelong musical identities of these respondents, giving them status as musicians in retirement, and bringing them into contact with others of their generation with a shared musical and educational heritage. For both respondents, their U3A leadership roles had replaced previously valued activities—in one case, retirement as a piano teacher [UK46, aged 72], and in the other, the loss of his wife, described as "an excellent pianist and I miss *sharing* music with her" [UK39, aged 81].

Studies of "positive ageing" have repeatedly shown the value of musical activities (Southcott, 2009) and lifelong learning (Dench & Regan, 2000) for maintaining wellbeing, vitality, and social connections into later life, and the sense of a culmination of a musical life is clear in these respondents' descriptions of "a wonderful life of music making" [UK46, aged 72] and a belief that "only hard work, in the end, brings satisfaction and deep enjoyment of music" [UK39, aged 81]. Jane Southcott's (2009) research with a "third age" choir illustrates the strengths of the "self-help" model embodied by the U3A, whereby activities for senior citizens are drawn from the extensive resources within their own age group, rather than imposed, however well-meaningly, by younger and more able-bodied musicians. These alternative educational settings, therefore, provide not only a valuable source of musical enjoyment for the respondents and others like them in the U3A groups, but also an insight on the under-researched topic of music in older age, showing how in these two cases—and others within the life history responses—music has helped (or even avoided) the transition from work into retirement, and has sustained friendships, social contact, and musical identity into the final phase of life.

5.3 Becoming Music-Makers

Having established that performance opportunities in school were amongst the most highly valued formative activities for the life history respondents (see discussion in Chapter 3), challenging questions are raised about the extent to which such activities prepared these young people for lifelong involvement in music-making. Younger respondents coming to the end of institutional education sometimes expressed anxiety about where they would find future opportunities for playing: "Having just done what may be my last orchestra concert at university it is quite a sad thought that it may have been my last, at least for a little while" [UK45, aged 20]. This sociology graduate had spent her school years being in staged productions, orchestras, and choirs, competing in festivals with county ensembles, then joining university groups during a non-music degree, and it is not surprising that at the time of writing she felt a little uncertain about how—and whether—she would be able to maintain that level of activity as she moved out of education and into employment. She would have been reassured to know that many of the life history respondents had succeeded in continuing their playing, by joining community groups, contributing to church music-making, playing with friends at home, continuing lessons and practice individually, or forming their own ensembles and directing or composing music for them. Nonetheless, it is undoubtedly true that making music outside school and university settings requires a different kind of motivation and commitment, no longer driven by teachers or contributing explicitly to learning, but demanding individual initiative and a new recognition of the value of music for wellbeing and satisfaction.

The contexts in which the life history respondents made music as adults fell into five broad categories (with some respondents occupying more than one of these):

1. Community settings (24 respondents): joining or establishing instrumental or vocal groups for adults

2. Educational settings (10 respondents): usually as teachers directing ensembles or accompanying pupils on the piano
3. Worship settings (11 respondents): church organists and worship band members contributing regularly to church services
4. Self-directed music-making (12 respondents): pop bands, chamber ensembles, and solo performers organising their own performance opportunities
5. Private music-making (8 respondents): individuals playing alone or friends making music informally in the home

This is an encouraging profile of music-making beyond institutional boundaries, showing that while schools play a valuable role in providing musical opportunities, many adults find other outlets for their playing in musical societies, churches, and more informally organised groups. For many of these respondents, there was a clear continuity between their childhood musical activities and the type of involvement they pursued in adulthood: memories of school choirs were linked with the impetus to join the local choral society, and helping a parent with music in church as a teenager had led in at least one instance to running worship groups as an adult (see Interlude J). Pianists, organists, and singers were well represented in the responses, with the keyboard players in demand as accompanists for exams, concerts, and church services, and the singers finding ready opportunities to join already established choirs. The motivations and experiences of the five groups identified above reveal some interesting features of adult participation, showing how personal satisfaction is balanced against a sense of group contribution, and revealing a high level of self-awareness in respondents' decisions to continue or cease their musical involvement from school years into adulthood.

The experiences of those adult musicians involved in community music settings complement previous research on musical participation (Pitts, 2005) by illustrating the dual benefits of making music among like-minded friends, often as a busy undercurrent to an already full life. Respondents' descriptions of the choral and orchestral repertoire they had performed showed that high standards and musical challenge were important in justifying the time they spent on musical involvement: "our chorus master at the Philharmonic is a superb musician and obviously an influence, encouraging us to work at the highest common denominator and assuming you have musical intelligence" [UK42, aged 62]. Some respondents had considered, or even tried, a professional career in music before arriving at their current amateur status, and tended to be sanguine about the benefits of their more informal pursuit of music: "Many friends who took up music professionally have told me I have had the best of both worlds. Being an amateur for many years enabled me to have even more joy in my music activities" [UK46, aged 72].

Only a few respondents expressed regret at not making music a more central part of their working and creative lives (Box 5.3.1), whilst others had been disillusioned by the realities of professional performing: "The major high-light—and major disappointment—was getting a full time job as a professional orchestral viola player at the age of 19, which was the pinnacle of my ambition at the time and turned out to be deathly boring and incredibly stressful, and knocked my confidence for six; it took seven years for me to recover my confidence in playing" [UK59, aged 33]. The ability and opportunity to make music in adulthood was generally seen as a privilege, sometimes difficult to fit around work and family commitments, but offering a dimension to life that was worthwhile and highly valued; as Tim says in Interlude D, "Talking to people who don't have a passion in life, as I have had for music, has made me realise how lucky I have been simply to have this driving force, always interesting, usually entertaining, often frustrating, sometimes deeply satisfying" [UKP73, aged 48].

As well as the intrinsic satisfaction of making music, many respondents gained pleasure from the ways in which their musical activities and skills benefited others, either by encouraging young people into music-making or by providing a service, such as accompanying pupils for exams or leading music in worship. This approach had led to some dilemmas in balancing quantity and quality of playing, with one pianist regretting "not having enough time to practise. I have been involved in a lot of music making but so much of it has been virtually sight read, through lack of time to commit to it. But that is a lot

---

Box 5.3.1

"Some years [after school], I was on a corporate team-building course when they showed an orchestra in rehearsal as an example of a team. I was totally surprised to find that I deeply wished I were in the orchestra instead of in business! There was a deep sense of regret there. I no longer play either cello (sold when we went to the US for study in 1977) or piano, so there is some loss there. I did consider taking up the cello again a few years ago when a friend offered me one, but decided the commitment to practice and rehearsal would put too much of a strain on our family life. Playing bass guitar at church only requires one evening a week and no practice in between; this I can manage! I hope to take up the piano again for fun within the next couple of years (when we have the funds to buy one!)." [UK58, aged 52]

---

to do with not being able to say 'no' when a new job opportunity has arisen!" [UK24, aged 65]. One suspects this pianist and others of having high standards when they make claims such as "I do play the piano and organ for church but have no technique" [UK20, aged 62]: perhaps, like the bass guitarist in Box 5.3.1, they are making music well within their capabilities—avoiding risk but nonetheless contributing musically within their local contexts. Such "functional" music-making can easily be devalued in comparison with achieving professional status, and yet the musical challenges that are created through being "always in demand" [UK3, aged 52] clearly bring their own satisfaction to adult musicians, as well as being of benefit to other players and listeners around them.

One respondent articulated explicitly the view that seemed to underpin many of the responses, writing of "recycling the benefits" of her own musical education: "as well as my full time (non-musical) job, I am musical director of a choir and a light opera group, do around 15 concerts a year and accompany another, work-based, choir and play for a number of church services and sometimes weddings and funerals! Most of that is unpaid but requires skills that are gradually declining in the society we are creating where such skills are not valued, but the value to the community is immense and irreplaceable" [UK25, aged 49]. Perhaps the sense of serendipity, rather than ambition, that was often a feature of involvement in music in worship settings, particularly, placed a limit on the claims that respondents were willing to make for their adult achievements: one even refuted the title that seemed to come with his role in church music, stating that "I have from time to time been asked to play the organ in church—another unexpected development from a schooldays opportunity. I refuse to be called an 'organist'—I correct folk who wrongly describe me so thus: 'a trombonist who plays the organ'" [UK54, aged 54]. Since music in worship is intended as a "facilitator of religious experience" (Miller & Strongman, 2002, p. 14) rather than a performance to be attended to fully and critiqued by its audience, playing in these settings perhaps provided a safe musical outlet for performers who would not otherwise choose to play in public, due to self-perceived limitations in their skills or available practice time. Despite their own self-deprecation, however, church musicians often felt appreciated by congregations and fellow musicians (see Interlude I), creating a positive context for their playing that affirmed current skill levels rather than challenging them with the demands of solo performance.

Gaining musical satisfaction in adulthood did not necessarily involve public performance, and the eight respondents who engaged in private music-making illustrate a largely hidden outcome of music education—adults who continue their playing as an adjunct to regular listening or concert-going, or

"One of my first opportunities to accompany was when singers from my mother's office came round for supper. My mother went to make the tea and, one night, I said to the baritone, 'I'll play that while my Mum is busy.' 'You can't play that', he said. I then proceeded to accompany him with the 'Road to Mandalay'. I also remember the Aberdeen Blitz when all the windows in the street were blown in, except ours, and my mother had everyone in for a cup of tea! Again while she was busy I sat at the piano and we all sang—I can't remember what but probably 'The Northern Lights of Old Aberdeen.'" [UK46, aged 72]

as a way of socialising with friends through informal chamber music playing in the home (see Interlude A). The private pursuit of music was often a retirement phase after a busy musical life, including some respondents who had withdrawn from public performance owing to ill health. Many of these older respondents recalled hearing their parents and their friends having "musical parties" [UK6, aged 65] in the home, and so had a role model for private music-making that was less prevalent in more recent decades (Box 5.3.2). While younger players, too, played "for pure enjoyment to unwind" [UKP80, aged 42], making music in private sometimes reflected perceived barriers to group involvement, including a lack of skill judged to result from a deficiency in education—"no choirs in Oxford will have me because I cannot sight read" [UKP79, aged 20]—or from having ceased learning before reaching a standard high enough for adult participation: "I wish I hadn't stopped playing the cello when I started secondary school so I could play in orchestras now, and I wish I had continued my singing lessons after starting secondary school" [UK48, aged 26].

Several respondents expressed a regret that "although I have played various instruments at different times I never achieved a really high standard on any of them" [UK53, aged 69]: in this case, the violinist in question had completed a music degree and "gave up playing the violin seriously after I finished university". Lapsed adult musicians who have attained, but not maintained, a high standard on their instrument seem to be a particularly challenging group to draw into adult participation, since they are self-critical of their current levels of playing in comparison to their previous peaks of success, and also aware of the effort and time that would be needed to return them to a standard they judged to be satisfactory (see Interlude K). As the discussion of adult learning later in this chapter will show (Section 5.4), some adults in this position gained greater pleasure from beginning a new instrument, so applying their residual learning to a new context, and recalibrating their expectations of musical achievement.

The group of 12 respondents classified above as being involved in "self-directed music-making" had taken a different route to adult participation, remaining outside institutional or organized groups and creating their own opportunities for performing with friends. This category included classical instrumentalists performing chamber music together, usually as a complement to a career as an instrumental or classroom music teacher, with an implied sense that maintaining their own performing skills and enjoyment of music enriched both their wellbeing and their work. Those most likely to pursue a self-directed route, however, were the popular musicians, who continued their habits of group learning from adolescence (see Chapter 3) by forming and joining bands as adults. Finding like-minded people to make music with was important to maintaining motivation and involvement: only one pop musician made music in private, describing himself as "Amateur drummer. Not a member of a band. Play style = leisurely" [UKP75, aged 27]. Others spoke of the value of a "vibrant, welcoming and forgiving musical scene" [UKP41, aged 35] for developing their playing skills and confidence, and felt that they were greatly influenced by the musicians they worked with: "I think the experience of rehearsing and performing together, collectively getting a set of material to sound as good as possible and going out gigging it, has a profound influence on how musicians play and think about music, though often in ways that are hard to define" [UKP73, aged 48]. Like the classical musicians, these players showed a high level of self-monitoring in judging their own musical credibility, offering evidence of their status and achievements in the form of recordings, prestigious gigs, and critical acclaim: "one of my old bands has just had a retrospective compilation CD released and will be featured on a label compilation released in Japan later this year" [UKP76, aged 50]. While popular musicians were more likely to generate their own opportunities for rehearsing, playing, and recording with other people, they shared with the other UK respondents a commitment to doing so at a level that brought pleasure to others as well as to themselves.

The experiences of these adult musicians, across the range of activities and contexts in which they make music, show that the continuation of music-making beyond school focuses not only on participation, but also on development and achievement. The respondents showed a reluctance to stagnate musically, expressing regret when their current levels of playing did not match those of their teenage years, when they had more time to practise—and often wishing that they had heeded parental exhortations to use this time to the full. They were careful not to let down their co-performers and listeners, seeking opportunities that were matched to the levels of skill and time that they had available, and talking modestly about activities that fell within those parameters. In interpreting respondents' judgements of their own activities, there is no objective measure of standards: research that sought to evaluate adult musicians' performance against their self-perception would be fraught with difficulties and probably of little benefit, and has certainly not been attempted here. The responses are revealing, however, in showing the level of self-awareness involved in adult music-making, as participants balanced their enjoyment of taking part with the success of their contribution. Self-awareness is shown to be a feature that both strengthens and inhibits adult musical participation, maintaining and motivating standards for some players and singers, but perhaps preventing others from becoming involved. Having explored respondents' experiences of maintaining and developing their existing skills, the next section considers another route into adult music-making—that of taking up a new musical challenge—which holds the potential to bring a different kind of satisfaction in lifelong musical engagement.

5.4 Becoming Adult Learners

The activities undertaken by the UK participants as adult learners fell into three categories: degree-level study, resuming instrumental lessons, and starting a new instrument. The 18 respondents who self-identified as adult learners were distributed across the age groups as shown in Table 5.3.

TABLE 5.3 Distribution of Learning Activity Across Age Groups

	C: LEARNING MUSIC			
AGE GROUP	ACADEMIC STUDY OF MUSIC	RESUMING INSTRUMENTAL LESSONS	LEARNING A NEW INSTRUMENT	NO. OF RESPONSES (TOTAL = 21)
18–25	[UK1] [UK2] [UK12]			3
26–35			[UK9] [UK59]	2
36–45	[UK43] [UK66] [UKP81]	[UK72]	[UK40]	5
46–55	[UK3] [UK26] [UKP77]	[UK62] [UKP76] [UKP77]	[UK26] [UK29] [UK61] [UK69]	8
56–65	[UK 11] [UK17]	[UK10] [UK57]	[UK11]	4
66–75				0
75+				0
No.	11	6	8	

Within this admittedly small sample, a trend towards increased self-development between the ages of 36 and 65 can be observed, with eight people within this category studying for university degrees in music, six resuming or continuing instrumental lessons, and six taking up a new instrument. While their activities can in no way be considered representative of a wider population, they do offer a prompt to considering the motivations of adult learners—in music and more widely—and the reasons for the apparent peak of activity in midlife, with the 46- to 55-year-old age group pursuing new learning in music most vigorously.

Among the life history narratives, attitudes to lifelong learning varied, and relative youth was no barrier to the feeling that "I regularly wish I could have learnt a musical instrument, especially the piano, but at the age of 31 I do not have the time or inclination to learn" [UK15, aged 31]. Respondents with this attitude also tended to have a low opinion of their school music education, describing it as "basically a skive lesson [that was] taken as a joke" [UK15, aged 31]. Others took the view that "there are always opportunities to start, no matter how old we are, and it's just a question of finances and prioritising now" [UK43, aged 38]; this attitude tended to be coupled with memories of a more vibrant musical education, where "school concerts—especially the Christmas ones—were magical" [UK43, aged 38]. Open-mindedness, and the possibility of continual development in music, seems therefore to be influenced not only by respondents' own childhood learning, but by the opportunities they witnessed in the school environment around them, and the consequent realisation that musical progress was something accessible to anyone, given sufficient effort and motivation. An attempt at learning in childhood, even when unsuccessful, seemed to enhance adults' receptiveness to music, increasing their pleasure as listeners (see Section 5.5) or holding open the possibility of future learning and development. That said, the greatest regrets expressed related to lack of progress in childhood, or a feeling of having started "too late to get any good at it" [UK40, aged 44]. Assumptions about the optimal age for learning an instrument (Gaunt & Hallam, 2009, p. 276) meant that adult learning was often undertaken not with an expectation of attaining a high performing standard, but in order to broaden existing musical interests, or to satisfy a lifelong desire to try a particular instrument.

One type of adult learner within this sample might be classified as an "extender", someone with already advanced musical experience choosing to learn a new instrument, often with the intention of broadening his or her performing opportunities into new genres or ensembles. For example, after graduating with a music degree as a viola player, one respondent [UK9] had taught herself the tenor horn: she joined a local brass band and described her experiences of getting "so much more satisfaction from playing badly in an

Box 5.4.1

"I took up the Double Bass at the age of 40, having always wanted to play it but been prevented when at school because my little brother was learning it and I might have been better than him. For some reason I thought it would be easier than the cello, which was the other instrument I'd always loved to listen to. How wrong can you be? Anyway, my teacher was very patient, but it was hard to be learning an instrument from scratch when in some ways I knew so much about music. I've now reached the stage where I can play away, with a bit of bluffing, in an amateur orchestra, and I have to say that playing in Elgar's Enigma Variations was one of those special moments for me. It was such a great feeling to be playing at the bottom of that great sound, like being the engine at the bottom of a great ship." [UK26, aged 52]

amateur band than I ever have from orchestral playing in a university orchestra" [UK9, aged 28]. Likewise, an accomplished pianist [UK26] began playing the double bass in order to participate in orchestral playing and to fulfil a childhood ambition which was another common motivation for taking up a new instrument in midlife. She offers a vivid description (Box 5.4.1) of the experience of being a beginner within your field of expertise— struggling afresh with the motor co-ordination of a new instrument, and the dissatisfaction of imperfect sounds and limited facility—and yet being within reach of a new world of musical experiences. As a teacher herself, this adult learner was appreciative of the patience of her double bass tutor, a contrast with the "quite terrifying" piano teacher encountered in her teenage years.

These adult beginners possess a more fully developed sense than their childhood counterparts of how much effort is involved in learning a musical instrument, and previous studies with adult learners have shown that they "may struggle to resolve a tension between the sophistication of a lifetime's engagement with music and the clumsiness of their attempts to articulate their musicality as they come face to face with the difficulties of actually playing their instruments" (Taylor & Hallam, 2008, p. 301). To balance this, adults learners also have a greater awareness of the rewards that come from that effort—the chance to play in new contexts, realising repertoire that they have previously appreciated as a listener, and belonging to new musical groups that might have different, more relaxed approaches to those encountered within educational contexts. Making music with others can be both a source of anxiety (Taylor, 2010) and of motivation (Cope, 2002), with much depending on the welcome and encouragement offered by teachers or fellow musicians.

Resuming the study of an instrument, or seeking vocal tuition after long experience singing in choirs, could be categorised as "consolidator" learning:

these adults were dealing with the unfinished business of lessons abandoned in childhood, or the sense that they could have achieved more in music given greater effort, opportunity, or encouragement. Again, the sense of learning for a purpose was predominant, and a group context for performance was a valuable motivation. One saxophonist [UK10] had followed up his teenage self-education by starting lessons around the age of 50, joining the small ensemble run by his teacher that "performed concerts for friends and relatives a couple of times a year and also did things in the street for charities" [UK10, aged 57]. Like the double-bassist above, he was aware of his own limitations as a player, and yet gained huge satisfaction from acquiring a new performing role: "the definite highlight has been joining the concert band and taking part in quite a lot of concerts and other gigs—this is very challenging but I can also see that I am improving slowly" [UK10, aged 57]. Two singers who had sought lessons to improve their choral singing both regretted coming late to tuition: "My only real regret is that I started singing lessons four years ago instead of 40. It turns out I have a good voice, but what I do with it is bad courtesy of lots of choral directors" [UK69, aged 53].

A high level of trust and appreciation of teachers encountered in adulthood was common: a pianist who had "always regretted giving up piano aged 13 because of pressure of school work and dislike of teacher" had found her adult teachers to be "inspiring in different ways" [UK11, aged 65]. Critical to these satisfactory relationships was a sense of definite progress, and a relaxed and supportive attitude: on re-reading his life history for Interlude F, Graham reported that he had subsequently started horn lessons with a teacher who "knows that I do music for the simple pleasure of doing something that takes me out of my daily life and constructs his lessons accordingly, with no pressure exerted" [UK64, aged 55]. Both "consolidators" and "extenders" were highly self-motivated and enjoyed making progress without pressure, delighting in achievements that, whilst outwardly less impressive than their other musical accomplishments, brought them fresh sources of challenge and satisfaction: "I am learning to play the guitar at night school. It's a very informal class, with a range of abilities and with a teacher whose enthusiasm is boundless. And after 18 months we're all playing simple tunes from tablature (including the ubiquitous 'Greensleeves')" [UK29, aged 54].

Another type of "extender" learning represented in the life history group was linked to academic study, and at the time of the survey included two university music lecturers learning new instruments related to their research interests, as well as the eight mature students pursuing higher education in music, ranging from diploma to doctoral level; several others described experiences of learning as a mature student earlier in their lives, and some of these additional examples are included in the discussion here. Ambitions for academic study were more often individually motivated, rather than pursued with a particular career aim in mind—though others who had been mature students in the past were able to see their experiences as part of a journey towards greater status or more direct employment as a musician. Pursuing a degree was often declared to be "for my own satisfaction" [UK39, aged 81], but in other cases was part of a more substantial life change: Matthew in Interlude I described his postgraduate course in composition as "creatively speaking one of the best years of my life so far and one which made me determined to be a full-time musician" [UK72, aged 45].

Among those currently studying, several were returning to a focus on music that had been deflected by parental influence or other factors when they made their initial choices about post-school employment or education. Christina (Interlude J) had been put off a musical career by a fearsome music college tutor, who during an audition had told her she "had double jointed fingers and would never be a cellist", resulting in her giving up the cello and forming the view that "musicians were pretty stuffy and I just didn't really want to turn out like them" [UK66, aged 40]. Returning to musical study in her late thirties, Christina had found a mentor who "restored my faith in myself and musicians generally", alongside a course leader she described as "a boundless source of energy and a real enthusiast for making music accessible to all" [UK66, aged 40]. Hers is a strong redemption story (Pillemer, 2001), as her own actions as an adult allow her to redress perceived unfairness or missed opportunities in her earlier music education. Another respondent had returned to piano lessons and Masters study in midlife, and in doing so "proved to myself that I was in fact a very capable all-round musician" [UK3, aged 52]. These respondents had successfully negotiated the risks of reviewing their skills and accepting feedback, known to be a challenging aspect of learning for mature students who are used to having competence and authority in other aspects of their lives (Young, 2000). Their reflections showed how a combination of their own resilience and their teachers' careful guidance had helped them make a successful transition back into musical learning; but this is difficult territory for both teachers and students, and the occasional mentions of short periods of adult learning—such as "drum lessons for a year" [UKP77, aged 49]—were the only hint that such experiences had not always lasted or fulfilled their purpose.

Finally, it is worth noting that although the oldest life history respondent to self-identify as an adult learner was aged 65, there were other reports to suggest that new opportunities might still be sought after this age, sometimes encouraged by younger family members. One respondent described giving her mother "a one-off drum lesson for her seventieth birthday—and she has since bought herself a drum kit" [UK37, aged 42], and another stated that he had "plans to re-start the piano when I retire" [UK64, aged 55]. A sense emerges from across this group of adult learners that despite the conventional wisdom that instrumental learning should be started in childhood, the motivation to acquire new musical skills remains strong, particularly when this is supported by an already active musical involvement.

Adult learners may have to overcome the limitations of reduced sensori-motor skills (Gaunt & Hallam, 2009, p. 276) and multiple demands on their time, and yet the high levels of determination and enthusiasm demonstrated by these respondents had allowed them to address past limitations in their musical learning, whether by reviving old skills or acquiring new ones. Peter Cope points out that learning through traditional music sessions and informal engagement in pop music is a more accessible route for some musicians than "the formality and precision of classical music [in which] the likelihood of success from a basis of self-tuition and informal learning is slim" (Cope, 2002, p. 103). The pop music respondents were well represented amongst the adult learners, though their involvement in degree-level study appeared to be career-driven rather than motivated by a desire to improve their playing. A more comprehensive understanding of adults' engagement in musical learning would need to encompass musicians from a wide range of genres, and to consider the link between their school music education and their adult participation, a relationship that some of Cope's Scottish session musicians had found problematic (p. 96). Currently there is little national or international documentation of the extent of adult participation in the arts, and although the value of such activities to the individuals involved and to society more broadly is increasingly being recognised in social and educational policies (McQueen & Varvarigou, 2010), there is still a concern that such opportunities are available only to those adults with the educational background and financial resources to access them.

5.5 Becoming Listeners and Concert-Goers

Fifteen of the life history respondents mentioned listening and concert attendance as being important to their current musical involvement—a relatively small proportion of the sample, but one that nonetheless replicates trends previously observed in classical music audiences towards a predominance of older, well-educated listeners (cf. Kolb, 2001). The median age of these respondents was 64 and, despite the inclusion of two avid pop listeners in their twenties, the greatest proportion of regular concert-attenders (60%) were in the 56- to 75-year-old age group. The majority of these older listeners had formed their listening habits in childhood, and had clear memories of being taken to concerts by their parents or wider family members. One listener, who described his current musical involvement as being "a very enthusiastic audience member for chamber music", recalled the childhood influences of "a grandmother who was from its inception a keen Edinburgh Festival goer: she suggested to me going to the very first UK revival of Monteverdi's *Vespers* of 1610 (York Minster, Walter Goehr); and the young me turned the offer down, for which I have always kicked myself" [UK7, aged 63]. Such recollections (or near-misses, in this case) of now-famous conductors and performers were not unusual amongst the older age group: one child had laughed out loud at a moment in Britten's *Saint Nicolas* and was able to apologise to the composer himself as he left, relieved to be told he "shouldn't worry as it was meant to be fun" [UK8, aged 68]. Looking back, these older respondents give the impression of a greater abundance of orchestral concerts, at which attendance was a normal and accessible part of family life, generating lasting memories: "sitting behind the percussion during 'The 1812' when aged 12 was amazing!" [UK11, aged 65].

One respondent recalled the wealth of musical opportunities available during her 1950s childhood in Sheffield, England (Box 5.5.1): 60 years later, there are still many accessible cultural and musical experiences for young people, but they are more diverse and less embedded in the home lives of the majority of the population. Separate children's activities, family concerts, or school workshops are now generally seen as a necessary step on the way to full involvement in other cultural provision—and yet there is limited evidence that such outreach activities are effective in

---

Box 5.5.1

"At that time the Hallé Orchestra used to give concerts every week in the City Hall and school children could get tickets for 1 shilling (5p in today's money!). The seats were on the platform and unreserved so we used to queue up beforehand and run down the corridor to get good seats [. . .] behind the percussion section and violins. I must have heard most of the mainstream classical repertoire during my teens and heard distinguished soloists like the violinist Ida Haendel and pianist Denis Matthews. The Hallé also occasionally gave special concerts for schools in the afternoons which we attended. The Central Library had a very good music library and we used to borrow miniature scores to follow the music. Sheffield was a great place to be in the 1950s if you were interested in classical music." [UK53, aged 69]

nurturing the next generation of concert-goers. Case studies of school concerts in Illinois (Bresler, 2010) and Madrid (Rusinek & Rincón, 2010) illustrate how teachers' unfamiliarity with the concert setting can limit their ability to prepare for and follow up the event in school, so leaving one-off attendance at a concert or opera as a valuable but momentary feature of the children's wider musical experience: "while teachers are insiders in their classrooms, their outsider position and identities in relation to musical performances limits how they can support and guide students' learning" (Bresler, 2010, p. 144). Bonita Kolb (2002) documents a generational change in which under-17s in the UK and US surveyed for a *Cultural Trends* report

Box 5.5.2

"In 1976, at the age of 25, I read Edward Heath's book, *Music*, in which he stated that no record can ever replace the excitement of a live event. As it happened there was a concert that evening only one mile from my home, so I went. It was Handel's *Judas Maccabaeus* and I was immediately hooked. Over the next year I travelled all over Northern Ireland, attending chamber concerts, orchestral, opera, etc.—indeed I saw/heard over 150 concerts. Since that time I have changed musical tastes, but I am still in love with music. [. . .] I think we need children to be exposed to such live events; do not tell them what they must expect; just expose them to the music—it will work on them." [UK23, aged 66]

stated that family was a stronger influence than school in their decision to attend a concert, whereas older respondents in that study had first been introduced to live music listening through school visits to concerts. Those life history respondents who remembered both were clearly in the most fortunate position, with the coherence between home and school experiences of concert-going providing a secure foundation for adult attendance.

Although patterns of concert attendance for older respondents were most often rooted in family habits, a few reported sudden conversions to live music in their twenties, usually after limited school music experiences, which in several cases included being "forced to listen to five minutes of classical music every day before assembly, a sure way to make us turn against such music" [UK23, aged 66; see Box 5.5.2 for the continuation of this story]. Encountering live orchestral music as a young adult was reported to be an overwhelming experience, but despite the impact of his own late discovery of live music, this lifelong listener urges the importance of introducing children to such experiences, not in the medicinal, controlled way of his own school listening, but through the vitality of a live event. His early experiences had given him sufficient interest in music to be reading *Music: A Joy for Life* (Heath,

1976)—though this interest could alternatively have been prompted by Edward Heath's status as UK prime minister from 1970 to 1974—but it took live music in quantity and concentration to turn this interest into a source of real pleasure.

Interlude L shows how Robert, now in his seventies, had also experienced the daily dose of classical music in school assemblies, though in his case played live by the music teacher, and making a much greater impression—"I often sought the teacher out to ask what she had played, writing the titles down in a little book so that I could watch out for the piece on a future occasion" [UK19, aged 74]. Robert's classical music education was unconventionally extended by working alongside a whistling lorry driver, who introduced him to "the most fabulous melodic lines I had ever heard [. . .] long chunks of the real classics, interspersed with scatology and sexual innuendo of the worst kind" [UK19, aged 74]. Subsequently given a concert ticket by the lorry driver, this young man's first experience of a live symphony orchestra was "unforgettable": wanting to prolong the evening, he missed the bus home and walked through the night "with Beethoven rolling round and round my head" [UK19, aged 74]. An ex-prime minister and a swearing lorry driver had performed the same function for these two respondents—sharing their passion for music, sending a novice listener to the live orchestral experience, and creating a memorable start to a lifelong engagement with music.

There are some striking differences between the listening habits of those younger respondents who classified themselves as concert-goers and the memories of young adulthood offered by regular listeners from the older age groups. For the under-forties in the life history sample, listening appeared to be a substitute for playing music, either because performing skills had lapsed or because a limited school music education had not included such opportunities. Older respondents were more likely to have a strongly committed attitude to listening, either coupling this with amateur playing or viewing their lifelong concert attendance and record-collecting as significant musical involvement in itself. Their confidence in listening as a culturally worthwhile activity is perhaps linked to their preference for classical music, which (particularly in the context of contributing to an academic study) is seen to have unarguable value, rather than being subject to the changing tastes and trends of popular music. Younger listeners had been brought up with an eclectic mix of parents' and friends' tastes, and an awareness of the multiplicity of musical experiences competing for their attention: little wonder, then, that their own tastes were tentatively declared and understood to be individual rather than universal. By contrast, older listeners were exposed to a narrower range of music in childhood, sharing tastes with the adults around them and finding the high status of classical music to be affirmed throughout their lives. Some of these values sit uncomfortably with contemporary notions of diversity and tolerance—to say unequivocally that classical music is of higher status than any other genre might now be considered a bold and culturally insensitive claim by many people; for the older respondents, however, this argument was an implicit part of their childhood and underpinned their lifelong support of (what they would almost certainly not call) the classical music industry.

5.6 Summary: Foundations for Lifelong Musical Involvement

The diverse routes into adult musical participation demonstrated by these 81 respondents offer only the broadest predictors of lifelong engagement, recognising the impact of significant adults and accessible opportunities for fostering a childhood interest in music. As the autobiographical memory research literature suggests (e.g., Bluck, 2003), similar events can have quite different effects depending on the context and personality of the individual, and will later be related differently according to life satisfaction and outcomes (McAdams et al., 2001). While childhood instrumental learning had led to continued engagement in music for the majority of these respondents, parental attitudes, teacher personality, and levels of attainment had varied markedly, even within this self-selected sample of musical enthusiasts. Some appeared to have overcome frustrating or potentially damaging experiences, reporting this as implicit evidence that their own commitment to music had been substantial enough to overcome discouragement and disappointment: "I had the off-putting kind of music teachers—heads of dept at both primary and secondary school, and piano teachers—and it was despite them rather than with their encouragement, let alone inspiration, that I did O Level and kept singing and playing" [UK28, aged 45].

There were a few stories in which respondents "fell into teaching by accident" [UK66, aged 40] or judged that "the combination of encouragement at home and at school more or less determined that I would do music in some form or another later on" [UK53, aged 69], but for the most part the respondents expressed a high level of agency in their narratives: they acknowledged with gratitude the people and opportunities who had helped them in their musical lives, but recognised that their own efforts had also played an important role. Theories of self-efficacy (Bandura, 1977) would suggest that this sense of agency was in itself a factor in the respondents' success in maintaining their musical involvement: young children have been shown to achieve more highly in music if they believe in their own capacity as performers (McCormick & McPherson, 2003), and these adults too had identified their musical efforts as being an aspect of their personal identity worth sustaining and developing into adult life. In doing so, they had pursued opportunities that had allowed this development to continue, and to be further reinforced by friends, pupils, and others around them. Conversely, the few within the study (and many more beyond) who believed that the decision to discontinue learning in childhood was the right one for their level of musical potential had maintained this view of themselves as musical consumers rather than creators: recalling childhood instrumental lessons, one lifelong listener mused that "if the organist [who taught me] had found a way to make my eyes and hands work together at the piano, then I might have benefited from more player-side appreciation of my listening . . . But I'm a very contented audience member and listener" [UK7, aged 63].

The lack of clear trends in the data is unsurprising, given the varied outcomes of these respondents' musical lives: similar diversity has been observed in Alexandra Lamont's (2011) larger sample of musically active adults, confirming that the responses here are representative of the constituency of engaged, nonprofessional musical enthusiasts. Studies with more homogenous groups have identified age-related markers of progress towards musical success (Manturzewska, 1990) and noted a similarity of learning experience among classroom teachers (Hargreaves & Marshall, 2003), typically taking a traditional route through academic qualifications and classical instrument learning, as many of the teachers in the life history study had also done. The greater narrative detail in the life history accounts, however, looks beyond the measurable evidence of qualifications, years of learning, and instruments played to the other factors that shape an adult musician's self-concept: attitudes absorbed from family members, teachers, and peers that have contributed to individual definitions of what musical education is and who it is for.

The responses show that there are multiple routes to adult engagement in music, but also many hurdles along the way: lack of opportunity or inclination, loss of confidence, self-perceived decline in skills, or a sense that chances missed in childhood can no longer be reclaimed. Many respondents appear to have lacked guidance about their potential musical futures, realising only later in life that they could have set their ambitions higher, and sometimes regretting that their foundational learning had imposed later limitations (see Duncan's reflections on "hard wiring" scales in Interlude F). They demonstrate that in their own cases "there is nothing stopping me doing something new" [UK50, aged 25], but these respondents speak from a position of security in the face of evidence that "participating in music activities is more likely if adults have been engaged with music earlier in life" (McQueen & Varvarigou, 2010, p. 168). In the classical music spheres negotiated by the majority of these respondents, barriers to lifelong engagement also include financial and educational status, with many of the activities undertaken requiring an investment of time, money, and self-confidence not accessible to a significant proportion of the population.

These considerations prompt the challenging question, "Lifelong learning—is it any more than privileging those who already have spent their lives as privileged individuals?" (Beynon, 2005, p. 7). Some of the wartime childhoods and large families of the older respondents would argue against this, as would the difficult family circumstances of a few brought up in homes "where praise and encouragement were in very short supply" [UK38, aged 42]. Nonetheless, the openness to learning and participation displayed by the majority of the respondents is indicative of a sense of self-worth provided by a secure home and successful adult life, and musical engagement in adulthood is often part of an already busy and fulfilling existence (Pitts, 2005). This makes the activities no less valuable and worthy of attention, but it does point to a social responsibility, rooted in education, to ensure that there are routes into lifelong musical participation for all sectors of society.

Interlude I: Matthew Redfearn [UK72]
Aged 45, left school 1982

Performance opportunities in school, followed by music at university as a mature student and a second career in music

My paternal grandfather played the violin well and the piano in a more limited way. He visited every Sunday and I have memories of him wandering around the house playing the violin ('Meditation' from *Thais* was a favourite) or sitting at the piano, playing one of several songs he'd written as a younger man. My maternal grandmother also played the piano well. When I was a young cornet player she would often accompany me, very competently, playing popular melodies from the classical repertoire and musicals. This gave me early experience of interacting with another musician and learning to play in time and in tune.

I can remember finishing my cornet practice one evening and on leaving the music room being completely overwhelmed by the music my father was playing in the living room (probably to drown out my cornet practice!). The music which moved me so much was a climax of one of the movements of Rachmaninov's Second Piano Concerto and I subsequently listened to that recording, with Sviatoslav Richter at the piano, repeatedly throughout my childhood. I explored my father's record collection thoroughly and in doing so was exposed to a wide range of musical styles: number one hits from the pop charts, musicals, revue shows, swing music, trad. jazz and light classical music. I have particularly fond memories of listening repeatedly to a recording of Flanders' and Swann's[1] revue show 'At the Drop of a Hat' with my

---

[1] Michael Flanders (singer) and Donald Swann (pianist) wrote and performed comic and satirical songs in the 1950s–60s; songs such as their famous "Hippopotamus Song" and "The Gas Man Cometh" can be found on youtube.com.

younger sister which reduced us to fits of laughter—all the more so as we grew up and understood more and more of the humour!

We never went to see concerts as a family but at the age of 5 I was taken by my father to a concert given by the Hammond Sauce Works Band[2]: this led directly to me asking if I could learn the cornet, which I started doing at my next birthday, aged 6. I had cornet and subsequently trumpet lessons at home with a visiting teacher from aged 6 to 18 years. The teacher had a brass band background which heavily influenced his repertoire choices for me. My older brother and younger sister both started learning the piano at a young age, my brother giving up whilst still of primary school age but my sister continuing until she left senior school having achieved ABRSM Grade 7. Their teacher visited the family home on Saturday mornings and sometimes played more advanced classical pieces during lessons, which I overheard and enjoyed. Although I didn't have formal piano lessons until the age of 17, having a piano around in the home certainly gave me an early appreciation of harmony and how it was notated.

Music-making was encouraged at my primary school: the headmaster would take the whole school for singing sessions, ably assisted by one of the infant teachers, who was a competent pianist and a warm and friendly teacher. I learned to play the recorder to a basic level with a class teacher in group sessions and had individual lessons learning folk guitar with a visiting teacher. In the last school concert in which I participated, I remember singing with the choir, playing in the recorder group, playing a duet with the guitar teacher and playing a cornet solo accompanied by my teacher. As I went up for my last performance of the evening, I heard a parent on the front row say "Blimey, he's here again", which was the first sense I had that I was doing something beyond the norm.

My experience of music at secondary school was less inspiring and this probably contributed to me not even considering studying music at a higher level, never mind considering music as a career option. There was one music teacher, teaching in a tiered, lecture theatre-style room with the aid of a blackboard, a gramophone and a grand piano. This teacher suffered from a recurrent illness through the whole of my secondary school years and so there was little development of the department during that time. The focus of the school was very much on 'rugby and results' rather than artistic endeavours, which at times seemed to be actively discouraged by staff. I was a

---

[2] One of many brass or silver bands associated with industries in the UK from the mid-19th century, often sponsored by local mines, and in this case by a condiments factory (see http://www.hammondsband.org.uk/history/history.shtml).

member of the school choir throughout senior school, singing hymns in four part harmony in assembly daily, sacred works in school services at Wakefield Cathedral and sacred and secular works at school concerts. I was also in the school wind band, continuing even when a conflict arose with attending a scout group and even though the ensemble never developed greatly in terms of standard or numbers participating. I was chosen to play first trumpet in a performance of *Noyes Fludde* as a first year, whilst a sixth former was put on second trumpet—which was good for my self-esteem as a player, although probably not for his! A joint orchestra with the nearby girls' school was directed by a rather limp high school mistress and played simplified versions of orchestral works in which the trumpet had even less to do than usual. Two factors kept me participating: enjoying listening to the orchestration when not playing (which was most of the time) and a pretty violinist with nice legs who sat directly opposite me. My early experiences of orchestral trumpet playing did not inspire me and, although I love listening to, writing and conducting orchestral music, playing the trumpet in an orchestra has failed to inspire me ever since.

After an unhappy time studying sciences in the sixth form, I began to doubt my decision to study biology at university, but I still hadn't been sufficiently inspired by, or trained in, music to consider that option instead. Instead the combination of my scientific training, some good 'A' level results and my desire to help people (springing from my Christian faith) led me to take a gap year and apply to study medicine. During this year, while working as a lab technician in the school I had just left, I decided I wanted to do a grade exam on my trumpet to establish my level of playing before going to university, and achieved a Grade 8 distinction, inspired by a teacher with a clever psychological approach that addressed my lack of confidence in my playing. I also become involved with making music at the church I was attending, growing further in confidence as the church musicians and congregation obviously appreciated my contribution to the sung worship and helped to give me a feeling of self-worth as a musician.

I regret now that having discovered that music was something which interested and motivated me during my gap year, I didn't face up to parental opposition and drop my plans to study medicine. Instead, supporting myself by working in medicine, I studied as a mature student, first a music foundation course, then a BMus, during which I discovered the thrill of composing and orchestrating. This was followed by postgraduate study in composition; creatively speaking one of the best years of my life so far and one which made me determined to be a full-time musician. During this time I also enjoyed valuable practical experience playing trumpet in a semi-professional big band, a semi-pro jazz quintet and a rapidly developing amateur concert band and co-founding a chamber orchestra to do scratch performances of new music alongside standard repertoire. At the age of 38 I achieved my dream of becoming a full-time musician when I was offered a post as music director of a large parish church in Sheffield, which I have subsequently combined with upper brass teaching in schools and privately; jobs which have used almost all the musical (and other!) skills I have ever spent time developing.

Interlude J: Christina Metcalfe [UK66]
Aged 40, left school 1985

Some off-putting instrumental learning experiences, overcome to pursue a second career and postgraduate study in music

I am a piano teacher who has returned to music after a degree in geography and a career in public relations, fundraising and event management. I never imagined I would become an instrumental teacher! I did consider music as a degree but I didn't want to be a teacher, and thought I wasn't good enough to be a performer, so I did geography instead. I continued with my piano playing all through university, and fell into teaching by accident, after I was approached by the Head of Music at my sons' school, who had noted that I was accompanying my children in their exams and that I had completed all my piano exams. That was five years ago and I have since gone on to do the CT ABRSM[1] and I am now in the last year of an MA in music psychology.

I auditioned for the Royal College of Music and Royal Academy in London at 13 and was told I had double jointed fingers and would never be a cellist (my second instrument). I went home and packed in the cello. My inspirational CT tutor was the person who changed that view of myself as a musician, and musicians in general, some 25 years later. I thought he might be very aloof like the woman I met, but he was the complete opposite and had so much time and understanding for what we were doing at grass roots level. Also influential was the CT course leader, who was a boundless source of energy and a real enthusiast for making music accessible to all. He inspired

---

[1] Certificate of Teaching, a professional development course run by the Associated Board of the Royal Schools of Music

me to try teaching without notation and this interest, coupled with his philosophy of music for all, has continued into my MA dissertation.

I first had piano lessons at the age of 4 and still clearly remember sitting at the grand piano with its shawl covering it like it was a delicate and prized object, almost a reverence about it. I developed a problem with my vision and my mum stopped my lessons a year or so later because she thought I was straining my eyes trying to read the music. I didn't have lessons again until I was 10 but I still have my first piano books and Fletcher[2] theory papers and sticky stars from those first lessons. In between time I would pick out tunes on the piano we had and dance to the test card[3] with my sister. I have recordings of me singing as a little girl. I did ballet and modern dancing and most of my pre teen years musical contact was through this I think. I remember music at my primary school consisted of singing traditional folk songs to a tape reel (might have been BBC programmes—not sure). I changed schools and music consisted of hymn singing, and playing glockenspiels and big xylophones.

At senior school we had singing lessons with our music teacher, as part of our normal timetable. He was a demanding and inspiring teacher and I consider myself lucky to have been taught by him at a state school. Otherwise class music was easy and I did well. I sang in choirs, singing madrigals to oratorios, and played cello in a youth symphony orchestra, school string quartet and jazz group. I learnt to play folk guitar at school but this clashed with my geography class and the teacher would get cross. So it is ironic that I ended up doing geography and later music at university! I also sang solos in Scout Gang Shows at Wimbledon Theatre. I loved musical theatre as a result and often went to see shows in London, wishing I could be up there on the stage.

My parents were very supportive of my music but did not make music themselves, despite my mother having played the violin to a high level. My mum did run the youth choir at church but did not play an instrument. I played guitar in this and sang. I remember my dad telling me I had to go and support my mum when I was having a teenage rebellion about it! I have run church music groups ever since leaving home so it obviously had an effect. It was here that I learnt to perform at the drop of a hat, be flexible and improvise, playing piano from guitar chords, improvising harmonies, etc. My sister

---

[2] The Leila Fletcher Piano Course, widespread in the UK and US from the 1950s onwards (http://www.leilafletcher.com/)
[3] The "test card" was shown in breaks between BBC programmes: see http://www.youtube.com/watch?v=Ncmg3bxtTBo for the music that Christina recalls, and the image of a girl playing noughts and crosses with a clown used most often in the 1970s.

played piano and flute and we would play piano duets, entering festivals together. I also played piano trios (6 hands on one piano) with two friends and we won the trio cup. I changed piano teacher at 16 and this affected my attitude, having loved my previous teacher. I went to a private school for sixth form and didn't feel I could ask my parents to continue paying for my lessons, having reached Grade 8, as it was difficult financially for them to send me to this school. So despite doing music A Level I did not have any more lessons. I regret this as I feel I should have gone on to diploma level, having done all 8 piano grades in 5 years, while also reaching Grade 5 cello in 3 years, and doing theory to Grade 5. I don't know how I fitted it all in. Now I look back and think I was actually very good especially when I see my pupils now. I didn't think so though and that stems from my music college auditions and especially the comment about my double-jointed fingers. I can still see that woman! I also thought musicians were pretty stuffy and I just didn't really want to turn out like them!

Last year I was teaching 25 pupils ranging in age from 6 to adult, both at school and from home. I also have taught theory to Grade 5 level. For two years I directed a keyboard group for pupils as a lunchtime activity which was accessible to all regardless of musical instrumental or reading experience and we performed at the summer school concerts. I accompany instrumentalists in ABRSM exams to Grade 8 standard. I run a music group for toddlers twice a week with a friend. I accompany the school choir; I play keyboards in a band, and sing in the church choir, playing guitar. The last two years I have had singing lessons in French and dabbled with the local town choir but the rehearsals finished at 11pm and they were very heavy going so I quit. (A true cultural experience: I have never sung in a choir where different sections openly criticised each other, tut tutting and declaring that the men were singing flat!) I performed in a staged concert last summer singing in French with my singing lesson group. Quite an experience!

To sum up I have an adult pupil, a school mum, who is about to take her Grade 1 piano having always wanted to play the piano all her life. I am very proud of her as she, like me, is living proof that you are never too old to learn and that music is for life.

6 | Rhetoric and Reality

THE REAL IMPACT OF MUSIC EDUCATION

6.1 Overview: Learning from Life Histories

THE DISCUSSION IN PREVIOUS CHAPTERS has explored the experiences of the life history respondents, using their own recollections and interpretations to highlight the significant people, influences, and events that have formed the foundations for their lifelong interest in music. Their musical life stories have been considered first from a generational perspective (Chapter 2), in which the slow pace of change in music education was shown to create an increasing divergence between home and school values, at the same time as changing technology made young people into independent consumers of music, bringing their own musical experiences, needs, and questions to the classroom.

Further consideration of the different locations for learning (Chapter 3) illustrated the characteristics of a supportive home and school environment, which both at their best provide opportunities for structured exploration of musical skills, offering guidance and encouragement while allowing young people to develop an intrinsic motivation for music. Self-directed learning, instrumental lessons, and extracurricular music-making were identified as bridging the gap between home and school in various ways, allowing greater responsibility in musical learning and offering a sustainable route into adult involvement. A focus on the Italian life history respondents in Chapter 3 allowed exploration of a more specialist music education system, showing how the limited provision of music in generalist schools created a divide between the minority who had been musically educated and the majority who felt that they had missed such opportunities. The contrast between this and the UK system raised questions about what it means to be musically successful, with the suggestion that a more inclusive definition left open more extensive possibilities for adult involvement and interest in music.

Chapter 4 examined the roles and characteristics of the adults who are most influential in the musical lives of young people, including parents who provide role models for musical attitudes as well as accomplishments, and teachers who might be memorable for a wide range of reasons, not all of them positive. The immediate impact of these interactions was set alongside their longer-term influence on respondents' own behaviour as teachers and parents, seeking to replicate or resolve the patterns set by their childhood mentors as they defined their own adult roles in supporting young people's musical development. Musical outcomes in adulthood were also the subject of Chapter 5, which compared the experiences and attitudes of respondents who had become performers, teachers, adult learners, or lifelong listeners. Respondents were shown to have followed serendipitous routes into adult musical involvement, and whilst these opportunities and their outcomes were highly valued by many respondents, they also illustrated the lack of guidance and direction available to young people seeking long-term engagement or employment in music.

The final two chapters of this book build upon the analysis of respondents' life histories by raising more speculative questions about what can be learned from their experiences, and how a life history approach can shed new light on research and practice in music education. The features that have been shown in the life histories to inhibit or promote musical learning will be evaluated alongside historical and contemporary research literature, in order to balance the claims made for music education against the realities as remembered by respondents. The potential long-term impact of current policies and practices will be considered, raising questions about the role of schools and families in supporting future generations of musically active young people—and about the place of lifelong outcomes in shaping aims and judging effectiveness in music education.

6.2 Historical Rhetoric and Remembered Reality

Throughout this book, and particularly in Chapter 2, reference has been made to the many claims that have historically been put forward for music education: as a civilising influence, a foundation for good use of leisure time, a source of creativity and expression, and a disciplined training in vocal or instrumental techniques. Writers on music education, perhaps driven by the subject's marginal status in the curriculum, have often argued vigorously for its benefits to young people—and sometimes lamented the failure of schools to fulfil this potential. Critiquing the aesthetic and utilitarian goals that have characterised past arguments for music in schools, Paul Woodford high-lights the need for "participatory democracy", whereby teachers engage thoughtfully with the purposes and practises of music education and can articulate their values and intentions to their students and beyond: "Teachers, after all, must be prepared to champion and explain their educational values to the public if they want to be held accountable for the attainment of realistic goals" (Woodford, 2005, p. 23).

In their initial training and ongoing professional development, teachers are rarely encouraged to critique and debate the requirements of the music curriculum (Jones, 2009), and yet the day-to-day decisions made in the class-room or instrumental studio are the lived reality of national policy. Learning and teaching exchanges are shaped by what sociologists would term "hab-itus", defined as "collective patterns of preference solidified around norms of behaviour and evaluative schema" (Wright, 2008, p. 397). Ruth Wright, in a case study of a secondary school in Wales, illustrates the different musical worlds (or cultural habitus) that teachers and students bring to the classroom and calls on teachers to challenge their own default positions in order "to lead [students] to discovery of new musical worlds at times when they are ready to engage positively with them" (p. 400). The life history responses show similarly how implicit messages about musical relevance and educa-tional opportunity have been absorbed during the school years: the content of lessons is recalled alongside a sense of how activities and knowledge were valued by the teacher who delivered it, and whether lessons were directed towards the "musically inclined children" [UK47, aged 62] or "managed to teach everyone in the school to read music to a basic level" [UK29, aged 54]. An understanding of whether music education has fulfilled its aims needs therefore to consider not only the statutory curriculum but also the effects of school culture and individual teachers' intentions. The life history respon-dents show the lasting impression made by all facets of school music experi-ence (policy, practice, and personality), gaining greatest benefit when those elements worked together. As Piers in Interlude B puts it, "If a teacher can persuade you that he or she is passionately committed to a particular musical work, you will learn. In education, nothing succeeds more powerfully than commitment" [UK47, aged 62].

The life history accounts offer a rare insight on retrospective perceptions of musical learning, and from the interludes and extracts in preceding chapters, the immediate effects of successful musical learning are clear: engagement in school, a growth in confidence and identity, a sense of achievement, and the sheer pleasure of musical involvement. These benefits emerge implicitly, evident in the vividness of memories, the continuity of musical activity from school days into adulthood, and the desire to encourage pupils, friends, and children to experience the same kind of musical enjoyment. Some respondents also reflected more directly on the contribution that music education had made to their personal and social development, with membership of youth orchestras particularly highlighted as a source of "lifelong friendships" [UK35, aged 52; see also Box 6.2.1]

Recalling their sometimes difficult teenage years, some respondents described music as "an escape" [UK38, aged 42], crediting their teachers with generating "confidence in myself" [UK33, aged 56] and seeing a close connection between their development as musicians and their emerging young adult identities. An American respondent described how "my band directors through the years have always been a major influence from the types of music we were encouraged to play, to the solos they suggested and the fact that no matter how poor any student was they always gave them 100% support in making them better musicians and people" [OUK49, aged 29]. Like the orchestral player in Box 6.2.1, this band member observed the wider benefits of musical encouragement for making young players not just "better musicians" but "better people".

Similarly, the lifelong choir member in Box 6.2.2 remembered gaining a distinctive musical identity amongst other girls who seemed otherwise more physically and psychologically assured. While such benefits cannot be guaranteed from music education, their effects on young people who might otherwise have left school lacking in confidence and direction were potentially life-changing—not just in the musical opportunities that were opened up, but also in the sense of security and personal validity that were a valuable byproduct of belonging to an ensemble, performing in public, or achieving other musical goals.

Amongst the responses there were also many illustrations of the lifelong benefits of a musical education for enriching leisure use and continued musical development in adulthood. Some respondents reflected directly on this, tracing their adult musical enjoyment to the influence of their school years: "what started for me with an inspirational music teacher has given me an adult life rich in musical enjoyment, both listening and performing in choirs" [UK56, aged 73]. Others identified some missed opportunities in these foundational years, one recalling a failed attempt at piano lessons and wondering whether if his teacher "had found a way to make my eyes and hands work together at the piano, then I might have benefited from more player-side appreciation of my listening"—before adding "but I'm a very contented audience member and listener" [UK7, aged 63]. Others had remedied such gaps in their musical education later in life, with one organist being taught by a Royal Air Force colleague to sing at sight during his years of compulsory National Service in the armed forces: "church choir experience was only as a treble, so he taught me. I owe him a great debt, as it has led to a lifetime of pleasure as a choral singer" [UK18, aged 76].

These adult experiences of music education sometimes revealed connections between different aspects of musical learning, as for the mature student for whom "it has been an eye-opener how much it helps my piano playing and appreciation of music to have increasing theoretical understanding" [UK11, aged 65]. It is possible that such connections and benefits are best perceived in hindsight: young people engaged in the immediate pleasures of participating in a band competition or a choir concert are unlikely to be further persuaded of the importance of their activities by a vision of their post-retirement selves engaged in continued music-making. Nonetheless, these long-term goals are valuable to the teachers and policymakers who influence school provision, and who need therefore to be aware of the potential impact of music education to change both individual lives and wider society: "The schooling of children in music can help to ensure the survival and even flourishing of certain genres and styles, and can affect the likely development of children's attitudes and values for music all their lifetimes long" (P. S. Campbell, 2002, p. 67).

Musical learning was also shown to have lifelong effects on personal relationships, both in the lasting friendships made through shared childhood experiences (Box 6.2.1) and in the connection with other like-minded people in adulthood: "My partner and I have been together for 34 years sharing music as one of the strongest bonds between us. Various friends have introduced me to music they love. And now my son introduces us to contemporary indie pop bands we might not otherwise have heard" [UK67, aged 49]. Where important life relationships lacked a musical element, this could have the converse effect on participation: "After school my musical activity died down—perhaps because my wife did not play an instrument (she later learned the guitar) so we could not share playing in an orchestra or quartet" [UK58, aged 52]. Another keen singer had accepted that "marriage and a growing family inevitably led to a more passive enjoyment of music, listening to the radio and records" [UK56, aged 73], although for those like Sue in Interlude C who "feel quite unhappy when I am not involved in some sort of singing activity" [UK13, aged 58], maintaining musical involvement alongside other commitments remained a priority. The contribution of musical activities to friendship and wellbeing, particularly in older age, is increasingly recognised (Hays & Minichiello, 2005): these life history accounts offer new evidence to show how the foundations for using music in "positive ageing" are built throughout the lifespan, as musical ambitions and attitudes are reviewed and fulfilled from childhood to retirement. The influences of parents and siblings are relatively well understood (e.g., McPherson, 2009), but there is some interesting future research to be done on how lifelong relationships contribute to the continued development of musical engagement—and how these adult experiences are in turn shaped by factors from childhood and adolescence.

While the life history respondents articulate many benefits of their musical experiences, earlier attempts to ask pupils to evaluate the aims and impact of music education have not always worked in the subject's favour. In studies from the 1970s to the 1990s in the UK, music consistently ranked as one of the least-preferred subjects in schools (see Ross, 1995), and a large-scale survey of arts education carried out in 2000 concluded that music was "the most problematic and vulnerable art form" at GCSE level (Harland et al., 2000, p. 568), chosen by a very small proportion of students and perceived to lack relevance by the rest. An alternative explanation for this low uptake was offered in a later study, which showed that while a healthy two-thirds of 8- to 14-year-olds enjoyed music, particularly its practical aspects, few would consider taking GCSE, for a variety of reasons: "music was seen as a highly specialist subject at this level, open only to those with considerable instrumental skill, and not relevant or necessary for careers in other kinds of music-related businesses" (Lamont, Hargreaves, Marshall, & Tarrant, 2003, p. 236). Although compulsory school music therefore provided enjoyment and engagement for the majority of students, its appeal was self-limiting, perceived to require substantial investment of learning outside school and so representing a risk to students with limited instrumental skills, and an impossibility to those without. Some evidence of such risk management is evident even amongst the life history respondents who, although a group with a self-identified interest in music, included a few who had either chosen or been advised by parents or teachers to concentrate on other subjects in school. Sue, for example, recalls in Interlude C how she could "remember stating to my father that I wanted to study music— but he apparently felt it was not a good career choice" [UK13, aged 58].

In the Italian setting considered in Chapter 3, these low expectations for the lifelong impact of music were even more in evidence, magnified by the gulf of experience between those respondents who had received a conservatoire training and those who had undertaken only "the weekly singing lesson hour" [IA8, no age given] with varying degrees of enthusiasm. Pupils receiving general music education in Italy are being trained to appreciate and interpret music, giving them "the competence necessary to become an autonomous and critical 'enjoyer' of musical culture" (Tafuri, 2001, p. 76). These aims are reminiscent of the "music appreciation" movement recalled by some of the older UK respondents (cf. Pitts, 2000, p. 13), many of whom experienced a pleasurable alignment between hearing music at home and having similar repertoire explained in greater depth by their teachers (see Section 2.3.1). For young Italians today, however, there is a gulf between their informally acquired musical knowledge and that presented in the classroom: Johannella Tafuri suggests that "adolescents have a symbolic investment in popular music and demonstrate disregard, and even contempt towards classical music ('the music of adults')" (ibid., p. 81). This disjunction demonstrates a need for school music to keep pace with the wider musical world, if not necessarily at the level of specific repertoire—which could be a minefield of adolescent tastes and affiliations—at least in the values and aims of musical education, which must be of demonstrable use in the musical communities inhabited by young people.

Those who did report a lifelong impact of Italian music education were predominantly members of choirs (again an echoing of earlier generations in the UK responses), although there was also a high proportion of regrets relating to "having given up so soon learning how to play an instrument and not having received an education in listening and in music in general from my early years" [IA11, aged 28]. The Italian respondents demonstrated lower levels of self-efficacy than the UK adult learners (see Section 5.4) who had addressed some of the shortfalls of their musical education in later life: low expectations and aborted attempts at learning had left the majority of this group of respondents feeling unable to pursue an alternative musical pathway as adults, so demonstrating once again that the values transmitted by musical education are as powerful as the opportunities provided.

The unforeseen benefits of music education experienced by the UK life history respondents have only a limited role to play in the debate about the purposes of music in the curriculum, since they lack the universal relevance of more familiar claims relating to skill acquisition, creative development, and cultural heritage. They are unreliable, too, in that no teacher could provide the assurance that participating in the school orchestra will lead to fulfilling adult relationships, nor that learning an instrument is necessarily an investment for future leisure use. Nonetheless, the repeated occurrences of such benefits show that the impact of music education can be lasting and valuable in a variety of ways. The life history approach to research is particularly helpful in identifying and celebrating these outcomes (see also Section 7.2), so offering a rounded picture of the long-term impact of music education. In acknowledging these lifelong effects of musical learning, however, teachers and researchers need to be cautious about using them to justify the place of music in schools, remembering that they are a supplement to—not a substitute for—the immediate, lived experience of musical engagement and skill development that is at the heart of the most positive life history accounts (and disappointingly absent from others).

6.3 Contemporary Rhetoric and Future Opportunities

One outcome of musical education not yet reviewed here is amongst the most prominent in contemporary rhetoric; namely, the idea that engaging in musical activities promotes transferable skills—typically taken to include group cooperation on a complex task, disciplined effort towards a goal, confidence in public expression, and sense of self-efficacy (Hallam, 2010, p. 9). One respondent outlined in detail the application of musical skills to other work contexts (Box 6.3.1), but for the majority these benefits were only implicitly evident in accounts of their musical accomplishments and highlights.

Gathering convincing evidence for the wider benefits of musical learning is notoriously difficult, since learning an instrument and participating in extra-curricular activities are likely to be associated with other factors, including parental support and adequate financial resources, as well as a positive family culture in relation to school engagement and attainment. Attempts to correlate academic success with levels of musical involvement have shown gains in literacy and numeracy for children who are musically active, although these were greatest amongst white, socioeconomically advantaged children, suggesting that family circumstances are a strong mediator for the effects of music learning (Southgate & Roscigno, 2009). Extracurricular activities can in turn raise teachers' expectations of those students who participate (Van Matre

> **Box 6.3.1**
>
> "While I earn most of my income from my 9–5 job, the musical upbringing I have had has influenced most of what I do, all the skills being transferable to the rest of my life from team working to analysis. If you can pull together a musical, audition the soloists, accompany the rehearsals, get your team to do direction, costumes, scenery, make-up, publicity etc. and produce the show to a budget on time, that is project management and replicated in most walks of life." [UK25, aged 49]

et al., 2000), reinforcing the increased school engagement and improved peer relationships that can also result from musical involvement (Mahoney, Cairns, & Farmer, 2003). However, such benefits are not guaranteed, cannot necessarily be directly attributed to the acquisition of musical skills—rather than simply the increased teacher attention and approval, for example— and nor are they unique to music. In themselves, therefore, they are not a sufficient case for supporting musical provision in schools—though they certainly add weight and illustrative examples to that case.

An essay-writing competition conducted in the US and analysed by Patricia Shehan Campbell and colleagues (Campbell, Connell, & Beegle, 2007) showed that adolescents themselves were conscious of the extra-musical benefits of their studies, noting that "the concentration required for learning music and the process of memorizing music pieces had honed those skills in other areas of their schoolwork" (p. 229). They were aware of the "Mozart makes you smarter" school of thought (D. Campbell, 2002), whereby classical music has been shown to cause short-term improvements in spatial-temporal reasoning and other brain functions (Rauscher, Shaw, & Ky, 1993). This discovery, mediated by the popular press, has brought the cognitive benefits of music to public attention, launching an industry of musical toys for babies and, in some US states, the sponsored distribution of classical music recordings to new mothers (Clarke, Dibben, & Pitts, 2010, p. 93). However, while these claims clearly increase awareness of the power of music to effect personal and developmental change, they should be seen as an adjunct to rigorous philosophical debate about the value of music in education, rather than its resolution.

> **Box 6.3.2**
>
> "Lack of proper teaching in early life and proper direction for practice. No real training in time and rhythm, in memory or performance skills. Too much reliance on sight reading. Too much glossing over difficult passages. Lack of performance opportunities to help in overcoming nerves." [UK57, aged 64]

Given these concerns about the potential appropriation or exaggeration of the claims for music's transferable benefits, it is worrying that these non-musical claims are prominent in contemporary discourse about the place of music in schools and society. Frances Rauscher, a neuroscientist studying the effects of music on the brain, has spoken out against the appropriation of scientific findings in educational justifications, stating that "Music education should not have to prove its value by showing that it has non-musical outcomes" (Rauscher, 2009, p. 251). The arguments for the value of music for its own sake are strengthened by the life history accounts in this book, which provide compelling evidence for the immediate and long-term transformative power of musical engagement. While the respondents illustrated the extra-musical benefits of their experiences through stories of gaining confidence, recognition, and identity through music, their views were underpinned with a sense of music being valuable in and of itself: specific repertoire, performances, and skills were identified as having contributed to "passion and enjoyment of music" [UK47, aged 62]—qualities valued in teachers and parents, and aspired to in childhood and adult life. The social and personal benefits of musical learning certainly have a lasting and often beneficial impact, but they should not be the primary focus of school music teaching, which should instead provide strong musical foundations for later self-education and lifelong exploration.

Many respondents looked back with regret at insufficient practice in childhood, lack of progress in instrumental lessons, or lost years with teachers who failed to inspire them musically (Box 6.3.2). This group of musically active adults had remedied such missed opportunities in later life, but the level of motivation and resourcefulness needed to correct the perceived inadequacies of music education after leaving school is much higher amongst these respondents than could be expected of the wider population. Classroom and instrumental music teachers therefore have a great responsibility to nurture not just an enjoyment of music but also the foundational skills needed to support lifelong learning. As David Myers asserted in his depiction of a crisis in long-term musical engagement, "the focus must be on engaging children in independent and authentic music-making that is consistent with their developmental capacities, and that will grow with them into and through adulthood" (Myers, 2005, p. 14).

One of the greatest challenges in ensuring that school music provision is meaningful to all students, not just those who are already primed by home experiences to be responsive to traditional approaches, is in admitting the limitations of schools and ensuring that young people are equipped to seek musical self-education from the wide range of resources that are open to them. Estelle Jorgensen proposes that teacher training needs to equip music educators better for "seeing the possibilities for music education inherent in the context of several institutions—the family, school, church, business, and music profession, among others—as a life-long rather than a school-age pursuit" (Jorgensen, 1997, p. 92). The life histories provide evidence that such resourcefulness in musical learning is a feature of many musical journeys, although the cultural assumption that school will be the primary source of such education means that these stories are often framed as being about compensating for poor teaching rather than engaging in a continuum of learning opportunities.

Some recent developments in UK music education have attempted to strengthen the connection between school music and the "wider art world" (Becker, 1982), either by making greater use of community musicians in schools or by seeking to emulate the learning practices of real-world musicians, rather than the teacher-directed approaches of conventional classrooms. The Musical Futures project (musicalfutures.org.uk) is amongst the most prominent of these movements, building on Lucy Green's analysis of how popular musicians learn (Green, 2002) to incorporate informal learning approaches in the classroom. In participating schools, students work in small groups to create arrangements and performances of recorded music and use an online media resource (numu.org.uk) to showcase and promote their own music. These approaches, intended to be interspersed with other, more formal lessons, change the teacher's role to one of "diagnosing, suggesting and demonstrating" (Green, 2008, p. 30), so placing greater autonomy on students, who were observed by their teachers to be "musicking", in the sense used by Christopher Small (1998) and David Elliott (1995)—"behaving less like novices and more like 'proper musicians'", as one teacher described it (Green, 2008, p. 60).

Through government and charitable funding, Musical Futures has provided resource packs, online materials, and professional development training, contributing to a view amongst participating teachers that their approaches to teaching have changed in ways that are sustainable in the long term (Hallam, Creech, Sandford, Rinta, & Shave, 2008). Barriers to participation were reported to include lack of time to plan new classroom projects, lack of resources, and concerns about how students would respond to the greater freedom of an approach in which teachers act as advisers rather than directors. The benefits of Musical Futures, as summarised by participating teachers, showed an encouraging integration of musical and personal development: the project "was perceived to have had a positive impact on pupils' attitudes towards music, self-esteem in relation to music, engagement and love of music and facilitated better group work and on task behaviour. It also engendered improved musical performances, enhanced musical skills and increased levels of attainment" (Hallam et al., 2008, p. 43). This close connection between musical and extra-musical benefits points to a strengthening of music education policy debate, where musical outcomes are presented as being valuable for their own sake as well as for their transferable effects. From this perspective, music holds a central place in school engagement and attainment but achieves this on its own terms rather than through its measurable effects on non-musical behaviour.

Another recent curriculum intervention has been the Wider Opportunities programme, which was set up in response to a government pledge to provide access to instrumental tuition for all children in junior schools (aged 7–11). Whole classes of approximately 30 children are taught by a specialist instrumental tutor alongside their class teacher, receiving one or two class lessons a week according to local policy, which also varies on whether children are permitted to take their instruments home to practise between lessons (Hallam & Creech, 2010). Instrumental skills are taught alongside notation, singing, and rhythm, and an evaluation of the pilot scheme reported that in the most effective cases, "the acquisition of technical and musical skills is also combined from the outset with opportunities to make music successfully in a large ensemble" (Ofsted, 2004, p. 6). This approach, while new to England, is long established in the band programmes of America and Australia, where the acquisition of instrumental skills is integrated with ensemble opportunities from an early stage (Campbell, 2008). The adoption of this approach in the UK marks a shift in policy from providing individual or small-group tuition for a few children, selected ostensibly by aptitude and interest but in recent years also being dependent on parental ability to pay for lessons; the two systems now run concurrently, although cuts to local education authority budgets mean that both have an uncertain future.

The long-term intentions of the Wider Opportunities scheme include greater accessibility of instrumental learning, with the pilot schools reporting beneficial changes in school culture as teachers, parents, and pupils all become more aware of the musical opportunities available to them. However, financing the continuation of lessons beyond the initial year of class learning remains a substantial obstacle to genuine accessibility, and the new pedagogy of whole-class teaching brings its own challenges: less successful lessons were reported to feature "poor posture, tuning and other aspects [which] went uncorrected, when it is essential to establish these effectively from the earliest stages" (Ofsted, 2004, p. 8). Teaching within a large-group context requires specific pedagogical skills if students are to acquire a secure foundation for future development as performers, and there are dangers (although undoubted value also) in the reported tendency towards "a greater emphasis given in most cases to the enjoyment and experience of making music rather than a strong focus on musical and instrumental skill development" (Bamford & Glinkowski, 2010, p. 4).

These two examples of recent changes in UK music education represent a move towards making musical learning more widely accessible: Musical Futures by connecting more closely with the musical world outside schools, and Wider Opportunities by opening up instrumental tuition to children of all abilities and circumstances. They illustrate how teachers' roles need to be reconsidered and supported, and highlight some of the barriers to change, as new resources are needed for new ways of teaching and practitioners feel understandably nervous about relinquishing their sense of control and expertise in order to learn alongside their students. Further challenges are inherent in changing one part of an educational system without considering its effects on students' other school experiences: teachers in the Musical Futures project, for example, reported an increased take-up for GCSE Music but noted that some of these new entrants "were not equipped with the necessary musical knowledge required in order to be successful" (Hallam et al., 2008, p. 7). Since musical success can be variously defined at different stages of education and in different contexts, this can create a barrier to progress through established systems, as the "knowledge gap" between compulsory school music, selective exams, and university education becomes ever greater and increasingly reliant on private instrumental tuition out of school. Consequently, the numbers of students engaging formally with music in schools decreases sharply at each potential dropout point (Bray, 2000), and music at higher levels is perceived to require special skills and sensibilities for which compulsory school music is not an adequate preparation (Lamont & Maton, 2008). Opening doors to musical participation requires that the route beyond is not a dead end: as François Matarasso has remarked in relation to community arts initiatives, "since they are part of a continuum of experience, positive outcomes can turn sour if the work is not built on" (Matarasso, 1997, p. ix).

Another, more radical attempt to achieve social equality through music is the El Sistema orchestra, founded in Venezuela in 1975, and recently adapted as the Sistema Scotland programme (Allan, Moran, Duffy, & Loeninga, 2010). The Venezuelan "system" is explicitly a way of life for its participating children and their families: "one of the most obvious reasons for the miracle is that El Sistema has the students for three or four hours a day, six days a week or sometimes more, for many years" (Booth, 2009, p. 80). Striving for musical excellence and lifting children out of poverty are seen as mutually reinforcing goals, and the 30-year success of the programme no doubt helps to increase parents' faith in its capacity to provide life-changing opportunities for their children. When the system transferred to Scotland, one music critic expressed concern that the connection between educational and cultural policy required to finance and support the project was unprecedented in Britain, warning that "if the El Sistema pilot schemes, to say nothing of any national project, take money away from existing music education and community music projects, then they have failed their own goals even before the first notes have been played" (Service, 2008).

Several years into the scheme, the dual goals of social change and musical excellence are in greater tension in Scotland than has been acknowledged in Venezuela, and evaluators of Sistema Scotland urge "the importance of ensuring that social inclusion programs do not themselves become instruments of exclusion" (Allan, 2010, p. 119). In the more individualist society of contemporary Britain, there is discomfort around associating classical music with social aspiration; in Venezuela, parents are persuaded of the value of this route out of poverty, and funding has been maintained through changes of government over three decades (Booth, 2009). While the funders of Sistema Scotland understandably seek evidence of impact to support the continuation of the scheme, project researcher Julie Allan suggests that they "would do well to avoid the pursuit of proof that changes in health, education and wellbeing are down to the arts activities that have been introduced" (Allan, 2010, p. 120). The life histories recounted in this book, though none so dramatic as that of Gustavo Dudamel, the Venezuelan slum child who became the conductor of the Los Angeles Philharmonic Orchestra (Vulliamy, 2007), show nonetheless that the effects of musical opportunity are far-reaching and life-changing. The El Sistema model perhaps offers an encouragement to be bolder in claiming the value of musical excellence as an agency for social change, while recognising that cultural and educational sensibilities in different countries might mean that a transfer of ideals, rather than methods, should be the focus of such a campaign.

When presenting the benefits of musical education to funders, policy-makers, and media who might otherwise marginalise the subject, it is tempting to reach for the prevalent arguments for extra-musical effects rather than attempting the more difficult task of articulating the specific qualities of musical learning. However, Elliot Eisner urges caution in this respect: "what we must search for are the justifications built upon what is distinctive—indeed, even unique—about music as a form of human expression" (Eisner, 2001, p. 20). All too often, such attempts at distinctiveness can sound like special pleading: to justify its place in the curriculum, music needs to be sufficiently similar to other subjects to take its place in a coherent, comprehensive education, but sufficiently different to offer developmental and aesthetic benefits that cannot be achieved elsewhere in school. The life history respondents demonstrate many of these benefits but also show the fragility of their claims, noting the missed opportunities for themselves and their peers that were sometimes caused by an unsympathetic teacher or a stultified curriculum, or indeed by a lack of engagement from a child for whom school music seemed remote or irrelevant.

In adult life, it is readily accepted that music serves different purposes according to temperament, interest, and level of skill (DeNora, 2000): one role of school music education must therefore be to ensure that all potential routes to future engagement are left open, so that the choices in lifelong participation lie with each individual, not with the limitations in his or her musical circumstances. The lifelong impact of musical learning may well be one of the distinctive claims that music can bring to the curriculum—but since its measurement lies well beyond traditional measures of school efficacy, there is a need for teachers, parents, and school managers to trust in the future investment of a high-quality musical education. Musical life histories offer one way of generating that evidence and a new perspective on the value of musical learning for providing lifelong opportunities.

6.4 Summary: Relevance and Timelessness in Musical Learning

The life history accounts analysed here offer compelling evidence for the lifelong impact of musical education, showing that the skills, values, and attitudes relating to music that are acquired in childhood have a lasting influence on adults' musical engagement. The "ideal" childhoods found amongst the responses were those where music was at the heart of all aspects of a child's life: music in schools was flourishing under an inspiring teacher; opportunities were available in and out of school to play instruments to a sufficient level of competence to gain recognition from peers, teachers, and family; and parents were supportive of the child's inclination towards music, absorbing this as part of the family's musical life through concert-going, ensemble playing, and encouragement of practice. Very few of the life history respondents were fortunate enough to experience such rich musical surroundings: many maintained a musical interest despite lacklustre teaching in school, finding satisfaction through their instrumental lessons instead, while others whose families did not have the resources or inclination to support instrumental learning became keen listeners, choral singers, or self-taught musicians, finding an outlet for their musical interests despite limited opportunities. These varied experiences offer hope for the resilience of musical potential, fully realised only in adulthood by some of the respondents—but they also show how education and home life can be a catalyst for musical discovery and development from which all children can and should benefit regardless of their home background and socioeconomic circumstances.

There are few clues to the ideal music curriculum amongst the life histories: these respondents had found many different aspects of their education useful (or otherwise), with the strongest impressions being left not by the particular skills they acquired in the classroom but by the enthusiasm of their teachers and the sense of sharing "a passion and enjoyment of music" [UK47, aged 62]. For many respondents, the specific skills and repertoire of school music had become obsolete in their later lives, but in the most positive cases they had retained a lifelong awareness of how to develop musically: they knew the effort involved in rehearsing for a performance as well as the rewards that resulted from doing so, and in their adult lives some had sought opportunities to replicate that experience in new contexts or had benefited from the additional insight this afforded to them as listeners and regular concert-goers. If they had been put off musical learning in school, this was most often through the negative attitudes of their teachers or the dislocation between the music of their home and friendship groups and the skills offered to them in the classroom. Their experiences show, therefore, the fine balance between curriculum content and delivery in ensuring an effective musical education: teachers are powerful musical role models for their students and hold the responsibility for making music an accessible and welcoming subject for the full range of students they teach.

A lifespan perspective on music education shows how difficult it is for teachers and curriculum designers to predict the skills that will be needed by future generations of musical creators and consumers. The diverse outcomes of the life history respondents' formative musical experiences also demonstrate that the long-term effects of musical learning are not directly predictable: amongst the older respondents, for instance, some childhood piano lessons had led to lifelong performing activity or to a late flourishing of a music teaching career, while others were judged to be best forgotten, although they still provided an additional dimension to respondents' concert listening or an increased inclination to encourage their own children to take music lessons. It is too soon to know, therefore, whether those students currently engaging in the self-directed listening and ensemble playing activities of the Musical Futures programme (Hallam et al., 2008) will have a significantly different lifelong musical experience than their contemporaries engaged in the more familiar composing, performing, and listening tasks of other British music classrooms (e.g., Mills, 2005). The clearest lesson offered by the life histories is that teachers and parents have a long-term responsibility for their children's musical attitudes and engagement, and that this factor should be present in making decisions about the school curriculum, the provision of instrumental learning, and the guidance offered to young people about their potential musical futures.

In early 20th-century debates about music education, writers taking a lifelong perspective saw school music as an arbiter of taste (see Chapter 2), emphasising the need to introduce children to high art and protect them from undesirable cultural influences. In our more pluralistic age, there is much greater recognition of the need for schools to build on young people's existing musical experience and informally acquired knowledge—and in doing so to broaden their musical horizons and provide training, encouragement, and opportunity to develop musically. John Paynter, a vociferous advocate of music education for all, urged music teachers to "teach from what is offered" (Paynter, 2002, p. 218), which in composing (or "making up music", as he preferred to call it) meant interpreting a child's musical understanding as presented in his or her creative work and then providing access to the knowledge and techniques through which that understanding could be advanced. This student-centred approach, also embodied by the Musical Futures programme (Hallam et al., 2008), makes great demands of the music teacher, who must encourage without interfering and build on pre-existing knowledge without belittling it—roles that may be in conflict with the external

> **Box 6.4.1**
>
> "My piano teacher was an elderly lady in poor health and over the years I spent with her she had a profound influence on me and we became great friends. Her pupils were brought up on a diet of Bach, Beethoven, Mozart, Haydn, etc., but providing you followed her advice and played scales, exercises and the classics she did not mind what other music you took to the lessons and she enjoyed listening to the pop music of the day. She was also a strong Methodist and loved it if you would play a few hymns. She was often ill and would ask some of her senior pupils to go in and teach the younger children. I loved doing this and believe it sowed the seeds for my future teaching career. The experience was invaluable." [UK55, aged 70]

measures of a "good" teacher imposed by school inspection regimes (Finney, 2011, p. 154). The life history responses illustrate powerfully, however, that these moments of connection between teachers, students, and musical discoveries have lasting value and should be at the heart of musical education, whether in the classroom or the instrumental studio (Box 6.4.1).

Those teachers recalled for the intensity of their musical enthusiasms demonstrate another aspect of teaching with a lifelong perspective, which is that not everything of value has to be in the curriculum: more important is that children are given a sense of the wealth of music—or art, literature, or other fields—that is there to be explored. David H. Hargreaves illustrates this with reference to the works of Shakespeare and Jane Austen, ruined for many adults by their heavy-handed treatment in schools (Hargreaves, 2004, p. 14). His appraisal of the school curriculum as a whole has some helpful parallels for music, which similarly has elements of both basic literacy and skills as well as the cultural and historical weight of repertoire:

> It is hard to acquire the basics [of literacy and numeracy] later in life if they are neglected during school years, and failure here incurs a heavy personal and social cost in adult life. But the same cannot be said of aspects of our cultural heritage, where there are many opportunities in adult life for discovering them through mature learning: jamming them into a compulsory curriculum for all at certain ages may damage the very motivation and enjoyment the compulsion is intended to achieve. (Hargreaves, 2004, p. 14)

Music in schools must provide both kinds of foundational learning: sufficient literacy and practical skill to ensure that all children have access to continued development in adulthood, and an introduction to the "cultural heritage" of music that is enticing but not overwhelming. Students leaving school with the sense that "I don't play an instrument, never have and think I never will as I believe I do not have the understanding of how to learn" [UK15, aged 31] should be a rarity—even if the proportion of the population that actively chooses (or is able) to invest the time and resources needed to pursue instrumental learning in adulthood remains small. Knowing music "from the inside", as a composer, ensemble player, instrumentalist, singer, or attentive listener, offers the potential for lifelong engagement in music and could provide teachers, students, and parents with a sense of the closer fit between school music and the wider musical world beyond.

Interlude K: Nikki Dibben [UK5]
Aged 37, left school 1987

Influential primary school and siblings, and enjoyment of singing throughout education; now a music lecturer who no longer performs

M y eldest sister learnt the clarinet at secondary school and I remember her practising in the living room with her music balanced on the fire guard while we were in the room too. I would have been about 4 or 5 at the time. I remember thinking it was an odd thing to do and asking her what it was and what she was doing; she explained that she was learning it so that she could be in the school band with her friends and travel to other places to play.

My elder brother and sisters used to listen to Radio 1 chart shows[1] so I was used to having pop music around. I loved *Top of the Pops*[2] and asked my Mum to make me a special dancing outfit. I think my siblings got pretty fed up with me dancing in front of the TV when they were trying to watch it. My eldest sister was very impressed with my knowledge of the charts when I was about 5 and I remember her testing me and feeling very proud when I got them right. So I think probably seeing older siblings valuing pop and involved in music themselves made it attractive to me as an activity.

The other most important influence was my primary school where we had a fantastic teacher who gave us lessons in music (choir singing, playing recorder, xylophones, reading music), played the piano in school assembly

---

[1] Radio 1 is the pop music radio station of the British Broadcasting Corporation (BBC), which broadcast at this time a regular "Top 40" singles chart, referred to as the "hit parade" by older respondents.
[2] A BBC television programme featuring performances of the top-selling pop music singles

where we sang hymns, and composed music-theatre pieces which we all participated in. I realised he was really good at the piano when another teacher replaced him one day (he was away) and it sounded awful! I loved the music theatre productions and always had a part in them. One year I was the lead and was *so* amazed and thrilled that our teacher not only played the piano for it but composed the music, and composed one song especially for me—or so it seemed at the time (he said that he had written it with my vocal range in mind). I think this made me come to see myself as a musical person with a good singing voice, because I was told that I had been specially chosen for my role because I could sing well and despite being bad at acting!

The highlights of my musical 'career' were those solo performances in music theatre pieces in primary school, a central singing role in a musical at secondary school, and in performances in higher education; also having singing lessons for four years at university where I learnt more about the connection between my body/voice and me as a person; and attending really incredible performances which have really made me feel alive.

I wonder why it is I've stopped being involved in music-making. I think it's because I always felt I was being judged when I made music. I had a bad mark at Year 1 level of my music degree which really shook my confidence, and I decided not to continue with performance in my degree. I carried on having singing lessons and performing though, so I don't think it was due to that. Partly it was because when I moved to a new city aged 26 I no longer had friends and contacts to perform with and never felt valued as a performer. I think I was never very confident as a performer, so as soon as my supportive network was removed I didn't have the ability or strength of mind to pursue it. I think also the performance opportunities which did seem available to me were associated with social contexts I felt repulsed by: church settings in which I felt hypocritical as a non-believer, or an educational institution (my university) whose values I disliked. And I didn't feel equipped to join any other musical group (e.g. jazz) because I felt I was too stuck in those previous styles.

I find it interesting that having loved the experience of playing so much I should find it so easy not to play now. It makes me wonder whether I am missing something I'm not aware of any more because it's gone. In some ways I feel the connection with my body which music used to provide is provided by my engagement in sport; and music still provides other aspects through listening. I think it's a bit sad that having spent ten years learning piano, many years singing, and five years learning flute I should now do none of them. But I remember how *hard* it is to play well and believe that it would take too much time and effort to get to a standard where my own playing would give me or anyone else any pleasure.

Interlude L: Robert Wardell [UK19]
Aged 74, left school 1946

Accidental discovery of classical music leading to lifelong listening and concert-going

No member of my extended family is in any way 'musical', none could play an instrument or ever went to concerts; we were very working class. My mother was a full-time waitress all her life, and although I suspect she never knowingly heard a note of Beethoven in her entire life she did have vague aspirations of feeling she ought to better herself. My father, on the other hand, (despite having two schoolteachers as parents) was a macho anti-culturalist, he lost an eye in the 1914–18 war and from his unspoken experiences loathed the Germans, so perhaps he associated them with 'high-culture'.

I left school in July 1946 at the age of 14 (the leaving age went up to 15 the next year) having had the worst education imaginable. We lived in Hull, deemed to be a bombing target, so that on 1st September 1939 I was evacuated, at the age of 7, to Beverley.[1] There was no bombing so at Christmas I came home; the bombing started so I went back to Beverley, but to a different foster-family; the bombing stopped so I came home again. This pattern went on through the war, so that between the ages of 7 and 12 I went to eleven different schools. None of my 'adopted parents' had any musical interests, my only contact with 'music' was that during the war, on Sunday nights following the 9pm news, the BBC played all the national anthems of the allies. I was especially struck by the Netherlands anthem, and although I don't think I have heard it since 1945 I can even now whistle or

---

[1] Both towns in the North of England: Hull is a river port and Beverley an inland market town.

hum it right through. There must have been a sub-conscious musical streak in my psyche somewhere!

The war ended with me having the luxury of 18 months at the same school. There was no school choir, no school orchestra or band, no instrumental teaching of any description. Culturally it was a desert. We had one 40 minute music period once a week. This consisted of lusty unison singing of Bobby Shaftoe, Molly Malone, Vicar of Bray[2] and so on with no aspiration to get beyond that. Once or twice the teacher played some records (78s) but whatever she played it did not resonate. However in our final term the Carl Rosa Opera[3] came to the New Theatre at Hull and a small group of us were taken to see *Rigoletto*, which I vaguely enjoyed.

What did leave a real impression was the tiniest thing: each morning the entire school assembled in the main hall, we said a prayer, sang a hymn (which I loved, having acquired a church-going habit whilst evacuated. The religion bored me to tears but I loved the hymns!). As we trooped in and out of assembly—in a very no-talking orderly fashion I might add, we got the cane if we dared speak, girls or boys—my great joy was that the music teacher 'played us in' and 'played us out' on the piano, with pieces from her classical repertoire. These included the Brahms A Flat Waltz (for me the most perfect piece ever written by anyone!), the Schubert *Marche Militaire*, Grieg's *In the Hall of the Mountain King* and Halvorson's *Entry of the Boyers*. I often sought the teacher out to ask what she had played, writing the titles down in a little book so that I could watch out for the piece on a future occasion. I think I filled two pages before I left.

Leaving school, virtually uneducated, I had four years of dull dead-end jobs before I joined the army as a regular soldier. But between the ages of 14–18 two musical influences did emerge. In 1947, out of the blue, my mother declared an interest in Gilbert and Sullivan just as the D'Oyly Carte[4] were coming to Hull. She took me to see *The Mikado* (my father stayed disapprovingly at home). Wow! This was magical! The next year, when D'Oyly Carte came again, we saw a further four operas in their weekly repertoire. There and then I began a love affair with G&S which has not just remained but has intensified: many, many years later I became a staunch life-member of the Sir Arthur Sullivan Society and in addition to all the Savoy operas I have some 20-25 CDs of Sullivan's non-Gilbert music which are in the repertoire

---

[2] All folk songs of the kind collected by Cecil Sharp and widely used in music education at this time

[3] A travelling opera company, still in existence: http://www.carlrosaopera.co.uk/history/index.asp

[4] A light opera company presenting the works of Gilbert and Sullivan (see Interlude F for more details)

of my frequently played discs. I think an introduction to G&S has been a stepping-stone for many non-musical children. Sullivan to Schubert is dead easy, if you can get to Sullivan in the first place.

Then in 1949, my last dead-end job, I became a 'lorry driver's mate'—long happy hours on the road sitting beside the driver, then helping him load and unload as necessary. I joined a one-lorry self-employed driver working between Hull and the far-flung wastes of East Yorkshire: the most unforgettable man I have ever met. He was educated, cultured, but you wouldn't have known! He told me the most outrageous filthy jokes, and sang the most obscene songs—but then would come a transformation. Walt would whistle, quite accurately, the most fabulous melodic lines I had ever heard: with my attuned but musically ignorant ears I would ask, "What's that, Walt?" He would answer, "Oh, that's Beethoven's Pastoral Symphony" or "that's the end of Brahms's First Symphony" and so on. Long chunks of the real classics, interspersed with scatology and sexual innuendo of the worst kind. No explanations other than the bald title, no attempt to educate me. He whistled. I listened. Then, sometime in early 1950, Walt tossed me a ticket for a Hull City Hall concert: the long-gone Yorkshire Symphony Orchestra were playing one of his favourites, the Emperor Concerto, and he thought I should hear it played properly. I sat by myself and it was an experience I shall never forget. I had intended to get the bus home, but I wanted to delay facing my disapproving father: instead I walked home with Beethoven rolling round and round my head. Totally unprepared for what I would hear, I never looked back.

In 1950 I joined the army as a driver, and in 1951 I was posted to Germany, where I spent many hours sharing a waiting room ready for assignments. The German drivers had their radio invariably tuned to a German classical music station: here I was introduced to Haydn, Brahms, lots and lots of Beethoven, Mendelssohn and Schumann. Later, as a senior NCO[5] I had my own room and a personal radio, and making up for lost time I began to devour classical music as if it was about to be rationed. On leaving the army I became a London tour guide, and by regular concert-going I added the symphonies of Bruckner, Elgar and Nielsen to my repertoire and, as I say, music became more than just a pleasure. I never, ever use it just as background for household chores. It's too good for that. Every week I have a 'concert' and listen, seriously, to CDs of a symphony, concerto, overture. My in-car entertainment consists of compilation tapes of the shorter pieces

---

[5] Non-commissioned officer, a senior army position

seldom heard properly, from Sousa marches to Strauss and Waldteufal waltzes, and lots of Sullivan, with and without Gilbert.

I bitterly regret the loss of music in schools (who plays Brahms and Schubert in assembly these days?); what lorry drivers in 2007 sing dirty songs, swig bottled beer, and whistle Beethoven at the same time? And if they did who would be there to listen?

7 | Chances, Choices, and Conclusions

7.1 Chances and Choices in Musical Education

THE LIFE HISTORIES PRESENTED IN this book illustrate the numerous influences on young people's musical development and offer examples of a range of routes into lifelong engagement with music—some of them actively encouraged by teachers or parents, others arrived at accidentally through encounters with musical enthusiasts later in life. They show musical education to be the product of chances and choices—a balance between access to resources, guidance and opportunities, and the self-directed or family-supported willingness to engage with those musical chances or to seek out alternatives. In contrast with the pattern of ambitious parents, an early start on an instrument, and thousands of hours of practice in childhood that is common to many professional musicians' life stories (Gembris, 2006), the music teachers, amateur performers, and lifelong listeners in this study showed more varied trends of musical engagement. Relatively few had experienced equally strong support in both the home and the school, although many had been influenced by—or reacted against—musical mentors, who were often valued as much for their musical enthusiasm as for their expertise. Amongst these variable chances and choices, questions are raised not about the ideal route into lifelong musical engagement, since there seem to be many possibilities, but rather about the ways in which the range of musical opportunities available to young people can be strengthened and supported:

1. How can provision of opportunities for musical discovery be strengthened in home, school, and community settings?

2. Where should the structured, purposeful acquisition of musical skills take place, and how can this best be supported?
3. Who is best placed to provide the guidance needed by young people to be fully aware of their potential musical futures?

The life histories show variation in these experiences between individuals but nevertheless offer some general principles that could help to guide future policy and research.

Firstly, the evidence from the life histories shows that opportunities for musical discovery are most effective when they occur in multiple locations and are reinforced by compatible attitudes and opportunities in the home, school, and elsewhere. A number of respondents recognised their good fortune in having supportive parents who provided them with instrumental lessons, and showed how the skills gained there had greater value in a child's life when they led to opportunities and recognition as a performer within school. This is an admittedly privileged route into musical engagement, and one that favours a focus on classical music, for which parental support and teacher recognition are key factors in sustaining motivation to practise (Hallam & Creech, 2010). While not all children will experience these musical choices—at least under current systems of paying for instrumental lessons—the principle of ensuring coherence between school music and young people's wider musical experience applies across other circumstances. Older respondents who recalled listening to light classical music at home, and then having these experiences deepened through schools' radio broadcasts or choral singing, demonstrate another kind of connection between musical worlds—albeit one that feels somewhat outdated for contemporary classrooms.

The multiplicity of musical and cultural experiences that young people now bring to the music classroom mean that teachers cannot make assumptions about where their educational offerings will fit in the broader musical experience of their students. Parental attitudes to music will range from those of highly skilled and experienced musicians, seeking to replicate opportunities for their children, through dismissive or disinterested, to outright opposition in the case of some cultural and religious groups (Harris, 2006). Music teachers in classrooms and instrumental studios have limited control over their students' musical backgrounds, but the life histories show that an influential mentor can play a huge role in allowing students to discover new musical perspectives and come to their own understanding of what music means in their lives. For the life history respondents, this had happened most immediately through active involvement in music: in extracurricular participation, band membership, and chances to create

"Without my parents' input and encouragement it's hard to say if I would have enjoyed music as much as I did in my teen years, when I not only took lessons (piano, theory, cello) but also played in orchestras (my mother often being the 'taxi' driver), sang in choirs and spent a lot of time composing music, most of which was never played. School music was very important too, as it was at school that I first sang in a choir (from age 11) and started to play an orchestral instrument (the cello and some percussion: timpani, snare drum, etc.). The school choir sang such works as the Mozart and Brahms Requiems, Britten's *St Nicolas* and his *Ceremony of Carols*, and the Haydn *Nelson Mass*. We also sang some madrigals, I remember." [UK58, aged 52]

music. Teachers demonstrated their enthusiasm for music through their energy and commitment, and those young people who were receptive to the opportunities made available were swept along through a busy school life of music-making and into lifelong engagement (Box 7.1.1).

There are many such optimistic memories amongst the life histories, celebrating the enthusiasm of teachers and the unfailing support of parents, and showing how these provide a fertile ground for the flourishing of young people's emerging musical identities. However, the recollections of classroom music lessons were often more muted, with respondents across the generations reporting limited benefits from lessons that were sometimes at odds with their passion for music outside the curriculum. While the first question outlined above, regarding provision of musical opportunities, can therefore be answered with reasonable confidence, the second, relating to the deliberate acquisition of skills, is more problematic. It seems entirely reasonable that young people's exposure to music will be different according to their family circumstances—but not that the opportunity to acquire musical expertise should be available only to those with financial and parental support. Classroom music therefore holds a central place in ensuring that all students are equipped with the strategies for learning musically, and with an understanding that musical opportunities can and should be universally accessible. The life history responses show some success stories, where an influential teacher had imbued a young musician with confidence and eagerness for learning, but the general trend is for those opportunities to have been dependent on engagement in music beyond the classroom.

The problems of mixed-ability classroom music teaching are readily acknowledged in the research literature (e.g., Wright, 2007), and it could be that for these musically high-achieving respondents, classroom lessons had faded in their memories compared to the highlights of ensemble member-ship and concert performances. Music teachers are sometimes accused of following a "sorting machine model" (Kelly, 2009, p. 88) of music education, selecting the most able students for tuition and neglecting the needs of the majority, with potentially damaging effects on the motivation of those who are selected and the self-esteem of those who are not. The UK life history respondents reported no such sense of being specially selected, with younger respondents more often seeing classroom music as lacking challenge and purpose, even whilst respecting their teachers for their provision of extracur-ricular activities. No wonder that researchers have repeatedly questioned the place of music in the curriculum (Ross, 1995) and that others have argued "very strongly that composing and performing are, jointly, the true basis of musical education" (Paynter, 2008, p. 168). The solution seems to be in en-suring that young people can readily perceive the purpose of their musical education, both for their immediate development as emerging musicians and, in retrospect, for the lasting impact upon the musical choices that they make in their adult lives.

There are of course other routes to the acquiring of musical skills, and the many accounts of self-teaching and independent exploration of music illus-trate the great capacity of young people's musical initiative and curiosity. Such exploration, though, tended not to take place entirely in isolation: the recognition of friends, family, and ideally teachers too was seen in retrospect to have sustained motivation and increased ambition, and in several cases had led to the seeking of formal tuition after a period of self-teaching (see Interludes D, G, and I). Although there are dangers in teachers being too quick to appropriate students' informal learning as part of the curriculum (Folkestad, 2006), their failure to recognise independently acquired exper-tise can be another factor in the separation of school music from other aspects of musical experience, causing the kind of resentment felt by the pop musician who was "banned from the music block for playing 'slap' bass after I sneaked in at lunch time" [UKP81, aged 44]. Where students felt that their teachers had "really embraced my passion and musical ability" [UKP74, aged 18], this appeared to have enhanced their sense of musical self-worth, so making them more receptive to opportunities in school.

Such connections are often missed by teachers or not offered up by stu-dents: Sheri Jaffurs writes of her dismay as a music teacher when a student whom she had taught for four years told her that he "composed songs at home with his family and also wrote songs for his band [. . .] I couldn't ima-gine him playing in a rock band. I had never thought of him as someone who was interested in music" (Jaffurs, 2004, p. 189). Jaffurs responded with an ethnographic study of her students' band and a reflexive critique of their learning styles and her own teaching habits, recognising that her own sense of unfamiliarity in the students' musical world was equivalent to "how they felt when I asked them to sing my songs" (p. 199). For classically trained teachers—and parents—there are huge challenges in embracing not just the musical preferences of the next generation but also their perspectives on the usefulness of music in their lives. Much hope is offered by the life history respondents' exchange of listening tastes with their parents and wider families, and with their appreciation of teachers' attempts to connect with their musical interests—such efforts are truly worthwhile and can help to shape musical attitudes and values for life.

On the third question outlined above, the life histories show that guidance on the long-term possibilities for musical engagement was absent or even obstructive in many cases: several respondents decided against studying music at university, fearing that it would lead inevitably to a career in teaching, and others were advised by their parents to keep music as a hobby while pursuing a more lucrative or reliable career choice (Box 7.1.2). For parents with limited previous experience of the professional world of music, its lack of job security would be an understandable deterrent in guiding their off-spring, and it is understandable that support given willingly for a fulfilling pastime might be withdrawn when it seemed to be encouraging a risky career choice (Borthwick & Davidson, 2002). Comparing the life history respondents with professional musicians suggests that making musical career decisions in mid-adolescence might already be too late: "if emotional ties with music and spontaneous vocal or instrumental musical activity do not develop before the age of 9, then the probability that exceptional musical abilities or natural ease of vocal or instrumental emotional expression will develop later is rather low" (Manturzewska, 1990, p. 133). While very few of the life history respondents had aimed for professional status as performers, some expressed regret that they had not been sufficiently guided in childhood to make this possible (see Section 5.1) and might have benefited from more readily available advice in school, where careers guidance in music is still often inadequate (Pitts, 2002). Teachers are undoubtedly right to focus

---

Box 7.1.2

"Although my parents let me do my grades and O Level music, they were dead against me carrying on with it as a career option. But my love of music has stayed with me, and even though they wouldn't let me do music A Level and go to music college, I've studied music and teaching as an adult. But it would have been easier if my parents had encouraged me." [UK43, aged 38]

mainly on the immediate goals of engaging their students in classroom and extracurricular music, and yet it is vital that these activities contain within them the future possibility of long-term musical interest and activity.

The desire to avoid charges of elitism in music education perhaps risks embracing instead a self-limiting outlook, where progression to the next phase of attainment is the exception rather than the norm, and young people are not made fully aware of the future directions that could be open to them. There is clear evidence that musical engagement is at its most vulnerable at points of educational transition, with many young musicians ceasing instrumental tuition on starting secondary school (Lamont et al., 2003) or losing performing confidence as they enter higher education in music (Burland & Davidson, 2004). Mentoring from older students, community musicians, and teachers themselves could help to overcome perceived barriers to future engagement, as demonstrated with disaffected teenagers (Finney & Tymoczko, 2005) and reluctant male singers (Hall, 2005). Clare Hall's class of 5-year-old boys were introduced to male singers aged 9 and 17, and their interactions showed the boys to be "most interested in learning about becoming older and being friends with the peer (social level), but they were also learning about many other things, namely the joy and usefulness of singing (affective level) and how to sing well (cognitive level)" (Hall, 2005, p. 16). John Finney and Michael Tymoczko's study showed that there are benefits for the mentors, too, in such exchanges, both in expanding their own musical and pedagogical horizons and in raising teachers' expectations of their level of responsibility and success (Finney & Tymoczko, 2005, p. 48).

The sustainability of peer modelling strategies within schools makes them a valuable resource for teachers, and where schools can also facilitate connections with professional and community musicians, there are further potential benefits in raising students' awareness of wider musical worlds (see Pitts, 2010). A large-scale study of community music partnerships in Australia noted the mutual benefits of school–community collaborations: "The school provides educational opportunities for community members to extend their musical skills. In turn, the participation of the community members in school events introduces the students to the benefits of intergenerational learning" (Bartleet, Dunbar-Hall, Letts, & Schippers, 2009, p. 156). The life histories illustrate how these "acts of hospitality" (Higgins, 2007)—exchanges between musicians of different traditions and experiences—are beneficial throughout the lifespan of musical engagement, encouraging coherence between the values of school, home, and the wider musical community and making the full range of musical opportunities visible and accessible to young people.

Christopher Small, who has long advocated the "de-schooling" of musical education (Small, 1977/96), proposes that a network of music centres would be a more effective location for such exchanges to take place, stating that "Classrooms are not good places for the gaining of significant musical experience. I am not saying that it never happens, but the odds are cruelly stacked against it" (Small, 2010, p. 288). He reports a change in the conservatoires of Spain, "which have in the past been content to deal exclusively with the conventional materials and methods of conservatoires but are now looking to expand their operations as centres of musicking for everybody in the town who wants it" (p. 289). Opting in to this proposed system, however, could bring barriers to access of the kind reported by the Italian life history respondents (see Section 3.5): better perhaps for schools to retain their position as a conduit of musical learning, but to do so with greater awareness of their place in the connected musical worlds of adult engagement, both professional and amateur, and the home lives of students, in all their diversity.

7.2 The Usefulness of Life History Approaches

This study has drawn on autobiographical narratives, colloquially termed "life histories", that have offered detailed and distinctive accounts of musical development as experienced across generations and circumstances. As explained in Chapter 1, the project used an adapted form of life history methodology, favouring a larger sample of written responses over the more usual method of in-depth interviewing but retaining the focus on "the complex interaction between individuals' lives and the institutional and societal contexts within which they are lived" (Cole & Knowles, 2001, p. 126). This large-scale adaptation of life history methods enabled the inclusion of many respondents' voices within the book, both through the interludes that presented individual stories in full and through the comparisons of different accounts as quoted in the chapters. Analysing the data from different perspectives—by generation (Chapter 2), by context (Chapters 3 and 4), and by outcome (Chapter 5)—enabled exploration of the many factors in respondents' musical decisions and journeys, an approach that was intended to preserve the coherence of respondents' accounts while also observing trends and patterns across the responses.

The ethical responsibilities of gathering and interpreting such personal research data are at the forefront of life history research, both in showing care for the respondents and others whom they mention within their accounts and in shaping an analysis that respects respondents' own interpretations of their experience. In this project, the greatest challenges of analysis and interpretation related to the music education contexts with which I was least familiar. The Italian respondents, for example, were almost unanimous in their negative views of general music education in their country, but for me as an English researcher to report this seemed disingenuous—so highlighting in contrast the extent to which my interpretations of the UK responses were informed by my knowledge of the practice and rhetoric of music education in Britain. While researching close to home brings its own risks of being unduly influenced by personal experience and already formed opinions, the reciprocal understanding necessary for life history research suggests that a degree of immersion in the context to be studied is desirable—and therefore that a broader international perspective on life histories in music education would best be achieved through collaboration between native researchers; perhaps a project for the future.

To understand further the process of constructing a musical life history, I undertook to write my own—included as a postlude to this book, but not in the analysis featured in the preceding chapters. I found that the process of writing rather than talking about my experiences generated a stronger urge to shape a narrative, thinking chronologically about the effects and outcomes of different decisions and sometimes being surprised by the prominence that quite small factors gained in this process. I no longer play the clarinet, for example, but as the starting point for my musical activities this assumed a critical place in the narrative; I thought about my sense (or lack) of musical ambition for the first time, noticing the serendipitous ways in which I have arrived at a current level of music-making that can be maintained alongside my academic work; and I felt a loyalty to the family and teachers who have influenced me that made me want to mention them all—though reading back through my account I note the absence of several piano teachers, opera conductors, and friends who could easily have been included had space permitted. Where I imposed a word limit on myself, several respondents were limited by the time they had to devote to writing, or by a feeling that they might have said too much. Christina, reviewing her edited text for Interlude J, remarked, "I did go on a bit didn't I, but I suppose I wanted to give you a full picture." Since writing an anecdote takes longer than telling it, written forms of life history research might inhibit respondents from including all that they can remember—although the opportunity to add extra detail or clarify connections between different events is more within the control of the writer.

My own life history also reveals my musical background and therefore the experiences and assumptions that I brought to this study—a process that life history researchers are strongly encouraged to engage with in order to empathise with their participants: "If we make explicit our own understandings, and know ourselves well enough, we are better able to understand what might be getting in the way of us listening to and understanding participants' experiences" (Cole & Knowles, 2001, p. 52). Readers might observe that my own very positive experiences of extracurricular music in secondary school, for instance, perhaps make me well disposed to respondents' accounts of similar activities and inclined to interpret an absence of such activities as being detrimental to developing musical interests. Certainly I noted both arguments within the life history accounts, along with reports of extracurricular music that was dull or dissatisfying—so placing my own experience within a broader spectrum where the opportunity (even compulsion) to participate was not always so fondly remembered. I read with interest respondents' accounts of the influence of siblings (not having any myself) and reflected on how my sharing of listening tastes within the home took place instead with my parents, so highlighting a comparison of family roles that proved fruitful for further analysis. I confess to having initially disregarded parents' proud accounts of their offspring's musical achievements, feeling a slight antipathy borne out of reluctant conversations in everyday life, before reminding myself that supporting the next generation in their musical development is indeed a valuable long-term outcome of music education—perhaps one of the most widespread and reliable, in fact, and one that therefore deserved due prominence in my analysis. Perhaps fortunately, given these confessions, life history accounts offer an intrinsic reminder to researchers to look beyond their own experience, since they contain a greater degree of respondents' own interpretations than is usual in many other methods of educational research.

One obvious disadvantage of the written life history method is that it favours highly literate respondents, and especially those with an interest in the topic of research: one respondent noted explicitly that "your subject is one that I feel passionately about, having experienced the love of my life by sheer accidental good fortune" [UK19, aged 74], whilst others gave unsolicited views on the importance of music education that showed their desire to support research that might promote this agenda. For largely sentimental reasons, my friends, former students, and colleagues are over-represented as the authors of interludes in the book and were not so prominent in the sample as a whole, of whom I knew 21 people (16%) personally. There was nonetheless a prevalence of university-educated respondents, accustomed to writing and articulating their views and willing to invest their time in an academic research project to an extent that would not be so likely in a wider cross-section of the population.

The level of non-completed responses was most evident in the phase of data collection that included the popular musicians: their responses tended to be shorter, as were the Italian responses, and several incomplete accounts had to be discarded. Due to the way that the project was advertised to the Phase 2 participants, all responses by the popular musicians were submitted through an online survey, a method that made non-completion more apparent than in the e-mail and letter submissions of Phase 1 and might also have discouraged more reflective writing by appearing in a format more often associated with quick, multiple-choice surveys. The questions may have seemed less relevant to pop musicians (though Interlude D shows that this was not always the case), and musicians with negative experiences of school music education, as these tended to be, may have been distrustful of a university-based research project. For these respondents—and for all those who considered participating but chose not to—a greater sense of connection was perhaps needed to secure their interest and trust. The Life Story Center at the University of Maine offers one example of how this might work (see http://usm.maine.edu/olli/national/lifestorycenter/): here respondents are guided in writing their own life stories and are able to search an online archive to see what others have contributed. A similar approach could work well for music education, offering the chance for participants to compare experiences in a public forum and build a communal sense of the effects and effectiveness of musical learning in different contexts. It is hoped that the companion website to this book will provide such an opportunity, and readers are invited to visit http://www.oup.com/us/chancesandchoices to read and contribute to the entries collected there.

Another challenge for life history research to tackle in the future is the documenting of the "non-impact" of music education, drawing on the experiences of adults who profess not to be interested in music, or who attribute their interest to sources other than childhood influences of home and school. While the life history accounts presented here were not without their negative portrayals of music in schools, they came from respondents who had remained musically active in adulthood: a wider sample would include further evidence of ineffective music teaching, as well as the perspective not represented in this book, that of the adult who enjoyed a good musical education at the time but has subsequently pursued other interests. Where non-musically active adults have previously been studied, clear differences in their experiences of school music have been found: Helen Gavin's study of musical memories reported that "In the musical group, all participants stated that school or teachers had been a source of encouragement in music, with the majority (95%) citing both teachers and facilities. In the non-musical group, by contrast, all participants found music at school unimportant, with 10 (33.33%) expressing hostility" (Gavin, 2001, p. 58). However, the likelihood of adult "non-musicians" reporting dissatisfaction with their formative musical influences is increased by the tendency of life narratives to be shaped by current perspectives, whereby "a memory may lose or gain affective intensity depending on its connection to an individual's present goals rather than to goals originally served by the remembered behaviors" (Singer, 1990, p. 537).

Adults for whom music is no longer a significant part of their identity are less likely to have rehearsed their stories of childhood musical discovery, having fewer opportunities to discuss musical interests with like-minded friends, and so constructing an unquestioned view of themselves as "not being musical". Theories of the life story "schema" propose that "the extent to which our social network provides us with interested listeners may affect the extent to which we elaborate our life story, and which parts of it become central to us" (Bluck & Habermas, 2000, p. 140). Since research on music in everyday life (DeNora, 2000) has shown the high level of musical sophistication that is widespread in the population, individuals with no musical life story to tell would be extremely rare. However, Alexandra Lamont (2011) has reported the difficulties of recruiting adults who are not musically active to participate in such research, and the life history approach is perhaps particularly problematic in seeking narratives and insight from people who might not previously have considered the impact of their musical education. Understanding non-participation is a limitation in research across arts, sports, and leisure engagement (Allender, Cowburn, & Foster, 2006), and whilst demographic information on the social and economic barriers to participation exists, this only partially explains the experiences and attitudes of the "self-excluders" who choose not to engage with a particular art form (Bunting, Chan, Goldthorpe, Keaney, & Oskala, 2008). Just as arts organisations seek to understand and convert the views of non-attenders to musical events (Winzenried, 2004), so the experiences of those people for whom music education seems not to have left a lasting impression would have some valuable and probably salutary insights to offer for music teachers and researchers.

The responses have also shown the powerful influence of parenting approaches and attitudes, and investigating the long-term impact of homes in which music is not strongly supported would be another sensitive but valuable area of research. Access to instrumental lessons generally implies a level of disposable income associated with higher socioeconomic status, though the life history respondents—particularly those writing about post-war childhoods of relative cultural and economic deprivation—show that music lessons were often a financial sacrifice made by parents with a strong determination to provide such opportunities for their children. More challenging for some was forging a path as a "first generation" musician, and here generational cycles of privilege and opportunity were more in evidence: parents who had not experienced the benefits of music lessons themselves were less likely to understand the effort, practice, and long-term engagement needed to achieve musical competence and so were less able to identify strategies for sustaining engagement and motivation beyond the early stages. None of these life history respondents talked about feeling inhibited from engaging in music by virtue of their family background, but a published autobiographical account by Alison Gangel (2011) of undertaking piano lessons in a Glasgow children's home illustrates the barriers to participation for those unfamiliar with the often-privileged world of classical music-making. On winning a scholarship to a Glasgow music conservatoire, Gangel describes feeling overwhelmed by the smartly dressed, well-spoken children who surround her there, and by teachers who offer only criticism—their praise intended to be implicit, but their corrections devastating to a young girl for whom her school-based piano teacher had been her only source of esteem and encouragement.

The impact of musical learning for adults disadvantaged by poverty, lack of education (Matarasso, 1997), and even homelessness (Bailey & Davidson, 2002) is increasingly being understood as a powerful tool for social rehabilitation. These interventions could be even stronger if experienced earlier in life, but Gangel's (2011) account shows that entry into a new musical world requires more than just instrumental skill, since this alone is not enough to bridge the gap between difficult family circumstances and élite musical education. Life history research might help to explore the family stories and attitudes that surround a child's first ventures into musical learning, providing insight on the barriers to musical engagement and strategies for how these could be overcome.

7.3 Recommendations and Future Directions

The research presented here has posed some challenging questions about the purpose of musical education and its place in the lives of all those who pass through school classrooms and instrumental studios. It has shown the value of a supportive, responsive, and coherent musical environment for young people, which is at its most effective when the musical opportunities of school, home, and the wider world coincide in clear and purposeful ways. It has also revealed how these opportunities are sometimes absent from formative musical experiences and has illustrated how later interventions, coupled with individual determination, can lead to effective musical learning at any stage of life. Musical education has been shown to have tremendous responsibilities in shaping lifelong values, attitudes, and skills while taking a modest place alongside the musical enthusiasms and role models that may be present to varying degrees in a child's home life. The complexity of formative musical experiences that are shown in the musical life histories suggest a need for a new emphasis on lifelong engagement as a valid aim for music education, and for a research agenda that recognises the diversity of musical lives within contemporary culture.

Teaching music with a view to lifelong engagement means focusing not only on the acquisition of skills and knowledge, but also on the forming of open-minded and receptive attitudes that allow for future musical learning and exploration. The life history respondents looked back with greatest respect on those teachers whose practice was based on a personal musical passion, while accommodating the different interests of their students. While this most often happened outside the classroom, the ideal would clearly be for this responsive approach to be at the heart of school music, and therefore accessible to all students. The stories in which respondents achieved their musical potential long after their school years show the importance of leaving open future routes into music by providing foundational skills and inclusive opportunities. Since parents, particularly those without a musical background, may not be aware of the possibilities for lifelong musical involvement, teachers have a mentoring responsibility to provide guidance not only for those students showing exceptional musical aptitude but also for all those whose future lives will be enriched by continued engagement with music.

One aspect of securing a place for music in schools involves demonstrating to students, parents, and policymakers the purpose of musical education. The recollections of learning an instrument, for example, illustrated benefits far beyond the ability to play specific repertoire, offering in addition the potential for increased confidence, recognition, and school engagement as well as a sense of musical achievement that had sustained adult involvement in fulfilling leisure activities as performers or listeners. Participating in extracurricular music, similarly, offered friendships and lasting memories that were looked back on with affection by many respondents. Recollection of classroom music, however, was often less vivid or favourable, so raising a perennial challenge of how to ensure that all students have access to meaningful musical experiences in school. Where dissatisfaction with school music existed, including in the Italian responses, this seemed to relate to self-limiting activities, undertaken without a sense of their future purpose or their relationship to the wider musical world. There are signs in both practice and research that this problem is being addressed, but it remains one of great urgency if music is to retain its rightful place in the school experience of all young people.

The life histories demonstrate with great clarity how musical learning is by no means confined to the school years, with respondents describing their experiences as adult learners, performers, and concert-goers and as the teachers and parents of the next generation of young musicians. However, for some within this group—and no doubt many in the wider population—finding opportunities to continue musical involvement had been difficult, either through their own lack of time and motivation or because they had been unable to identify appropriate activities that fit with their other commitments. This dilemma presents an opportunity for arts organisations to reconsider their target markets, for instance by focusing ticket offers for concerts not just on students, as is usual, but on young adults and those in middle age who are outside educational settings. Likewise, while community initiatives to provide playing and singing opportunities for older people are extremely laudable, encouraging school and university leavers to join amateur ensembles would help them to make the transition into adult musical life and establish habits of cultural engagement that might in turn inform their own parenting and their support for the arts and education.

These practical recommendations for supporting lifelong musical engagement also present a new challenge for researchers, to document and interpret the range of musical lives that lie between everyday listening (DeNora, 2000) and the career trajectories of professional musicians (Manturzewska, 1990). The "ordinary" musical lives represented by the respondents in this book show the depth and diversity of musical engagement that exists in contemporary society—even while offering a reminder that such opportunities are not as readily available to all as they should be. Further work needs to be done on extending the life history approach to other musical groups, to other countries and educational systems, and to those who have become disengaged from music through lack of opportunity or support. The chances and choices that contribute to musical life histories need to be continually questioned so that researchers and practitioners might understand the place of music in education, in society, and in a wide range of musical lives.

Postlude: Stephanie Pitts
Aged 37, left school 1992

Supportive home and school environments, followed by career as a university music lecturer

Some of my strongest memories of primary school are related to music: I can remember being singled out in a junior school choir rehearsal as being the only person watching the conductor—and being slightly startled by that, as I'd assumed everyone else was doing the same. I started clarinet lessons at the age of 7, the choice between oboe, flute and clarinet being dictated by the fact that my second cousin had an instrument that I could borrow: I still remember the trip to my great-grandpa's house to collect it, and the thrill of opening the slightly musty case and seeing this mysterious instrument in pieces. When I left that junior school in Yorkshire to move house for my father's next Royal Air Force posting, my clarinet teacher wrote in my autograph book that she hoped one day to see my name 'up in lights'. That was my first glimpse of the possibility of a musical career, and for a little while I wanted to be Emma Johnson, the clarinettist who won Young Musician of the Year in 1984. The clarinet turned out not to be the right instrument for me, though I made it to Grade 8 with a kind of plodding inevitability. Meanwhile my mum had bought a piano, choosing it because it went well with the furniture, and subsequently discovering that my dad's claims to be able to play had been slightly exaggerated. I started piano lessons at around the age of 10, and this time I was instantly hooked, liking the sense of completeness that came with being able to play a whole piece rather than counting bars of rests, and enjoying sight-reading, and later accompanying—which came to be the skills I developed most fully as an adult.

My parents were always very supportive of my music-making: both of them I think had untapped musical potential, and both my grandmas had been musical; one singing alto with church choirs and choral societies in Leeds, and the other playing piano and later owning an electric organ, which I was always expected to play when we went to visit. Asking after my musical activities was a regular feature of visiting relatives, and on one occasion resulted in me fainting on great-grandpa's hearth while trying to demonstrate my prowess on the clarinet—in my excitement I must have forgotten to breathe in. We listened to a fair amount of music at home too: the Top 40 on Radio 1 while having tea on Sundays, and records from my parents' 1960s teenage collections, then later bootleg cassettes that my dad brought back from his trips to Hong Kong. I still recognise pieces of classical music that I didn't realise I knew, and then date them back to that time of listening to unreliably labelled tapes.

Secondary school really secured my interest in music, though it took me a year or so to admit that I played any instruments and put my hand up to have lessons. Once I'd declared my interest I became fully absorbed in music department activities; a group of us used to hang around in the music block at break and lunchtimes, and I joined every ensemble going, playing in end of term concerts and being increasingly in demand as an accompanist, including for my teacher, with whom I did a number of violin and piano recitals in the sixth form. The real turning point came when the second music teacher was away ill for a number of weeks leading up to the Christmas production one year: I took over his repetiteur duties at chorus rehearsals, and was very reluctant to relinquish them when he came back. He left for another school a year or so later—I hope not because of my teenage usurping of the piano stool—and from then on I was always busy, playing for lessons, exams, concerts, rehearsals, loving the sense of involvement and probably also rather liking the way that teachers and friends were impressed by my skills.

I'd been having piano lessons with my music teacher's wife, but I stopped these after reaching Grade 8, which probably limited my technical ability in the long term, meaning that I didn't put in the work to become a really accomplished solo performer. However, I have stayed busy as an accompanist and rehearsal pianist all through my life, so I don't regret that choice, or at least not often. Meanwhile I'd accidentally discovered the cello, after being challenged to play the bass line of a trio I'd written for GCSE music: I still wonder if my teacher meant me to improve my composition rather than start scraping on a cello, but if so I'm glad I didn't take the hint, choosing instead to have a crash course of lessons and join first the school's second orchestra, then the more advanced one, and even venturing out to play for a local opera orchestra (rather recklessly in the week of my A level exams, as I recall). I'd also started playing the organ at a local church—I know I was 'only fifteen' when I started doing that, as the older members of the choir pointed this out frequently, but they were very supportive in their way, and I felt a real sadness when I left that community to go to university, returning to play for Christmas services for several years after moving away.

I decided to do a music degree and went to York, where I felt hugely out of my depth as a pianist, though my confidence was rescued by a very understanding piano teacher, with whom I also lodged in my third year, and who encouraged me to keep performing at a time when it would have been very easy to retreat to the library and decide to be an academic. I did that too, largely through the influence of John Paynter, who made me passionate about research and writing, and deflected me from my original intention of a career as a school music teacher. At his insistence I embarked on a PhD, moving to Sheffield where I was aware of a more inclusive musical environment than at York: the students seemed a little less super-confident, or maybe I was just older and less bothered about what other people thought of me. The local opera group found me, and playing for weekly rehearsals became a very enjoyable way of paying the grocery bills, as well as leading to numerous concerts and to other connections with singers and musical societies in Sheffield. I also got involved in playing for a local church: I said I'd do that for six months while they found themselves a 'proper' organist, and I'm still there about ten years later.

Nowadays I spend most of my time talking and writing about music, as a university lecturer, but I still gain enormous pleasure from playing, particularly from the recitals I do with a trumpeter friend, and from occasional opportunities to play chamber music. I had some more cello lessons a few years ago, and enjoyed the new lease of life that gave to my playing. I'm not sure I'd ever do the same on the piano—I'm happy with what I can do, and with the chances I have to make music with friends and give concerts a few times a year. I'm grateful that while I've never been enormously ambitious musically, I've never been short of encouragement and opportunities, from parents, teachers and friends—music's always been there, and I wouldn't want to be without it.

GLOSSARY OF ENGLISH EDUCATIONAL TERMS AND SYSTEMS

School Structures

Children in England typically attend *primary school* (ages 4–11), sometimes split into *infant* (ages 4–7) and *junior* (ages 7–11) schools, covering *Key Stages* 1 and 2 of the *National Curriculum* (http://www.education.gov.uk/). At the age of 11 they transfer to a *secondary school* to complete compulsory schooling to age 16, and may stay to do A Levels in a school or further education college. This optional stage of schooling (ages 16–18) is still colloquially referred to as "sixth form", using pre-National Curriculum terminology for the numbering of school year groups. Music is compulsory until the age of 14, at the end of Key Stage 3.

State and Private Schools

The majority of schools in Britain are government funded and referred to as *state schools*. If parents opt to pay for education, children attend *private schools*, most of which choose to follow the National Curriculum, although they are not obliged to do so.

School Music Examinations

Music is examined in secondary schools at the age of 16 through the *General Certificate of Secondary Education (GCSE)*, a system that replaced the *'Ordinary' Level (O Level)* and *Certificate of Secondary Education (CSE)* in 1988.

A small proportion of students then take *'Advanced' Level (A Level)* music at 18+, a programme now separated into two year-long stages, referred to as *AS* and *A2*.

Graded Performance and Theory Examinations

Music examinations run by the *Associated Board of the Royal Schools of Music (ABRSM)* and other music colleges are paid for privately by parents as part of instrumental tuition. These systems of exams run from Grades 1 to 8, followed by diplomas in performance or teaching for advanced students.

Universities and Conservatoires

Undergraduate degrees in music can be taken in *universities* or *conservatoires*, with the former traditionally more weighted towards academic studies and the latter towards performance. There are currently nine British conservatoires (one each in Glasgow, Birmingham, Manchester, Cardiff, and Leeds, and four in London), each with a junior department offering instrumental tuition to exceptional school-aged students through Saturday schools and ensembles.

REFERENCES

Allan, J. (2010). Arts and the inclusive imagination: socially engaged practices and Sistema Scotland. *Journal of Social Inclusion, 1* (2), 111–122.

Allan, J., Moran, N., Duffy, C., & Loeninga, G. (2010). Knowledge exchange with Sistema Scotland. *Journal of Educational Policy, 25* (3), 335–347.

Allender, S., Cowburn, G., & Foster, C. (2006). Understanding participation in sport and physical activity amongst children and adults: a review of qualitative studies. *Health Education Research, 21* (6), 826–835.

Anttila, M. (2010). Problems with school music in Finland. *British Journal of Music Education, 27* (3), 241–253.

Atkinson, R. (1998). *The life story interview.* Thousand Oaks, CA: Sage.

Austin, J., Renwick, J., & McPherson, G. E. (2006). Developing motivation. In G. E. McPherson (Ed.), *The child as musician: A handbook of musical development* (pp. 213–238). Oxford: Oxford University Press.

Bailey, B., & Davidson, J. W. (2002). Adaptive characteristics of group singing: perceptions from members of a choir for homeless men. *Musicae Scientiae, 6* (2), 221–256.

Baker, D. (2006). Life histories of music service teachers: the past in inductees' present. *British Journal of Music Education, 23* (1), 39–50.

——— (2005). Peripatetic music teachers approaching mid-career: a cause for concern. *British Journal of Music Education, 22* (2), 141–153.

Baker, F., & MacKinlay, E. (2006). Sing, soothe and sleep: a lullaby education programme for first-time mothers. *British Journal of Music Education, 23* (2), 147–160.

Bamford, A., & Glinkowski, P. (2010). *"Wow, it's music next": Impact evaluation of Wider Opportunities programme in music at key stage two.* Leeds: The Federation of Music Services.

Bandura, A. (1977). Self-efficacy: toward a unifying theory of behavioral change. *Psychological Review, 84* (2), 191–215.

Barone, T. (2001). *Touching eternity: the enduring outcomes of teaching.* New York: Teachers College Press.

Bartleet, B., Dunbar-Hall, P., Letts, R., & Schippers, H. (2009). *Sound links: community music in Australia*. Brisbane: Queensland Conservatorium Research Centre.

Becker, H. S. (1982). *Art worlds*. Berkeley: University of California Press.

Bennett, D. (2008). *Understanding the classical music profession: the past, the present, and strategies for the future*. Aldershot: Ashgate.

Bennett, D., & Hannan, M. F. (Eds.) (2008). *Inside, outside, downside, up: conservatoire training and musicians' work*. Perth: Black Swan Press.

Bernard, R. (2009). Uncovering pre-service music teachers' assumptions of teaching, learning, and music. *Music Education Research, 11* (1), 111–124.

Beynon, C. (2005). Lifelong learning in music: privileging the privileged? *International Journal of Community Music, 2* (1). Retrieved 15 February 2007, from http://www.intjlcm.com

Biasutti, M. (2010). Investigating trainee music teachers' beliefs on musical abilities and learning: a quantitative study. *Music Education Research, 12* (1), 47–69.

Bluck, S. (2003). Autobiographical memory: exploring its functions in everyday life. *Memory, 11* (2), 113–123.

Bluck, S., & Habermas, T. (2000). The life story schema. *Motivation and Emotion, 24*, 121–147.

Booth, E. (2009). Thoughts on seeing El Sistema. *Teaching Artist Journal, 7* (2), 75–84.

Borthwick, S. J., & Davidson, J. W. (2002). Developing a child's identity as a musician: a family 'script' perspective. In R. MacDonald, D. J. Hargreaves, & D. Miell (Eds.), *Musical identities* (pp. 60–78). Oxford: Oxford University Press.

Bowman, W. (2001). Music education and post-secondary music studies in Canada. *Arts Education Policy Review, 103* (2), 9–17.

Boynton, S., & Kok, R. (2006). *Musical childhoods and the cultures of youth*. Middletown, CT: Wesleyan University Press.

Bray, D. (2009). *Creating a musical school*. Oxford: Oxford University Press.

——— (2000). An examination of GCSE music uptake rates. *British Journal of Music Education, 17* (1), 79–89.

Bresler, L. (2010). Teachers as audiences: exploring educational and musical values in youth performances. *Journal of New Music Research, 39* (2), 135–145.

Bresler, L., & Thompson, C. M. (2002). *The arts in children's lives: context, culture and curriculum*. Dordrecht: Kluwer.

Brockman, J. (2004). *When we were kids: how a child becomes a scientist*. London: Jonathan Cape.

Bunting, C., Chan, T. W., Goldthorpe, J., Keaney, E., & Oskala, A. (2008). *From indifference to enthusiasm: patterns of arts attendance in England*. London: Arts Council England.

Burland, K., & Davidson, J. W. (2004). Tracing a musical life transition. In J. W. Davidson (Ed.), *The music practitioner: research for the music performer, teacher and listener* (pp. 224–250). Aldershot: Ashgate.

Burt, R., & Mills, J. (2006). Taking the plunge: the hopes and fears of students as they begin music college. *British Journal of Music Education, 23* (1), 51–73.

Burwell, K. (2005). A degree of independence: teachers' approaches to instrumental tuition in a university college. *British Journal of Music Education, 22* (3), 199–215.

Calouste Gulbenkian Foundation. (1982). *The arts in schools: principles, practice and provision*. London: Calouste Gulbenkian Foundation.

Campbell, D. (2002). *The Mozart effect*. London: Hodder & Stoughton.

Campbell, P. S. (2008). *Musician and teacher: an orientation to music education*. New York: W. W. Norton.

——— (2002). The musical cultures of children. In L. Bresler & C. M. Thomspon (Eds.), *The arts in children's lives: context, culture and curriculum* (pp. 57–69). Dordrecht: Kluwer.

——— (1998). *Songs in their heads: music and its meaning in children's lives*. New York: Oxford University Press.

Campbell, P. S., Connell, C., & Beegle, A. (2007). Adolescents' expressed meanings of music in and out of school. *Journal of Research in Music Education*, 55 (3), 220–236.

Chaffin, R., & Lemieux, A. F. (2004). General perspectives on achieving musical excellence. In A. Williamon (Ed.), *Musical excellence: strategies and techniques to enhance performance* (pp. 19–39). New York: Oxford University Press.

Chua, A. (2011). *Battle hymn of the Tiger Mother*. London: Bloomsbury.

Clarke, E. F., Dibben, N. J., & Pitts, S. E. (2010). *Music and mind in everyday life*. Oxford: Oxford University Press.

Cole, A. L., & Knowles, J. G. (2001). *Lives in context: the art of life history research*. Walnut Creek, CA: AltaMira Press.

Conway, C., & Hodgman, T. M. (2008). College and community choir member experiences in a collaborative intergenerational performance project. *Journal of Research in Music Education*, 56 (3), 220–237.

Cooper, H., Valentine, J. C., Nye, B., & Lindsay, J. J. (1999). Relationships between five after-school activities and academic achievement. *Journal of Educational Psychology*, 91 (2), 369–378.

Cope, P. (2002). Informal learning of musical instruments: the importance of social context. *Music Education Research*, 4 (1), 93–104.

Côté, J., Baker, J., & Abernethy, B. (2007). Practice and play in the development of sport expertise. In G. Tenenbaum & R. C. Eklund (Eds.), *Handbook of sport psychology* (3rd ed., pp. 184–202). Hoboken, NJ: John Wiley & Sons.

Cox, G. (2002). *Living music in schools 1923–1999*. Aldershot: Ashgate.

——— (1999). Secondary school music teachers talking. *Music Education Research*, 1 (1), 37–46.

Cox, G., & Stevens, R. (Eds.) (2010). *The origins and foundations of music education: cross-cultural historical studies of music in compulsory schooling*. New York: Continuum.

Crafts, S. D., Cavicchi, D., Keil, C., & the Music in Daily Life Project (1993). *My music*. Hanover, NH: University Press of New England.

Creech, A. (2010a). The music studio. In S. Hallam & A. Creech (Eds.), *Music education in the 21st century in the United Kingdom: achievements, analysis and aspirations* (pp. 295–313). London: Institute of Education.

——— (2010b). Learning a musical instrument: the case for parental support. *Music Education Research*, 12 (1), 13–32.

Custodero, L. A., & Johnson-Green, E. A. (2003). Passing the cultural torch: musical experience and musical parenting of infants. *Journal of Research in Music Education*, 51 (2), 102–114.

Davidson, J. W., & Burland, K. (2006). Musician identity formation. In G. E. McPherson (Ed.), *The child as musician: a handbook of musical development* (pp. 475–490). Oxford: Oxford University Press.

Dench, S., & Regan, J. (2000). *Learning in later life: motivation and impact.* Retrieved 1 June 2011, from Department for Education, UK Government: http://education.gov.uk

DeNora, T. (2000). *Music in everyday life.* Cambridge: Cambridge University Press.

Dibben, N. (2006). The socio-cultural and learning experiences of music students in a British university. *British Journal of Music Education, 23* (1), 91–116.

Dionyssiou, Z. (2011). Music learning and the formation of local identity in the Philharmonic Society Wind Bands of Corfu. In L. Green (Ed.), *Learning, teaching, and musical identity: voices across cultures* (pp. 142–155). Bloomington, IN: Indiana University Press.

Eden, D., & Saremba, M. (2009). *The Cambridge companion to Gilbert and Sullivan* (pp. 190–200). Cambridge: Cambridge University Press.

Eisner, E. (2001). Music education six months after the turn of the century. *Arts Education Policy Review, 102* (3), 20–24.

Elliott, D. (1995). *Music matters: a new philosophy of music education.* New York: Oxford University Press.

Ericsson, K. A., Krampe, R., & Tesch-Römer, C. (1993). The role of deliberate practice in the acquisition of expert performance. *Psychological Review, 100,* 363–406.

Finney, J. (2011). *Music education in England, 1950–2010: the child-centred progressive tradition.* Farnham: Ashgate.

Finney, J., & Tymoczko, M. (2005). Secondary school students as leaders: examining the potential for transforming music education. *Music Education International, 2,* 36–50.

Fletcher, P. (1987). *Education and music.* Oxford: Oxford University Press.

Folkestad, G. (2006). Formal and informal learning situations or practices vs. formal and informal ways of learning. *British Journal of Music Education, 23* (2), 135–145.

———— (2005). Here, there and everywhere: music education research in a globalised world. *Music Education Research, 7* (3), 279–287.

Fornäs, J., Lindberg, U., & Sernhede, O. (1995). *In garageland: youth and culture in late modernity.* London: Routledge.

Fraser-Thomas, J., & Côté, J. (2009). Understanding adolescents' positive and negative developmental experiences in sport. *The Sport Psychologist, 23,* 3–23.

Fraser-Thomas, J., Côté, J., & Deakin, J. (2008). Examining adolescent sport dropout and prolonged engagement from a developmental perspective. *Journal of Applied Sport Psychology, 20* (3), 318–333.

Frego, R. J. (1995). Uniting the generations with music programs. *Music Educators Journal, 81* (6), 17–19.

Gangel, A. (2011). *The sun hasn't fallen from the sky: a memoir.* London: Bloomsbury.

Gaunt, H., & Hallam, S. (2009). Individuality in the learning of musical skills. In S. Hallam, I. Cross, & M. Thaut (Eds.), *The Oxford handbook of music psychology* (pp. 274–284). Oxford: Oxford University Press.

Gavin, H. (2001). Reconstructed musical memories and adult expertise. *Music Education Research, 3* (1), 51–61.

Gembris, H. (Ed.). (2006). *Musical development from a lifespan perspective*. Frankfurt: Peter Lang.

Gladwell, M. (2008). *Outliers: the story of success*. London: Penguin.

Goodson, I., & Sikes, P. (2001). *Life history research in educational settings*. Buckingham: Open University Press.

Gouzouasis, P., Guhn, M., & Kishor, N. (2007). The predictive relationship between achievement and participation in music and achievement in core Grade 12 academic subjects. *Music Education Research, 9* (1), 81–92.

Gouzouasis, P., Henrey, J., & Belliveau, G. (2008). Turning points: a transitional story of grade seven music students' participation in high school band programmes. *Music Education Research, 10* (1), 75–90.

Graham, R. (2009). The function of music education in the growth of cultural openness in the USA. *Music Education Research, 11* (3), 283–302.

Green, L. (Ed.) (2011). *Learning, teaching, and musical identity: voices across cultures*. Bloomington, IN: Indiana University Press.

———— (2008). *Music, informal learning and the school: a new classroom pedagogy*. Farnham: Ashgate.

———— (2002). *How popular musicians learn*. Aldershot: Ashgate.

Guardabasso, G. (1989). Music education in Italy: what is going on? *International Journal of Music Education, 13* (1), 35–36.

Haddon, E. (2005). *Making music in Britain: interviews with those behind the notes*. Aldershot: Ashgate.

Hale, N. V. (1947). *Education for music*. London: Oxford University Press.

Hall, C. (2005). Gender and boys' singing in early childhood. *British Journal of Music Education, 22* (1), 5–20.

Hallam, S. (1998). *Instrumental teaching: a practical guide to better teaching and learning*. Oxford: Heinemann.

———— (2010). The power of music: its impact on the intellectual, personal and social development of children and young people. In S. Hallam & A. Creech (Eds.), *Music education in the 21st century in the United Kingdom: achievements, analysis and aspirations* (pp. 2–17). London: Institute of Education.

Hallam, S., Creech, A., Sandford, C., Rinta, T., & Shave, K. (2008). *Survey of Musical Futures: a report from the Institute of Education, University of London for the Paul Hamlyn Foundation*. Retrieved 24 January 2011, from http://www.musicalfutures.org.uk/resource/27229

Hallam, S., & Creech, A. (2010). Learning to play an instrument. In S. Hallam & A. Creech (Eds.), *Music education in the 21st century in the United Kingdom: achievements, analysis and aspirations* (pp. 85–104). London: Institute of Education.

Hargreaves, D. H. (2004). *Learning for life: the foundations for lifelong learning*. Bristol: The Policy Press.

Hargreaves, D. J., & Marshall, N. A. (2003). Developing identities in music education. *Music Education Research, 5* (3), 263–273.

Hargreaves, D. J., & North, A. C. (2001). *Musical development and learning: the international perspective*. London: Continuum.

Harland, J., Kinder, K., Lord, P., Stoot, A., Schagen, I., & Haynes, J., with Cusworth, L., White, R., & Paola, R. (2000). *Arts education in secondary schools: effects and effectiveness*. Slough: National Foundation for Educational Research.

Harris, D. (2006). *Music education and Muslims.* Stoke-on-Trent: Trentham.

Hays, T., & Minichiello, V. (2005). The meaning of music in the lives of older people: a qualitative study. *Psychology of Music, 33* (4), 437–451.

Heath, E. (1976). *Music: a joy for life.* London: Sidgwick & Jackson.

Henley, D. (2011). *Music education in England.* Retrieved 18 February 2011, from Department for Education, UK Government: http://publications.education.gov.uk

Hennessy, S. (2000). Overcoming the red-feeling: The development of confidence to teach music in primary school amongst student teachers. *British Journal of Music Education, 17* (2), 183–196.

Herbert, T. (1998). Victorian brass bands: class, taste and space. In A. Leyshon, D. Matless, & G. Revill (Eds.), *The place of music* (pp. 104–128). New York: The Guilford Press.

Hickey, M. (2003). *Why and how to teach music composition: a new horizon for music education.* Reston, VA: Music Educators' National Conference (MENC).

Higgins, L. (2007). Acts of hospitality: the community in Community Music. *Music Education Research, 9* (2), 281–292.

Hildebrandt, D. (1985). *Pianoforte: a social history of the piano.* (H. Goodman, Trans.) London: Hutchinson.

Holt, J. (1978). *Never too late: my musical life story.* New York: Merloyd Lawrence.

Horne, C. (2004). *Contemporary jazz UK: twenty-one lives in jazz.* London: Perspectives in Jazz.

Hoskyns, J. (2002). Music education: a European perspective. In G. J. Spruce (Ed.), *Teaching music in secondary schools: a reader* (pp. 51–62). London: Routledge.

Howe, M. J. A., & Sloboda, J. A. (1991). Young musicians' accounts of significant influences in their early lives: 2. Teachers, practising and performance. *British Journal of Music Education, 8* (1), 53–63.

Howe, M. J. A., Davidson, J. W., & Sloboda, J. A. (1998). Innate talents: reality or myth? *Behavioral and Brain Sciences, 21,* 339–442.

Jaffurs, S. E. (2004). The impact of informal music learning practices in the classroom, or how I learned how to teach from a garage band. *International Journal of Music Education, 22* (3), 189–200.

Jones, P. (2009). Hard and soft policies in music education: building the capacity of teachers to understand, study and influence them. *Arts Education Policy Review, 110* (4), 27–32.

Jorgensen, E. R. (2008). *The art of teaching music.* Bloomington, IN: Indiana University Press.

———— (2003a). What philosophy can bring to music education: musicianship as a case in point. *British Journal of Music Education, 20* (2), 197–214.

———— (2003b). *Transforming music education.* Bloomington, IN: Indiana University Press.

———— (1997). *In search of music education.* Urbana, IL: University of Illinois Press.

Kaiserman, P., & Price, D., with Richardson, J., Pacey, F., & Hannan, F. (No date). *A guide to personalising extra-curricular music.* London: Musical Futures/Paul Hamlyn Foundation. Retrieved 1 March 2007, from http://musicalfutures.org.uk

Kelly, S. N. (2009). *Teaching music in American society: a social and cultural understanding of music education.* New York: Routledge.

Kertz-Welzel, A. (2004). Didaktik of music: a German concept and its comparison to American music pedagogy. *International Journal of Music Education, 22* (3), 277–286.

Kinney, D. W. (2010). Selected non-music predictors of urban students' decisions to enroll and persist in middle school band programs. *Journal of Research in Music Education, 57* (4), 334–350.

Kirchhoff, C. (1988). The school and college band: wind band pedagogy in the United States. In J. T. Gates (Ed.), *Music education in the United States: contemporary issues* (pp. 259–276). Tuscaloosa, AL: University of Alabama Press.

Kokotsaki, D. (2010). Musical involvement outside school: how important is it for student-teachers in secondary education? *British Journal of Music Education, 27* (2), 151–170.

Kolb, B. M. (2001). The decline of the subscriber base: a study of the Philharmonia Orchestra audience. *Market Research, 3,* 51–59.

——— (2002). The effect of generational change on classical music concert attendance and orchestras' responses in the UK and US. *Cultural Trends, 41.*

Lamont, A. (2011). The beat goes on: music education, identity and lifelong learning. *Music Education Research, 13* (4), 369–388.

Lamont, A., Hargreaves, D. J., Marshall, N., & Tarrant, M. (2003). Young people's music in and out of school. *British Journal of Music Education, 20* (3), 229–241.

Lamont, A., & Maton, K. (2008). Choosing music: exploratory studies into the low uptake of music GCSE. *British Journal of Music Education, 25* (3), 267–282.

Lamont, A., & Webb, R. (2010). Short- and long-term musical preferences: what makes a favourite piece of music? *Psychology of Music, 38* (2), 222–241.

Lave, J., & Wenger, E. (1991). *Situated learning: legitimate peripheral participation.* New York: Cambridge University Press.

Lum, C. H. (2008). Home musical environment of children in Singapore: on globalization, technology, and media. *Journal of Research in Music Education, 56* (2), 101–117.

MacDonald, R., Hargreaves, D. J., & Miell, D. (Eds.) (2002). *Musical identities.* Oxford: Oxford University Press.

MacDonald, R., Miell, D., & Wilson, G. (2005). Talking about music: a vehicle for identity development. In D. Miell, R. MacDonald & D. J. Hargreaves (Eds.) *Musical communication* (pp. 321–338). Oxford: Oxford University Press.

Madsen, C. K., & Kelly, S. N. (2002). First remembrances of wanting to become a music teacher. *Journal of Research in Music Education, 50* (4), 323–332.

Mahoney, J. L., Cairns, B. D., & Farmer, T. W. (2003). Promoting interpersonal competence and educational success through extracurricular activity participation. *Journal of Educational Psychology, 95* (2), 409–418.

Mantie, R., & Tucker, L. (2008). Closing the gap: does music-making have to stop upon graduation? *International Journal of Community Music, 1* (2), 217–227.

Manturzewska, M. (1990). A biographical study of the life-span development of professional musicians. *Psychology of Music, 18,* 112–138.

Marsh, K. (2011). The permeable classroom: learning, teaching and musical identity in a remote Australian Aboriginal homelands school. In L. Green (Ed.), *Learning, teaching, and musical identity: voices across cultures* (pp. 20–32). Bloomington, IN: Indiana University Press.

Marshall, S. (1963). *An experiment in education*. London: Cambridge University Press.

Matarasso, F. (1997). *Use or ornament? The social impact of participation in the arts*. Stroud: Comedia.

McAdams, D. P. (2001). The psychology of life stories. *Review of General Psychology, 5* (2), 100–122.

McAdams, D. P., Reynolds, J., Lewis, M., Patten, A. H., & Bowman, P. J. (2001). When bad things turn good and good things turn bad: sequences of redemption and contamination in life narrative and their relation to psychosocial adaptation in midlife adults and in students. *Personality and Social Psychology Bulletin, 27* (4), 474–485.

McCarthy, M. (1999). *Passing it on: music and the narrative of Irish culture*. Cork: Cork University Press.

McCormick, J., & McPherson, G. E. (2003). The role of self-efficacy in a musical performance examination: an exploratory structural equation analysis. *Psychology of Music, 31* (1), 37–51.

McPherson, G. E. (2009). The role of parents in children's musical development. *Psychology of Music, 37* (1), 91–110.

McPherson, G. E., & Davidson, J. W. (2006). Playing an instrument. In G. E. McPherson (Ed.), *The child as musician: a handbook of musical development* (pp. 331–351). Oxford: Oxford University Press.

McQueen, H., & Varvarigou, M. (2010). Learning through life. In S. Hallam & A. Creech (Eds.), *Music education in the 21st century in the United Kingdom: achievements, analysis and aspirations* (pp. 159–175). London: Institute of Education, University of London.

Miller, J., & Baker, D. (2007). Career orientation and pedagogical training: conservatoire undergraduates' insights. *British Journal of Music Education, 24* (1), 5–19.

Miller, M. M., & Strongman, K. T. (2002). The emotional effects of music on religious experience: a study of the Pentecostal-Charismatic style of music and worship. *Psychology of Music, 30* (1), 8–27.

Mills, J. (2005). *Music in the school*. Oxford: Oxford University Press.

Mills, J., & Smith, J. (2006). Working in music: becoming successful. In H. Gembris (Ed.), *Musical development from a lifespan perspective* (pp. 131–140). Frankfurt: Peter Lang.

Moffitt, K. H., & Singer, J. A. (1994). Continuity in the life story: self-defining memories, affect, and approach/avoidance personal strivings. *Journal of Personality, 62* (1), 21–43.

Morrison, S. J. (2008). Of school bands, orchestras, and jazz ensembles. In P. S. Campbell, *Musician and teacher: an orientation to music education* (pp. 165–186). New York: W. W. Norton.

Myers, D. E. (2005). Freeing music education from schooling: toward a lifespan perspective on music learning and teaching. *International Journal of Community Music (Volume D)*. Retrieved 26 May 2011, from http://www.intljcm.com/articles/Volume%204/Myers%20Files/Myers.pdf

Niblett, E. (1955). *School music: an instructional handbook*. London: Blandford Press.

North, A. C., Hargreaves, D. J., & O'Neill, S. A. (2000). The importance of music to adolescents. *British Journal of Educational Psychology, 70*, 255–272.

North, A. C., & Hargreaves, D. J. (2008). *The social and applied psychology of music.* Oxford: Oxford University Press.

O'Flynn, J. (2011). Performance, transmission, and identity among Ireland's new generation of traditional musicians. In L. Green (Ed.), *Learning, teaching, and musical identity: voices across cultures* (pp. 252–266). Bloomington, IN: Indiana University Press.

Ofsted [Office for Standards in Education, UK] (2004). *Tuning in: Wider Opportunities in specialist instrumental tuition for pupils in Key Stage 2.* London: Ofsted. Retrieved 19 December 2011, from http://www.ofsted.gov.uk/resources/tuning-wider-opportunities-specialist-instrumental-tuition-for-pupils-key-stage-2

Papageorgi, I., Creech, A., Haddon, E., Morton, F., De Bezenac, C., Himonides, E., Potter, J., Duffy, C., Whyton, T., & Welch, G. (2010). Perceptions and predictions of expertise in advanced musical learners. *Psychology of Music, 38* (1), 31–66.

Parncutt, R. (2006). Prenatal development. In G. E. McPherson (Ed.), *The child as musician: a handbook of musical development* (pp. 1–31). New York: Oxford University Press.

Paynter, J. (2008). Making progress with composing. In J. Mills & J. Paynter, *Thinking and making: selections from the writings of John Paynter on music in education* (pp. 144–175). Oxford: Oxford University Press.

——— (2002). Music in the school curriculum: why bother? *British Journal of Music Education, 19* (3), 215–226.

——— (1982). *Music in the secondary school curriculum.* Cambridge: Cambridge University Press.

Paynter, J., & Mills, J. (2008). *Thinking and making: selections from the writings of John Paynter on music in education.* Oxford: Oxford University Press.

Peretz, I., Cummings, S., & Dubé, M. (2007). The genetics of congenital amusia (tone deafness): a family-aggregation study. *American Journal of Human Genetics, 81,* 582–588.

Philpott, C. (2010). The sociological critique of curriculum music in England: is radical change really possible? In R. Wright (Ed.), *Sociology and music education* (pp. 81–92). Farnham: Ashgate.

Pillemer, D. (2001). Momentous events and the life story. *Review of General Psychology, 5* (2), 123–134.

Pitts, S. E. (2010). Musical education as a social act: learning from and within musical communities. In J. Ballantyne & B. Bartleet (Eds.), *Navigating sound and music education* (pp. 115–128). Newcastle-upon-Tyne: Cambridge Scholars Publishing.

——— (2009). Roots and routes in adult musical participation: investigating the impact of home and school on lifelong musical interest and involvement. *British Journal of Music Education, 26* (3), 241–256.

——— (2008). Extra-curricular music in UK schools: investigating the aims, experiences, and impact of adolescent musical participation. *International Journal of Education and the Arts, 9* (10).

——— (2005). *Valuing musical participation.* Aldershot: Ashgate.

——— (2002). Changing tunes: musical experience and self-perception amongst school and university music students. *Musicae Scientiae, 6* (1), 73–92.

————— (2000). *A century of change in music education*. Aldershot: Ashgate.

Pratt, G., & Stephens, J. (1995). *Teaching music in the National Curriculum*. Oxford: Heinemann.

Radocy, R. F. (2001). North America. In D. J. Hargreaves & A. C. North (Eds.), *Musical development and learning: the international perspective* (pp. 120–133). London: Continuum.

Rainbow, B., with Cox, G. (2006). *Music in educational thought and practice*. Woodbridge: Boydell.

Rauscher, F. (2009). The impact of music instruction on other skills. In S. Hallam, I. Cross, & M. Thaut (Eds.), *The Oxford handbook of music psychology* (pp. 244–252). New York: Oxford University Press.

Rauscher, F., Shaw, G., & Ky, K. (1993) Music and spatial task performance. *Nature*, *365*, 611.

Reimer, B. (2003). *A philosophy of music education: advancing the vision*. Upper Saddle River, NJ: Prentice Hall.

————— (1989). *A philosophy of music education* (2nd ed.). Englewood Cliffs, NJ: Prentice Hall.

Richardson, M. (1948). *Art and the child*. London: University of London Press.

Riley, M., & Laing, D. (2006). *The value of jazz in Britain*. Retrieved 3 March 2008, from London: Jazz Services: www.jazzservices.org.uk

Robinson, T. (2010). *How popular musicians teach*. University of Sheffield: Unpublished PhD thesis.

Ross, M. (1995). What's wrong with school music? *British Journal of Music Education*, *12* (3), 185–201.

Rowe, V. C. (2008). *Patterns and consequences of gender interactions in instrumental music lessons*. University of Surrey, Roehampton: Unpublished PhD thesis.

Rusinek, G., & Rincón, C. (2010). Attending musical performances: teachers' and students' expectations and experiences at a youth programme in Madrid. *Journal of New Music Research*, *39* (2), 147–158.

Sadie, S. (1979). Sir Robert Mayer at 100. *The Musical Times*, *120* (1636), 457 and 474–475.

Salaman, W. (1983). *Living school music*. Cambridge: Cambridge University Press.

Scholes, P. (1935). *Music, the child and the masterpiece*. London: Oxford University Press.

Service, T. (2008, June 25). El Sistema might not be a quick fix in the UK. *The Guardian*. Retrieved 19 December 2011, from http://www.guardian.co.uk/music/tomserviceblog/2008/jun/25/thenewsthatelsistema

Silverman, D. (2001). *Interpreting qualitative data: methods for analysing talk, text and interaction* (2nd ed.). London: Sage.

Singer, J. A. (1990). Affective responses to autobiographical memories and their relationship to long-term goals. *Journal of Personality*, *58* (3), 535–563.

Sloboda, J. A. (2005). *Exploring the musical mind*. New York: Oxford University Press.

Sloboda, J. A., & Howe, M. J. A. (1992). Transitions in the early musical careers of able young musicians: choosing instruments and teachers. *Journal of Research in Music Education*, *40* (4), 283–294.

————— (1991). Biographical precursors of musical excellence: an interview study. *Psychology of Music*, *19* (1), 3–21.

Small, C. (2010). Afterword. In R. Wright (Ed.), *Sociology and music education* (pp. 283–290). Farnham: Ashgate.

——— (1998). *Musicking: the meanings of performing and listening.* Hanover, NH: Wesleyan University Press.

——— (1977/96). *Music–society–education.* London: University Press of New England.

Smilde, R. (2009a). *Musicians as lifelong learners: 32 biographies.* Delft: Eburon Academic Publishers.

——— (2009b). *Musicians as lifelong learners: discovery through biography.* Delft: Eburon Academic Publishers.

Soto, A. C., Lum, C., & Campbell, P. S. (2009). A university-school music partnership for music education majors in a culturally distinctive community. *Journal of Research in Music Education, 56* (4), 338–356.

Southcott, J. E. (2009). And as I go, I love to sing: The Happy Wanderers, music and positive ageing. *International Journal of Community Music, 2* (2 & 3), 143–156.

Southgate, D. E., & Roscigno, V. J. (2009). The impact of music on childhood and adolescent achievement. *Social Science Quarterly, 90* (1), 4–21.

Stebbins, R. A. (1992). *Amateurs, professionals, and serious leisure.* Montreal: McGill-Queen's University Press.

Stewart, L. (2006). Congenital amusia. *Current Biology, 16* (21), 904–906.

Stokes, W. R. (2005). *Growing up with jazz: twenty-four musicians talk about their lives and careers.* New York: Oxford University Press.

Strachan, L., Côté, J., & Deakin, J. (2009). "Specializers" versus "samplers" in youth sport: comparing experiences and outcomes. *The Sport Psychologist, 23,* 77–92.

Strand, K. (2006). Survey of Indiana music teachers on using composition in the classroom. *Journal of Research in Music Education, 54* (2), 154–167.

Suzuki, S. (1970). *Nurtured by love: a new approach to education.* London: Bosworth.

Swanwick, K. (1999). *Teaching music musically.* London: Taylor & Francis.

——— (1979). *A basis for music education.* London: Taylor & Francis.

Tafuri, J. (2001). Italy. In D. J. Hargreaves & A. C. North (Eds.), *Musical development and learning: the international perspective* (pp. 73–86). London: Continuum.

Tarrant, M., North, A. C., & Hargreaves, D. J. (2002). Youth identity and music. In R. A. MacDonald, D. J. Hargreaves, & D. Miell (Eds.), *Musical identities* (pp. 134–150). Oxford: Oxford University Press.

Taylor, A. (2010). Participation in a master class: experiences of older amateur pianists. *Music Education Research, 12* (2), 199–217.

Taylor, A., & Hallam, S. (2008). Understanding what it means for older students to learn basic musical skills on a keyboard instrument. *Music Education Research, 10* (2), 285–306.

Tomes, S. (2010). *Out of silence: a pianist's yearbook.* Woodbridge: Boydell Press.

Torff, B., & Winner, E. (1994). Don't throw out the baby with the bathwater: on the role of innate factors in musical accomplishment. *The Psychologist, 7* (8), 361–362.

Trehub, S. E. (2006). Infants as musical connoisseurs. In G. E. McPherson (Ed.), *The child as musician: a handbook of musical development* (pp. 33–49). New York: Oxford University Press.

Turton, A., & Durrant, C. (2002). A study of adults' attitudes, perceptions and reflections on their singing experience in secondary school: some implications for music education. *British Journal of Music Education, 19* (1), 33–50.

Van Matre, J. C., Valentine, J. C., & Cooper, H. (2000). Effect of students' after-school activities on teachers' academic expectancies. *Contemporary Educational Psychology, 25,* 167–183.

Vincent, C., & Ball, S. J. (2007). 'Making up' the middle-class child: families, activities and class dispositions. *Sociology, 41* (6), 1061–1077.

Vulliamy, E. (2007, July 29). Orchestral manoeuvres. *The Observer.* Retrieved 19 December 2011, from http://www.guardian.co.uk/music/2007/jul/29/classicalmusicandopera1

Wang, G. (2009). Interlopers in the realm of high culture: "music moms" and the performance of Asian and Asian American identities. *American Quarterly, 61* (4), 881–903.

Webster, P. (2007). Computer-based technology and music teaching and learning: 2000–2005. In L. Bresler (Ed.), *International handbook of research in arts education* (pp. 1311–1328). Dordrecht: Springer.

Weigel, D. J., Martin, S. S., & Bennett, K. K. (2007). Mothers' literacy beliefs: connections with the home literacy environment and pre-school children's literacy development. *Journal of Early Childhood Literacy, 6* (2), 191–211.

Winzenried, R. (2004, January–February). *Stalking the culturally aware non-attender.* Retrieved 7 September 2009, from Symphony: http://www.americanorchestras.org/images/stories/symphony_magazine/jan_feb04/04jf_cana.pdf

Woodford, P. (2005). *Democracy and music education: liberalism, ethics, and the politics of practice.* Bloomington, IN: Indiana University Press.

Woods, P. (1993). *Critical events in teaching and learning.* London: Falmer Press.

Wright, R. (2007). Addressing individual needs and equality of opportunity in the music curriculum. In C. Philpott & G. J. Spruce (Eds.), *Learning to teach music in the secondary school* (2nd ed.) (pp. 193–208). Abingdon: Routledge.

——— (2008). Kicking the habitus: power, culture and pedagogy in the secondary school music curriculum. *Music Education Research, 10* (3), 389–402.

York, N. (2001). *Valuing school music: a report on school music.* London: University of Westminster & Rockschool Ltd.

Yorke Trotter, T. H. (1914). *The making of musicians.* London: Herbert Jenkins.

Young, P. (2000). 'I might as well give up': self-esteem and mature students' feelings about feedback on assignments. *Journal of Further and Higher Education, 24* (3), 409–418.

Young, S. (2008). Lullaby light shows: everyday musical experience among under-two-year-olds. *International Journal of Music Education, 26* (1), 33–46.

INDEX

teacher training 30, 40, 91–92, 129, 161, 169

toddlers 131, 158

uncles 60, 85, 108

university 80, 88, 93, 95, 123–124, 129, 132–133, 138, 141–142, 154, 156–157, 171, 179, 188, 192–193, 197, 201

ensembles 46, 70, 88, 117, 134

war (World War II) 26, 37, 41, 62, 72, 151, 180–181
   post- 41, 126, 194

whistling 31, 148, 180, 182–183

Wider Opportunities scheme 95, 170–171

worship 119, 135–137, 154. *See also* church